BARBARA WOOTTON

BARBARA WOOTTON

SOCIAL SCIENCE
AND PUBLIC POLICY

◆

ESSAYS IN HER HONOUR

Edited by
Philip Bean and David Whynes

TAVISTOCK PUBLICATIONS
LONDON AND NEW YORK

First published in 1986 by
Tavistock Publications Ltd
11 New Fetter Lane, London EC4P 4EE

Published in the USA by
Tavistock Publications
in association with Methuen, Inc.
29 West 35th Street, New York, NY 10001

Printed in Great Britain
at the University Press, Cambridge

Photoset by
Rowland Phototypesetting Ltd
Bury St Edmunds, Suffolk

British Library Cataloguing in Publication Data

Barbara Wootton: social science
and public policy:
essays in her honour.
1. Social sciences
I. Bean, Philip   II. Whynes, David
III. Wootton, Barbara
300   H85

ISBN 0-422-79690-5

Library of Congress Cataloging in Publication Data

Main entry under title:
Barbara Wootton – social science and public policy.
Bibliography: p.
Includes index.
1. Economics – Addresses, essays, lectures.
2. Social policy – Addresses, essays, lectures.
3. Welfare state – Addresses, essays, lectures.
4. Crime and criminals – Addresses, essays, lectures.
5. Wootton, Barbara, 1897–   – Addresses, essays, lectures.
I. Bean, Philip.
II. Whynes, David.
III. Wootton, Barbara, 1897–   .
HB171.B248 1985   330   85-27650

ISBN 0-422-79690-5

CONTENTS

LIST OF CONTRIBUTORS

LORD MCGREGOR OF DURRIS is Chairman, Advertising Standards Authority, London.

PETER TOWNSEND is Professor of Social Policy, University of Bristol.

MERYL ALDRIDGE is a Lecturer in the Department of Social Administration and Social Work, University of Nottingham.

DAVID WHYNES is a Lecturer in the Department of Economics, University of Nottingham.

JOAN MITCHELL is Professor of Political Economy, University of Nottingham.

RAYMOND PLANT is Professor of Politics, University of Southampton.

ADRIAN SINFIELD is Professor of Social Policy, University of Edinburgh.

PHILIP BEAN is a Senior Lecturer in the Department of Social Administration and Social Work, University of Nottingham.

J. C. SMITH is Professor of Common Law, University of Nottingham.

HOWARD JONES is Professor of Social Administration, University College, Cardiff.

TERENCE MORRIS is Professor of Social Institutions at the London School of Economics and Political Science.

DAVID DOWNES is a Reader in the Department of Social Science and Administration, London School of Economics and Political Science.

D. J. WEST is Professor Emeritus of Clinical Criminology, University of Cambridge.

GORDON TRASLER is Professor of Psychology, University of Southampton.

ANTHONY E. BOTTOMS is Wolfson Professor of Criminology, University of Cambridge.

WILLIAM MCWILLIAMS is Research Fellow, Institute of Criminology, University of Cambridge.

LOUIS BLOM-COOPER is a Barrister-at-Law.

PREFACE

It is doubtful whether anyone working in the field of social science has remained untouched by the influence, either direct or indirect, of Barbara Wootton. In a long and distinguished career she has written on a great diversity of economic, social, and political matters, making especially significant contributions in the fields of criminology and social policy. Both her academic and her public activities have earned her considerable acclaim and it is with the greatest of pleasure that we offer this collection of essays as a tribute to one of the foremost critical minds of our generation.

This having been said, devising a book in Barbara's honour proved to be no easy task. The scope and volume of her written output has been prolific. Moreover, Barbara Wootton is very much a polymath and has moved across the academic boundaries with ease, probing into areas in which others feel uncomfortable, always asking relevant and pertinent questions. In fact, she seems not to have recognized at all those tidy academic boundaries which other social scientists have been so eager to construct. Such characteristics hardly assist editors hoping to encapsulate her work in a single volume.

Had our aim actually been to cover each and every aspect of Barbara's life and ideas it would have been possible to produce quite a number of books, all of them different. We have tried to do less than this in producing a collection of papers covering a limited number of topics. The selection of these topics has been conditioned by several factors, probably the most significant being editorial interest pure and simple. Indeed, editorial bias must be regarded as inevitable because the project was motivated in the first place by our own personal interests in specific aspects of Barbara's work. The fact that one of us is a criminologist and the other an economist naturally predisposes us towards such areas. We were also particularly keen to include contributions from those who had worked or been otherwise associated with Barbara at various points in her career. In briefing our contributors we tried to act in what we take to be the spirit of Barbara Wootton; we asked them to write in a critical fashion, to develop and extend the arguments. Furthermore, we encouraged them to do this unflinchingly, Barbara herself having little time, we felt, for either fawning eulogy or irrelevance to contemporary circumstances. We accordingly hope that the completed volume represents both an accolade and an academic discourse in its own right.

In one sense our editorial task was made lighter by the large number of distinguished contributors readily offering their services. It is a reflection of Barbara's eminence and of the affection in which she is held that so many authors were eager to write; yet she herself founded no 'school', she has belonged to no fashionable academic clique, nor has she actively encouraged devotees. Over and above the quality of her work, most people, on a personal basis, see her as a rare scholar, and one whose fundamental humanity intrudes at every level. If she could be categorized within a single tradition it would perhaps be as a Benthamite. She has retained a fierce faith in the ultimate triumph of rational argument and, as she once said in a letter to us, happiness is to be preferred to unhappiness and there's an end to moral philosophy. To this tradition she has remained faithful throughout, and has been recognized as such by contemporaries who, whilst not necessarily sharing her outlook, see Barbara as representing something of the tradition which is valuable.

We were extremely glad when Lord McGregor of Durris consented to write the Introduction to the collection, dealing in detail with Barbara's life and work. As a friend and colleague of more than forty years' standing he is able to write with some authority. Lord McGregor also compiled the Bibliography at the end of the book. We have grouped the remaining essays into two sections, the first covering a number of Barbara's interests at the earlier stages of her career. The fields are economics and social policy, and several papers deal with the evolution and improvement of the Welfare State, a subject which has remained close to Barbara's heart. The second section comprises essays on criminological themes, criminology being an area towards which she turned increasingly in later life.

Our one regret in compiling this collection has been our inability to include papers by the many other friends, colleagues, and admirers of Barbara Wootton. We must offer our apologies to all those who feel a special attachment and whom, out of ignorance, we omitted to approach.

We hope that they can feel that those tributes which we have included can stand for us all.

Philip Bean
David Whynes
University of Nottingham
June, 1985

1
CHAMPION OF THE IMPOSSIBLE
Lord McGregor of Durris

Barbara Wootton was born into an academic family in Cambridge in 1897, a quarter of a century after religious tests in the university had been abolished and only fifteen years after fellows had been permitted to marry and retain their fellowships. Both her parents were classical scholars. Her father, James Adam, only son of an Aberdeenshire farm servant and author of *The Religious Teachers of Greece*, was Senior Tutor of Emmanuel College but died prematurely when she was 10. Her mother, a banker's daughter, taught at Girton. Barbara Adam had two brothers. The younger was a scholar at Balliol when he joined the army during the First World War. He was killed in 1916. The elder became a professor of chemistry and a fellow of the Royal Society. She recollects 'the intense concentration upon academic success and particularly upon classical studies' which pervaded her childhood. 'Even the cat was called Plato' (Wootton 1967: 17). Barbara's nanny had moved on from the Keyneses to whose kitchen she was often taken during her morning walk, there to overhear the cook's regular lamentations over 'the lay-about habits of Mr Maynard', never up before midday.

Despite the reduced circumstances which followed her father's death, her childhood ran in the conventional grooves of an upper middle-class family in the Edwardian years. When her father died her two brothers had already won scholarships to Winchester. She did not go to school at all until the age of 13½, and then to a day school in Cambridge. Before that, she was taught at home by her mother. There was little sympathy between daughter and mother, 'an extremely intellectual woman, as well as what is commonly called a strong character', with many academic, linguistic, and musical accomplishments. Apart from being a strong advocate of female suffrage, Mrs Adam was conservative in outlook, almost every social change filling her with foreboding. Her daughter remembers

> 'how she walked restlessly from room to room in anguish at the prospect that the first Old Age Pensions Act would allow old people without other means to receive a pension of as much as 5s. a week; while a few years later the obligation to stamp insurance cards for her servants produced an almost more severe psychological trauma.'
>
> (Wootton 1967: 20)

As in many other similar childhoods, devotion to a nanny provided the emotional warmth lacking in the parental tie. The nanny stayed with the family for more than thirty years and was maintained in retirement by her last charge until she died in very old age.

In the second year of the First World War, Barbara Adam went into residence at Girton at the age of 18 to read classics. Two years later she married John Wesley Wootton. The honeymoon had to be cancelled because he was recalled to his regiment in France at short notice, and so the bride had just one day and a half with her husband. He was killed in action five weeks later. Almost half a century afterwards, in delicate and beautifully phrased passages in her candid autobiography, Barbara Wootton recounted those happenings. Before she reached her twenty-first birthday, she had suffered the death of her father, a brother, and her husband. Her response to such experiences says much about her resoluteness of character and principles of conduct:

> 'In ten years I had learned little about life, much about death. . . .
>
> My troubles were, of course, in no way unusual. What had happened to me happened also, in one form or another, to thousands of my contemporaries; and that fact served at least to hold in check any temptation I might otherwise have had to dramatise my tragic situation. . . . My upbringing, too, had left no room for self-pity: none of the adults in our family circle would ever have dreamed of using misfortune or unhappiness as an excuse for shortcomings. Whatever happened, one was expected to go ahead and make the best of whatever the next job might be. In this the attitude of our elders, though somewhat exacting, was, I think, much to be preferred to the contemporary practice of encouraging the young to dwell upon any early misfortunes . . . and to use these as explanations of, if not as excuses for, their own subsequent deficiencies. To the young, particularly, it should be the future not the past that counts. [We should] encourage children from the earliest possible age, however wretched their backgrounds, to believe that they are, or at least soon will be, masters of their fate.'
>
> (Wootton 1967: 51)

And so she went straight back to her undergraduate course in classics, 'to translating English poetry into the metres of ancient Greece and Rome', a pursuit which she had come to loathe as futile and irrelevant. She had no taste for extending her knowledge of dead civilizations while the only living civilization that she knew was crashing about her ears. In the event, a violent attack of tonsillitis put paid to her degree examination though she qualified for an aegrotat.

However, one valuable accomplishment did derive from early training in Greek and Latin. It taught her fastidiousness in the use of the English language and shaped a prose style which is plain, clear, elegant, and sometimes reminiscent of the wit and savagery of Hazlitt. A characteristic example appears in *Social Science and Social Pathology* (1959: 273) in the course of a critical examination of the silly and arrogant language then used by social workers. She quotes from a standard text an account of the claimed ability of social workers

> 'to understand the person in need, not only at that particular moment in time, but also the pattern of personality, the major experiences and relationships which make him the person he now is: with conflicts of whose origin he may be unaware; with problems whose solution may lie less in external circumstances than in his own attitudes; with tensions, faulty relationships, inabilities to face reality, heightened into forms which he cannot alter without help. . . . [The social worker] must enter into his problems as he sees them, his relationships as he experiences them . . . and see him, or his different selves, as they appear to him himself. Yet, at the same time she must also be clearly aware of the realities of the situation and through her professional skill in relationships enable him to come to a better understanding of himself and others.'

'It might well be thought', was Barbara Wootton's demure comment, 'that the social worker's best, indeed perhaps her only, chance of achieving aims at once so intimate and so ambitious would be to marry her client.'

Barbara Wootton sets exacting standards of communication for her fellow social scientists. In all disciplines the essential requisites of effective communication are precision and intelligibility. On both counts much of the modern literature of the social sciences achieves a very low score. Too many of the practitioners belong to the class of writers who, as Virginia Woolf once remarked, hold their pens in brass fingers.

In autumn, 1918 she began to read economics at Girton. She had introduced herself to the subject by acquiring the works of Alfred Marshall, in her enthusiasm even going to the length of carefully annotating every line of his *Principles of Economics*. She says that she worked extremely hard and with a zest that she had never known before. The result was a

First with a special mark of Distinction. This had never been awarded before and was never again conferred on a candidate because the recently introduced regulations under which she sat were changed some years later. At this point in her career, Barbara Wootton experienced her first taste of rejection on the ground of her sex. Despite the mark of Distinction, she was not, as a woman, entitled to write the letters BA after her name, as were all the men on the list under her. After a short while on a research scholarship at the London School of Economics, she became a fellow of Girton and Director of Studies in Economics. Her lectures there were so successful that she was invited by the Economics Board of Studies to give a course of lectures for the whole university on the economic functions of the state. Again, being the wrong sex turned out to be a drawback. A woman could not be a member of the university. Nevertheless, the General Board of Studies, responsible for publishing the official list of lecturers, could not prevent the economists from inviting a woman, although it could not stomach her name appearing on its list of lecturers. The economists overcame this obstacle by a gesture of kindly and gallant intent though really of such unfeeling arrogance that Lady Wootton resents it to this day. The *Cambridge Reporter* announced that Mr Hubert Henderson would discourse on the economic functions of the state but his name carried an asterisk with a footnote which read 'The lectures will be given by Mrs Wootton'.

In 1922, in search of real life, she left Cambridge to become a research officer in the Trades Union Congress (TUC) and Labour Party Joint Research Department. But she did continue to teach part-time at Westfield College and at Bedford College as well as in adult education to which she had become committed whilst a don at Girton (Wootton 1967: 63). After four years, she became aware of limitations in the real life of the Joint Research Department, though she remained 'absolutely whole-hearted in my devotion to the Labour Movement and my adherence to socialism', a position from which she has never deviated. So she moved on to the principalship of Morley College for Working Men and Women. She stayed there for less than two years, then accepted the offer of a newly established post as Director of Studies for Tutorial Classes in the University of London. This offered a number of attractions; for one thing, unlike Morley College, the university did not discriminate against women either by paying them less or by imposing a marriage ban on them.

The London Society for the Extension of University Teaching was a voluntary body which went back to 1876, when H. H. Asquith and F. W. Maitland were among the seven teachers of the first classes to be launched. A generation later, in 1903, the Workers' Educational Association (WEA) was founded by a group of trade unionists and co-operators to articulate the educational aspirations of labour. At that time university extension lectures in London, often with a vocational content and followed by a written examination, were enrolling more than 15,000 students a year in fifty-nine centres. By contrast, the aims of the WEA were to give its student members access to democratically organized liberal, not vocational, education to the end that, by the acquisition of knowledge and training of the mind, they might deploy more effectively such political and economic power as they had been able to grasp. By the inter-war years, the University of London had become the leading university in the provision of adult education.

In the first phase of the Association's development, the subjects studied were chiefly economics and economic history though the range widened later. The central medium of teaching was, and remained, the university tutorial class which comprised not more than thirty students, meeting regularly for twenty-four weeks for each of three years under a tutor appointed by a university. The tutor was paid by the university and a high proportion of the fee was reimbursed by the Board of Education under arrangements devised by Sir Robert Morant in the early years of this century. Students were required to undertake a course of reading prescribed by the tutor and to write fortnightly essays. Classes met every week for two hours: the tutor gave a lecture which was followed by a sustained period of questions and discussion. Such classes could be testing for tutor and students alike. During his time as staff tutor in London from 1922 to 1925, G. D. H. Cole created the advanced tutorial class, which continued for a fourth year and often involved work at a very high level.

In 1928, at the beginning of Barbara Wootton's service with the Extra-Mural Department of the university, two committees were established under an Extension and Tutorial Classes Council, the one to oversee extension work, the other to be responsible for tutorial classes. Thus, the two sides of the university's provision for adult education were institutionalized. As Director of Studies for Tutorial Classes she was, in effect, the academic head of the tutorial classes side of the work which extended also to running Saturday and summer schools. As many of the classes had been gathered together by the WEA, the director had to work closely and sympathetically with that body. The director was also required to teach a number of classes herself. In the 1920s and 1930s, members of university staffs, particularly left-wing social scientists, were often drawn to become tutors of tutorial classes. These gave teachers of the social sciences the best possible training in their craft together with a powerful incentive to master it. If the teacher could not hold the interest of his or her class, its members melted away by the third meeting when the register was made up, and with them went the fee. Such classes were exercises for tutors in presenting relevant ideas and information. It has to be said, too, that the fees paid to tutors were substantial and attractive to part-timers. Even today, no single step would do more to improve the quality of teaching within university departments of the social sciences than to impose upon their members, whenever possible, a compulsory requirement to take adult classes.

Barbara Wootton remained Director of Studies for Tutorial Classes for seventeen years, a longer period than she spent in any other post. She enjoyed the work, and was highly respected as Director by the WEA and the university. When she resigned, the University Extension and Tutorial Classes Council paid tribute to 'her high academic standards, her wide intellectual sympathies, her administrative skill and her keen interest in adult education' (Burrows 1976: 86). Her influence remained after her departure. In 1943, she wrote a paper for the university based on her experience. Many of her assessments and recommendations were debated during the next thirty years. She emphasized that 'we should unremittingly insist on work which makes considerable demands on the student'; any reduction in these demands would 'debase our intellectual currency and imperil the standards of the future'. She approved the idea of hybrid appointments combining internal and extra-mural teaching and she complained of the lack of suitable accommodation for adult classes (Burrows 1976: 89–90).

But there is more to Barbara Wootton's career in adult education than these sober and unexceptionable recommendations. In 1934 she married one of her students. At the time, George Wright was driving a cab for his living though he had just been awarded a full-time scholarship at the London School of Economics. After the war, he was on the headquarters staff of the Labour Party, he had a responsibility for trade union education and became an alderman of the London County Council before his early death from cancer. He was a man of political affairs, and Beatrice Webb's usual perception failed her when she wrote to the bride about a wedding present and sent her congratulations on taking 'a partner in research'.

For many working-class people like George Wright, seeking to make a reality of democracy, the adult class offered the only means of acquiring the education and knowledge without which the power to change society could not be extracted from the electoral system in central or local government. For such folk, the tutorial class was a finishing school where they learnt to apply their minds chiefly to economics, widely interpreted, and to the economic and social history of the industrial revolution. It was for such audiences that leading historians such as the Webbs, the Hammonds, R. H. Tawney, G. D. H. Cole, H. L. Beales, and Henry Hamilton wrote and often taught. Between the wars there was a tutorial class interpretation of economic history just as there had been a Whig interpretation of political history. Thirty years ago Professor F. A. von Hayek saw this as one of the steps on the road to serfdom. He pointed to 'one supreme myth which more than any other has served to discredit the economic system to which we owe our present-day civilization . . . it is the legend of the deterioration of the position of the working classes in consequence of the rise of "capitalism".' Such teaching lay at the heart of what Professor von Hayek described as 'a socialist interpretation of history which has governed political thinking for the last two or three generations' and which he blamed for 'the widespread emotional aversion to "capitalism"' (Hayek 1954: 5–10).

It is not fanciful to attribute a significant political influence to those then engaged in adult education, particularly in teaching tutorial classes. In the years before the Second World War, they helped to give the Labour Party historical letters of credit, a framework for its programme of social reform, and faith in future possibilities of social amelioration. The social development of industrialism came to be thought of as an evolution towards a welfare society. In schools and universities the 'socialist interpretation of economic history' which troubled von Hayek went almost unchallenged. A good deal of it, and of the economics which went with it, passed into the education of citizen soldiers during the Second World War. One of Barbara Wootton's staff tutors in London in the 1930s, W. E. (later Sir William) Williams, became head of the Army Bureau of Current Affairs which adopted the procedures and outlook of adult education. In the history and content of that form of education lies more than a small part of the explanation of the landslide Labour victory of 1945.

Barbara Wootton began to publish books in the early 1930s. Her first was a collection of short stories, *Twos and Threes* (1933), followed in 1936 by a novel, *London's Burning*. These are not successful as fiction. The style is stiff and uneasy and the language stilted, in marked contrast with the relaxed flow of prose in the scholarly books. The first of these, *Plan or No Plan*, came out in 1934; ten more followed, the last in 1978 when she was 81. She also produced *In a World I Never Made* in 1967, part autobiography and part sociological reflections on the worlds in which she had moved.

In 1944 she transferred from extra-mural work to a readership at Bedford College which carried the headship of the Department of Economics, Sociology, and Social Studies. The personal title of Professor of Social Studies was conferred on her four years later. She led a remarkably friendly and hard-working department which did very well by its students. Indeed, this member cannot remember hearing cross words or experiencing abrasive relations, though working in it turned out to be a commitment to engage in unending argument. Unhappily, relations between the department and most of the rest of the college were very sour and strained. The immediate cause of trouble was the acceptance by the University Grants Committee of the recommendations made in 1946 by the Committee on the Provision for Social and Economic Research, under the chairmanship of the economic historian J. H. Clapham, that earmarked grants should be made available for expanding research in the social sciences. Professor Wootton regarded development of empirical social research as a top priority for her department and always spoke of field research as being to the social sciences what a laboratory is to a department engaged in one of the natural sciences. She therefore used her department's 'Clapham money' to set up a research unit under the direction of Mrs, later Professor, Margot Jefferys with the intention of embarking on a series of inquiries. But the sociologists reckoned without the obscurantism and spite of heads of other departments with seats on the College Academic Board. Led by Professor, later Dame, Lillian Penson, a group of them insisted that earmarked grants offended against the principles of university autonomy and academic freedom, and the research unit had to be disbanded because the college refused to accept the grant which had been allocated to the department. This episode came as a great shock to Professor Wootton and was a main factor in precipitating her resignation as head of the department in 1952. She attributed the attitude of her academic colleagues to 'a compound of hostility, jealousy and ignorance – in what proportion I should not like to say' (Wootton 1967: 103). To these qualities she could have added the intellectual obtuseness and natural intolerance of those chiefly involved. Part of the hostility stemmed from the contempt in which sociology was held by many teachers of traditional disciplines throughout universities in Britain at that time. In fact, the subject existed in no more than a handful of places and the characterization 'sociologist' was widely regarded as a synonym for socialist or as a description of a person who habitually addressed mixed audiences on the subject of sex. Whatever the explanation of the treatment of the department by Bedford College, it must be said that nothing changed after her resignation or under her successors.

Thus it was that Barbara Wootton applied for a five-year research fellowship which the Nuffield Foundation had created for an assessment of the fruitfulness of social research. Bedford College provided accommodation but that was all; when the fellowship was over, she was 60 and she retired. Shortly afterwards, the findings of the research were published in her seminal *Social Science and Social Pathology*.

Barbara Wootton has never felt easy within the walls of universities. She admitted that 'although I have spent nearly all my professional life in academic circles of one sort or another it is not a world to which I have ever really felt that I belonged' (Wootton 1967: 195). Whether the explanation lies in her early experiences in Cambridge or in her method of work is hard to say. Certainly she is an iconoclast. She has rarely in her academic pursuits worked closely with anyone other than a research assistant and her writing and research have owed little to the influence or practices of conventional scholarship. But if she has never felt that she belongs to the world of the universities, that world certainly feels that she belongs to it. She has received more than a dozen honorary degrees including degrees from Cambridge, where she was trained, and from London where she taught.

We must now turn from the bare bones of Barbara Wootton's academic career to examine what she sought to achieve in research and writing, although it is not a purpose of this introductory chapter to discuss her substantive contributions to the fields of study which she cultivated as a social scientist. That task falls to the other contributors to this volume. Barbara Wootton never held a post which had 'social scientist' in the title. When the University of London established a chair for her, it was intended that her title should be Professor of Sociology. She refused this because she had no patience with the theoretical sociology taught to undergraduates in London. When the present writer joined her department in 1947, he was told 'you will have to teach the rubbish for the degree'. She could not take Social Science as a title because that was generally used to describe those who trained social workers, so she had to fall back on Social Studies. 'What I now like to call myself', she wrote after she had retired, 'is a "social scientist", by which I mean one who is concerned with the application of scientific method to the problems of human society' (Wootton 1967: 210). Nevertheless, Lady Wootton thinks that social studies necessarily and properly

'have a strong practical bias. The student in this field who is motivated by pure intellectual curiosity is himself something of a curiosity and indeed also something of a luxury. Generally speaking, the justification of social research is simply and solely that, by enlarging our knowledge, we shall become able to make social improvements.'

(Wootton 1967: 204)

On this view, it is desirable to maintain some balance between the amount of research and its application to actual situations. 'Sometimes it is difficult not to suspect', she suggests, 'that research itself can become a mechanism of escape, and that, ill-equipped though my generation was, there may have been something wholesome in our impatience to exchange learning for doing' (Wootton 1967: 205).

She has no exaggerated view of the present possibilities of a social science but sees future growth in the application of scientific method to social questions.

'The level of probability obtainable in the human sciences is necessarily lower than that to which the chemist or physicist can aspire; but that is a distinction not of kind but of degree. Specialisation notwithstanding, those who use the same tools and the same categories of thought and who speak the same language fundamentally understand and respect one another. That this mutual understanding should now extend not only to the physicists, the chemists and the biologists, but even to those who, like the economists and sociologists, hover on the fringes of scientific respectability, is indeed encouraging; but best of all is the dawning recognition that all are engaged in different aspects of a common enterprise.'   (Wootton 1967: 213)

She is a thoroughgoing utilitarian who emphasizes the necessity of disentangling questions of value from questions of fact. She gives as an example of her approach the question of whether sparing the rod will spoil the child.

'In order to answer the question whether sparing the rod spoils the child one must know what sort of child it is desired to produce, as well as what are the effects of using, or not using, the rod. If the ideal child is the one who is polite, respectful to his teachers, industrious and obedient . . . then some judicious beating might not come amiss; but if a higher value is set on adventurousness, leadership and initiative, sparing the rod might be more effective than using it. But, be that as it may, scientific enquiry can only throw light on the effects of beating or not beating; it cannot define what constitutes spoiling.'

(Wootton 1960)

Lady Wootton insists that the creation of a scientific attitude to social questions and, in particular, the acceptance of such an attitude by the general public will at the end of the day depend on the ability of social scientists to deliver the goods. During her working life, social science goods have been few in number and the delivery very erratic, certainly too erratic for the public to confer a degree of respect upon social scientists comparable to that paid to their colleagues in laboratories. In her view, the first condition on which the delivery of goods depends is to ask the right questions. First, social scientists must ask answerable questions. They must exclude the permanently unanswerable questions which relate to all basic moral, aesthetic, and theological valuations. These are not areas in which discussion can be grounded on evidence that can be tested. Second, the answerable questions must be sensibly selected; for this purpose, 'sensible' means most importantly that the questions chosen must have answers which are directly or indirectly of some practical social importance. Given the limited resources available at this stage in their development, the social sciences cannot afford much in the way of pure, as distinct from applied, work. Third, social scientists must choose manageable topics of inquiry. This means that they must not ask questions which are too large or attempt to generalize about fields that are too heterogeneous. It is not a manageable question, for example, to ask 'What are the causes of crime?' All that can result from such a question is that, as knowledge increases, delinquents appear to become more and more like other people.

> 'What we have overlooked is the fact that delinquents are much too heterogeneous a collection of people for any striking generalisations to be made as to the difference between them and the rest of us. Their one distinguishing feature is that they are known to have broken the law; but, since very many of us have at some time or another broken some law or other, even this hardly amounts to a noteworthy peculiarity. If we are to arrive at useful generalisations, we must concentrate attention, not upon delinquents in general, but upon much smaller and more homogeneous groups of offenders who commit the same kinds of crimes in the same kinds of circumstances or with the same degree of frequency.' (Wootton 1960)

Moreover, Lady Wootton insists that a manageable inquiry is one which does not tackle tasks that are too difficult. She thinks that too many social investigators are strongly tempted to run before they can walk. Causation is the most difficult field of inquiry and the task is nearly always beyond the powers of the investigator. It is not only that the causes of the simplest social phenomenon are always extraordinarily complex but also that the social scientist is expected to produce answers at a much deeper level than those which will serve for ordinary purposes. For example, she argues, in daily life

> 'if you ask why a particular house was broken into on a particular day, it may be a sufficient answer to say that a young man of criminal habits happened to be passing, and that this particular house looked an easy one to break into and out of without being detected. This is generally enough.' (Wootton 1960)

But the social scientist has to go on to explain why this particular young man does not share the inhibitions about stealing or breaking into other people's houses which prevent many of us from behaving likewise. That attempt will take him 'to deeper and deeper levels; and at these levels he is all too apt to drown'.

If we are frank with ourselves, she urges, we have to admit that nearly all the generalizations

> 'that have been made as to the causes of social phenomena are either so superficial and obvious as not to be worth making ("people steal because they are short of money") or have to be qualified to a degree which virtually deprives them of all content ("people steal because they have not been loved in infancy").'   (Wootton 1960)

However, inability to explain why things happen does not preclude the possibility of predicting sometimes what will happen. Prediction techniques have been useful in connection with the treatment of offenders, in fields of vocational and personnel selection, and in many other areas. Lady Wootton regards prediction as the most successful achievement of the social sciences, and the one on which they should now concentrate.

To ask answerable questions is one thing, to decide which questions to ask is another. Barbara Wootton's questions have been directed to a wide variety of subject matters which fall within several academic disciplines. These include economics, sociology, social administration, criminology and penology, and social philosophy. Her work and activities in the real world and her intellectual pursuits have always been functionally related. The origins of all her major writing have lain outside her study or the library. Her first academic book, *Plan or No Plan* (1934), stemmed from a visit to the Soviet Union which in turn led to her discussion of *Freedom under Planning* (1945). Her experience as an arbitrator on the Civil Service Arbitration Tribunal led to *The Social Foundations of Wage Policy* (1955) and her subsequent book on *Incomes Policy; an Inquest and a Proposal* (1974). She also sat as a lay magistrate for nearly half a century and for some sixteen years as a Chairman of Juvenile Courts in London. During that period of service, 'I reckon on a rough calculation . . . that I must have heard about 10,000 cases of juveniles and rather less than half that number' of adults (Wootton 1978: 16). These many instances of the administration of criminal justice raised

> 'questions which forced themselves upon my attention as a magistrate . . . which first set me thinking about what is really known about the subject of criminality, its nature, its causes and the ways in which it can best be handled; while on the other hand eight years experience as Head of a University Department training students for social work provoked

much reflection both about socially unacceptable behaviour in general, and about the changing attitudes of the community towards "deviants" who indulge in this.'   (Wootton 1959: 7)

One result was her major work on *Social Science and Social Pathology* (1959); other contributions to this field of study were her Hamlyn Lectures on *Crime and the Criminal Law* (1963) and her last book, *Crime and Penal Policy* (1978).

Serving as a magistrate made up only one part of a long career of public service which has given rich experience and pervasive realism to her research and writing. She has been a member of four Royal Commissions, on Workmen's Compensation (appointed in 1938), on the Press (in 1947), on the Civil Service (in 1954), and on the Penal System (in 1964); and of four Departmental Committees, the first of these being the Colwyn Committee of 1924 on National Debt and Taxation, for which she wrote every word of the Minority Report (Wootton 1967: 65). The others were on Shop Hours (appointed in 1946), on the Business of the Criminal Courts (in 1958), and on Criminal Statistics (in 1963). She has also been a member of the Council on Tribunals, of the Home Office Penal Advisory Council, of the Advisory Committee on Drug Dependence, and was Chairman of its Hallucinogens Sub-Committee which produced a much publicized report on cannabis in 1968, and the Advisory Council on the Misuse of Drugs. She sat on the University Grants Committee, was a governor of the BBC, a member of the National Parks Committee, and the first Chairman of the Countryside Commission. No wonder, then, that she was one of the four women who were among the first life peers to be created in 1958 under the Life Peerages Act, or that she was the first woman peer to sit on the Woolsack as a Deputy Speaker, or that she became a Companion of Honour in 1977. Had she done nothing else, her record of public work alone would have been a formidable achievement. She once remarked that the main committee room in the Home Office was the cell in which she had served a life sentence.

The 'beginning of the end of my career as an economist' was marked by the publication of *Lament for Economics* in 1938, written as a counterblast to the narrow view of Lionel Robbins on *The Nature and Significance of Economic Science*. Barbara Wootton's indictment was framed with the intention of demonstrating that the subject would have to be revolutionized if it were ever to become useful. She did 'not believe that the study of economics should be undertaken in a spirit of indifference to its practical utility as a means of improving the conditions of human life' (Wootton 1938: 16). She proposed a new foundation of inquiries which would liberate economists from the restrictions imposed by the analysis of market processes and extend their inquiries to 'the problems of achieving an optimum distribution of scarce means in any given situation – it being understood that this problem includes that of formulating and evaluating the ends to be pursued, as well as exploring the possible methods of achieving these ends, when known. In short, this is the question that we now face: to what field other than the continued elaboration of economic theory ought the student who is interested in social affairs to direct his energies?'   (Wootton 1938: 267)

The field to which such a student was advised to direct his energies was very broad. Economists should develop the regular habit of testing their theories against empirical data and become involved in demographic and sociological studies of existing social situations and trends. Research ought to be promoted 'into the nature of social ends in modern communities and the means by which these may best be formulated'. Once the social ends have been determined, it is desirable to assess the possibilities and to define the means of achieving them. Well might Barbara Wootton concede that 'the fertility and value of economic studies', so conceived, 'depends upon a ruthless disregard of present boundaries and definitions' (Wootton 1938: 261) to enable the disillusioned economist to move into territory colonized by the other social sciences. And that is exactly what she did herself. She has never confined herself to particular subject areas though she thinks that the social scientist will

'one day learn to respect boundaries and to restrict himself to a particular discipline such as sociology, social psychology, anthropology. . . . That time, however, is not yet. For the application to social problems of such basic scientific tools an exact observation and empirical testing of hypotheses is still so new, and so little understood or appreciated, that there remains much to be done by those whose primary concern is with the method itself.'   (Wootton 1967: 210)

The Social Foundations of Wage Policy (1955) illustrates impressively how the recommendations of *Lament for Economics* could be implemented in practice, and how the traditional theory of wages of the conventional economists could be tested against an empirical and sociological inquiry into the influences which affect the determination of wages and salaries. It is a safe prediction that the last has not yet been heard of a thirty-year-old book which helped to put incomes policy on the agenda of social and economic discussion long before events forced it into political controversy.

Thus, the earlier discontent with the narrowness and irrelevance of theoretical economics was reinforced by a later but rapidly widening knowledge and experience of policy-making in the real world. In this way, the pre-war economist became the post-war social scientist who shifted the discussion of every major social problem which she tackled to a new plane. Nevertheless, the great social scientists whose work rises above the limitations of time and place need more than intellect if they are to persuade their fellow citizens to change established attitudes to social problems and their solutions. They need the imagination to sense the directions of change. They need, too, that rarest of qualities, an instinct for the future. Social imagination and a feeling for the future Barbara Wootton carries in her bones.

There has to be as well a fire at the centre. With her it has been the making of social improvements in order to reduce or eliminate artificial and dehumanizing inequalities. She has been driven in all her work by a passion for equality by which she means equal respect for every human personality – her definition of democratic socialism, to which she has always remained faithful. Throughout the world in her lifetime, she watched 'the great dilemma – the inescapable choice between the inefficiency of the old order and the human suffering involved in the revolutionary measures by which alone the new order could be established. For me the price of that suffering is too heavy to be paid' (Wootton 1967: 184). A revolutionary in ideas, she has remained a democrat in politics.

She ends her autobiography by challenging the conventional wisdom that holds politics to be the art of the possible.

> 'In half a century of public and professional life I have not found it so. The limits of the possible constantly shift, and those who ignore them are apt to win in the end. Again and again I have had the satisfaction of seeing the laughable idealism of one generation evolve into the accepted commonplace of the next. But it is from the champions of the impossible rather than the slaves of the possible that that evolution draws its creative force.'   (Wootton 1967: 279)

Among British social scientists in this century, Barbara Wootton has been the most doughty and successful champion of the impossible.

REFERENCES

Burrows, J. H. (1976) *University Adult Education in London. A Century of Achievement.* London: University of London.

Hayek, F. A. von (1954) *Capitalism and the Historians.* London: Routledge & Kegan Paul.

Wootton, Barbara (1938) *Lament for Economics.* London: Allen & Unwin.

—— (1959) *Social Science and Social Pathology.* London: Allen & Unwin.

—— (1960) Unpublished. Lady Wootton delivered two lectures in the series of Charles Beard Memorial Lectures at Ruskin College, Oxford.

They were not published in the form in which they were delivered, though the substance was distilled into Wootton, Barbara (1962) *The Future of the Social Sciences*. Canberra: Australian National University. The quotations from the unpublished lectures have been made with the author's permission.

—— (1963) *Crime and the Criminal Law*. London: Stevens.

—— (1967) *In a World I Never Made*. London: Allen & Unwin.

—— (1978) *Crime and Penal Policy*. London: Allen & Unwin.

PART ONE

ECONOMICS AND
SOCIAL POLICY

2
SOCIAL PLANNING: IDEOLOGY AND INSTRUMENTS
Peter Townsend

Planning must be said to be the central unresolved problem of the management of British society in the 1980s no less than in the 1970s. Philosophically and ideologically it is something which Mrs Thatcher and her ministers have consistently rejected, albeit with faint reservations on the part of ministers like Peter Walker. Hayek inveighed against planning as totalitarianism in *The Road to Serfdom* (1944), and this appears to have been imprinted on the government's collective political consciousness. In practice too, Mrs Thatcher's ministers have done their best to abort, suppress, and weaken the merest expressions of planning. It would be possible to cite in illustration the presentation of the public expenditure White Papers, also the Green Paper (Cmnd 9319), the reorganization of local government, the cuts in statistical information and research services, the monitoring of the annual deployment of money and staff in the National Health Service, the review in 1985 of social security, and many more.

Governments should not *plan*, Mrs Thatcher's ministers believe. Planning uses public-sector resources and these must in principle be cut. Planning brings anti-market and anti-Conservative values to the surface. Planning necessarily involves a larger and larger role for government. Planning necessarily reduces the power of businesses and corporations. On the other hand, these ministerial beliefs have embarrassing and unsustainable implications for administration. They represent the politics of ignorance and irrationality. The significance of economic and social trends, the social and political effects of government measures, the lessons that may be drawn from comparing British experience with experience elsewhere in the world, and the implications of discoveries of the social sciences, are cavalierly ignored or undervalued. Petty prejudice and philistinism rule even when they masquerade as a philosophy of anti-egalitarianism, as in the work of Sir Keith Joseph (Joseph and Sumption, 1979).

The problem is not much better understood within the Labour movement. Planning has never been perceived as the antithesis of the market and therefore no proper consideration has ever been given to its implications for state institutions or a comprehensive set of state policies. Planning is the limited conception of isolated strategies and programmes to deal with different problems, whether town and country planning, the extension of the motorway network, better allocation of resources to hospitals, and so on. The possibility of restructuring society through different stages of a strategic programme has not been taken seriously. Partly this is a failure of the analysis of power. The election of a Labour government may be a necessary but certainly is not a sufficient step in achieving a transformation of society. The problems of handling a run on sterling and resisting the international money market, reconciling social aspirations with industrial as well as economic realities, and re-educating public opinion in favour of unselfish as opposed to selfish or acquisitive values are only three of the immense problems of the consolidation of a government committed to socialism.

Socialists in Britain are deeply ambivalent. They are of course aware of central state planning in parts of the East European block (see, for example, Ellman 1979). But consciousness of the various forms of that planning is hazy, and unfavourable opinions are fostered by the western media. People are deterred by examples of oppressive state bureaucracy, restricted ranges of goods in the shops, excessive uniformity of standards of housing, dress, and everything else, and the intolerance shown towards dissidents. These negative impressions of socialist states have also been deepened by knowledge of the misplaced enthusiasm of past supporters of state socialism and by the disappointed expectations of those who hoped for too much too quickly. The Webbs are an embarrassing case in point. They believed that Stalin's Russia represented the dawn of a new civilization.

So the possibility in Britain of the development of an alternative form of planning under democratic socialism has gained little momentum. It gains neither from constructive, detailed criticism of communist and state socialist models of planning, nor from the robust exchanges of an internal dynamic. State management of industry and public services has been conceived from the start in a fragmented way: the public and private sectors have not been brought under comparative systematic scrutiny by government institutions and that is why they have not been co-ordinated. Nationalized industries have been encouraged to emulate their private-sector equivalents and the criteria of their success which have been adopted are the competitive criteria of the market. The same might be said of other Labour ventures inside and outside industry. An obvious example is comprehensive schooling. Even now few socialists insist on measuring the success of comprehensive schools in terms of the principles of comprehensive schooling. The rest lamely allow competitive A level measures to prevail.

Early in this essay I am, therefore, presenting two arguments designed to establish the theme of this chapter. British government badly needs a fully-fledged ideology, and not merely the mechanisms, of social planning. And democratic socialism needs it even more.

BARBARA WOOTTON'S WORK ON PLANNING

How can the idea of 'planning' take better root in British democracy? I have been interested in conceptions and methods of social planning all my adult working life. My first job in the early 1950s was with a research organization called Political and Economic Planning (which is now embodied in the Policy Studies Institute) and my first task there was to review the success of the implementation of the Beveridge Plan. (The consequent published research paper was entitled *Poverty: Ten Years after Beveridge*). The paradoxes of planning in Britain have remained with me and a fair amount of my written work has attacked general as well as specialized themes related to planning (for example, Townsend 1972, 1975, 1980). Strangely, as in retrospect it seems, I first met Barbara Wootton in the offices of Political and Economic Planning in 1953, when the Nuffield Foundation was financing her to undertake a massive review of the social sciences. In 1959 this review was published as *Social Science and Social Pathology*. It was the first of her books which I read properly from cover to cover. I came to her work on planning only recently (though in the early 1960s I read *The Social Foundation of Wage Policy* (1955), which is a superb example of the application of the principles of planning to a chaotic set of human practices). As she explains in her autobiography, her academic research and writing largely arose as a by-product of outside interests. Her observations on state planning in the Soviet Union, *Plan or No Plan*, were published in 1934, slightly before the huge report on Soviet Communism by Sidney and Beatrice Webb in 1935, and have stood the test of time better. From the writing of that book, and for the next forty years, planning became a major and a more conscious theme in her work. Thus, the subject occupies a significant part of her short and succinct book *Contemporary Britain* (1971). Again, planning may be said to be the organizing principle of her beautifully composed and original book, *Incomes Policy: An Inquest and a Proposal* (1974), as well as of *The Social*

Foundation of Wage Policy (1955). Most of all the theme of planning pervades her treatment of social-science method and the ideology of democratic socialism. And it is for her work on these two that we are most indebted to her. Her views on methodology are largely represented in *Testament for Social Science* (1950) and punctiliously illustrated and applied in *Social Science and Social Pathology*. These books will be familiar to many social scientists. Less familiar will be her book *Freedom under Planning* (1945), written in anger after she had seen Hayek's manuscript of *The Road to Serfdom*. I found her book a revelation. It is acutely pertinent to the controversies and conditions of the 1980s. In taking Hayek apart intellectually the book provides contemporary ammunition for the discussion of the influences of the new right. What I find invaluable is her insistence on the conjunction of freedom and planning and her emphasis, all too rare in political, industrial, academic, and professional discussion of 'planning' since the Second World War, on the necessary ideological basis of approaches to that concept.

How then might contemporary ideas of 'social planning' be constructively reviewed, on the basis of Barbara Wootton's ideas and values? In the next pages I will build an argument for a more informed and committed approach to social planning on the part of government, with some illustrations of what might practically be expected to result. Barbara Wootton showed that the ideological arguments of the authoritarian right do not have to be merely confronted but patiently and systematically met and tamed. She showed that anxieties about freedom under planning must not be dismissed but treated seriously and, in so far as they turn out to be justified, solutions found to them. Sometimes the solutions would be necessarily complex. The exercise did not have to be conceived as one of compromise between fundamentally incompatible concepts. In a number of quite basic senses individual and social freedom could be enlarged through more constructive planning. But what had to be recognized was that vested interests were as liable to distort and pervert the different schemes and instruments of planning as they had been to create the problems which planning was conceived in the first place to meet.

It is this thoroughgoing, 'self-critical' methodology, and not just the limitation of the potentialities of the ideas and instruments of planning by the institutions of capital or the state, which seems to me to be important to understand.

THEORETICAL CONTEXT OF PLANNING

There are a number of possible starting-points for analysis. One is to try to explain how the meanings, instruments, and practices of planning in any particular society or set of societies have come to be developed. Any careful exposition of these will help us not only to understand any short-comings in present approaches but to obtain a shrewder appreciation of what might be done to make improvements. I believe that any account of the history of planning must be thought of as a small part of the much larger task of providing a theory of economic and social development. Revealingly, development theories are currently applied by social scientists more readily to poorer societies than to rich societies. Something, however, needs to be said about the theories which have been extremely influential, implicitly more than explicitly, in shaping meanings as well as practices of planning as much as other features of modern rich societies.

Whatever the degree to which social scientists are conscious of the influences upon them, they draw on intellectual frameworks of thought to examine particular issues. There is a much closer relationship between the social sciences and political or state management than is usually allowed. Approaches to theory in the universities and research centres often reflect the values and predispositions of those in the Establishment for a number of different reasons, for example sponsorship of research, patronage, unconscious reproduction of prevailing cultural values, constitutional control of organizations, the nature of personal job contracts, and the socialization of intellectuals within particular educational systems. Scientific and intellectual work can, of course, outstrip or rise above conventional influences. Quite how this happens is of endless fascination. It means that new sets of ideas come to challenge or at least modify the orthodoxies of the day. The extent of their newness is often exaggerated because of the convenience of that liberal value to ruling élites. Thus there is a process of institutionalization of 'new' ideas. They prove less original than they initially appear to be, as they tend to be qualified and narrowed down in the process of being put into practice. They are also used as new cover for old orthodoxies. None the less, social scientists influence the state just as the state greatly influences in general as well as in particular the social sciences. Examples are the influence of *laissez-faire* economists on the construction of the 1834 Poor Law, the influence of J. M. Keynes on the management of the economy and therefore the construction of the post-war Welfare State, and the influence in recent years of monetarists and neo-monetarists in weakening public-sector services, producing greater social inequality and more dependency, and re-establishing the paramountcy of market values.

This is not the place for an extended discussion of the different economic, sociological, political, and philosophical theories which share similar social values and assumptions and help to shore up or, alternatively, question the developing institutions of the state. But it is necessary to illustrate how general social-science theories have inhibited an adequate approach to planning in a democracy such as Britain. There may be said to be three sets of theories which could be invoked to try to account for the particular development of social institutions in Britain. These are liberal-pluralism, Marxian theories, and radical social policy analysis. How they are deployed to explain the emergence and growth of the statutory social services is illustrated in *Table 1*. No doubt each step in the illustration of different theories could be discussed at considerable length. My purpose here is only to convey enough to demonstrate how different they are in ideology, scope, and specialized preoccupations.

Table 1   *Three bodies of theory used to explain social development*

Liberal–pluralism
The public social services
(i) are a by-product of industrialization and economic growth – helping some of the casualties and using surpluses for collective good;
(ii) are temporary measures to help resolve temporary dislocations of the market;
(iii) give conditional help to the poor who cannot earn a living and who are unable to provide privately for themselves;
(iv) help errant individuals and families to mend their ways;
(v) equip citizens with the basic rights and facilities upon which to build by their own private efforts and compete in the market;
(vi) can become an unnecessarily and undeservedly high part of market costs;
(vii) substitute for absent family support.

Marxian theories
The public social services:
(i) are a major instrument of social control;
(ii) incorporate labour into the state;
(iii) create the conditions for the reproduction of labour;
(iv) maintain the non-working population at cheapest cost;
(v) represent gains in living and working conditions wrung out of a reluctant state by united working-class action.

Radical social policy analysis
The public social services:
(i) are the publicly visible part of the real range of social policies which have been institutionalized to structure society;
(ii) are inadequate attempts to meet need;
(iii) compensate for the social costs of 'diswelfare' (brought about by industrial, economic, technological, and social change);
(iv) represent attempts to assert collective over individual interests;
(v) symbolize the pursuit of equality;
(vi) involve the reorganization of private relationships.

Each of the theories has potentiality for different interpretations of the functions of 'planning' (see for example Townsend 1983, 1984; Mishra 1981; Walker 1984) Liberal-pluralism depends on a variety of inputs. For example, monetarist and neo-Keynesian theories contribute to liberal-pluralism. They could be said to correspond with different wings of neo-classical economic theory – one which is orientated towards restoring the hypothetical conditions of a pure market, and one which accepts a continuing, rather than temporary, role for the state in intervening to humanize the market and preserve a suitable balance of the mixed economy, but in the end accepts that the market plays the fundamental creative role in the development of the economy. A great deal remains to be done to establish a truly radical economics in Britain. There are radical economists, whose work has much in common with radical social policy analysis, whether Marxian or non-Marxian, but they are relatively few in number and are not able to exert much influence over current state policies.

In what ways do the limitations of these theories help us to understand the inadequate treatment of social development and social planning? Monetarists argue that the modern economy tends towards equilibrium: that there is a built-in tendency towards stability in prices, employment, and wages. If government and unions allow the market to work, then prices will be stabilized and wage rates will arbitrate the demand for and supply of labour. The supply of and demand for goods will achieve equilibrium at particular prices. Borrowing and lending will be balanced by interest rates. Monetarists are concerned to argue for slow growth in the money supply and for the government to ensure only that businesses can operate unimpeded, and in particular to refrain from exerting any control over the price mechanism. (For a penetrating and up-to-date review, see Desai 1981.)

Any study of such precepts reveals a lot about the social values or prejudices and the implications the theory holds for the structure of society (see also Bosanquet 1983). Liberal-pluralism is deeply or traditionally conservative in holding to the beliefs that social order and stability are produced by monetarism, that social inequality is an inevitable and, moreover, tolerable result of individual freedom, that the market entrepreneur is a figure to be venerated, and that capitalism is a system preferable to any other. Firm belief in the virtues of free-market capitalism has promoted a monetarist ideology which seeks to supplant the ideology which has prevailed for many of the post-war years and is represented by the Welfare State, a measure of egalitarianism, and a self-confident and strong working class. Monetarism is seen as arresting economic decline. Keynesian ideas and values are rejected as a different economic doctrine is believed to be needed. The state's emphasis on the protection of the weak, it is believed, has to give way to the promotion of the strong and productive, if Britain is to become more prosperous. Entrepreneurs have to be freed to obtain greater wealth. The private sector has to be extended and private social services have to be restored or developed at the expense of public services. The state and the unions have to be cut down to size. These interrelated beliefs are bound to have their effect on shaping ideas about the management of society and about planning.

The social criticisms of monetarism which I have stated or implied do not mean that previous economic orthodoxies are immune from criticism. It might be argued that Keynesianism never represented a sufficient or a radical alternative to the classical theories of the nineteenth century. The central Keynesian argument is that it is wrong to suppose that the market tends towards equilibrium. On the contrary, the modern economy is unstable and every government has to intervene to manage levels of demand by means of taxation and public expenditure policies. Keynes proposed an economic arrangement (spending to increase demand) which reconciled political democracy with the economic market-place. However, to argue that the state should only intervene to regulate and control some of the worst excesses of a predetermined and largely independent 'market' implies a very limited, if not negative, approach to social development and planning. Thus the emphasis is on reducing unemployment and not on defining and constructing employment. It is on taxation to mitigate an inequitable wage system and not on defining and controlling that wage system in the first place. It is on providing incentives to invest in the social interest rather than on taking social control over resources available for investment.

Such theories have to be considered to understand how ideas about social development and planning originate and take a particular form. Our capacity as a nation to plan for social development has been greatly restricted by the different theories making up what I have called 'liberal-pluralism'.

SOCIAL POLICY AND PLANNING:
REALITY AND POTENTIALITY

The effects on social policy and social planning may now be examined. During the twentieth century a broad definition of social policy, and therefore a broad understanding of the scope of state action to control social development, have never become established. Discussion of social health, social objectives, and social relationships has been subordinated to the management of the economy and in large measure has been left to institutions external or peripheral to the state. Some problems are felt to be properly within the province of church, the family, or charities. Thus debates about the Welfare State are generally restricted to the five principal public social services – education, housing, social security, health, and welfare (or, in today's idiom, the 'personal social services'). In much economic theory, social development and particularly the management of the public social services are perceived as auxiliary or secondary to the management of the economy and of the state. Some social services received by the rich (such as employer-subsidized pensions, housing, and welfare, or education subsidized through charitable trusts) are not recognized as such. The social assumptions as well as the social effects of the management of the economy are rarely discussed in any detail. This has led to the perception of social services as casualty rather than preventive services, or as giving 'support' to a social structure determined elsewhere. The functions of economic, state, and professional institutions in creating and changing social relationships are poorly recognized and rarely discussed.

These short-comings can be illustrated by attempting to provide a comprehensive or ideal definition. There have been moves in recent years to encourage a broader conceptualization of social policy. The principal feature has been an attempt to escape narrow nationalism, parochialism, and historicism. I do not say escape can be final, but the attempt can help us better to understand present activities as well as to make them more interesting. The attempts help to put the management of society into some cross-national and historical perspective. If *all* societies have social policies, then we will be ready to accept that some produce certain effects better than others, and that they can weaken as well as strengthen, and dismember as well as unite. There can be retrogression as well as progression. I grew up in a scholastic world in which each new piece of legislation was regarded as enlarging human welfare. This was during a period when the edicts of liberal-pluralism were even more influential than they are now. There was a basic assumption within liberal-pluralism that the Welfare State would be created and consolidated. However, once any piece of legislation is examined to find whether it may 'diminish' human welfare this introduces a radically different conception of social policy. A search for external criteria or standards by which to judge events has to be set in train.

An effort has to be made, therefore, not just to ventilate criticisms of existing ideas about social policy but to express the alternative standpoint or standards from which such criticisms can respectably be made. The study of social policy may therefore be said to include the study of the *goals* a society has chosen to pursue; the *values* a society has chosen to uphold; the *means* a society has chosen to employ; the *needs* a society has chosen to recognize; the *definitions* and *measurement* of problems which society has chosen to purvey. There is an elaborate conjunction of goals, values, perceptions, and means, rooted in organizations, agencies, services, laws, regulations, professions, unions, methods of training, recruitment, accreditation, and the communication of information and values – in short what might be called the policy system. There may be *other* goals which society's condition suggests should be pursued, or which are pursued in other societies. There may be other means, other needs, other definitions, other measures. If social policy is properly regarded as what is, then social planning can be regarded as what might be.

Social policy is the institutionalized management of services, agencies, and organizations to maintain or change social structure and values. In this sense all societies have social policies. Such policies arise subjectively, collectively, and culturally, and are therefore proper objects of study. Policy analysis is the task of unravelling and evaluating the policy of a society, or, more correctly, the policies of different social groups and agencies, with government and industry being the predominant agencies in advanced industrial societies. Planning, by contradistinction, may be said to be that system of thought, preparation, and organization which maintains or changes existing, institutionalized, policies. If planning is conceived as the search for alternative policies, it is not just the more efficient or cost-effective way of managing policy, nor just the application of scientific method to policy making. It is the definition of goals, at best, on the basis of measured needs among (and between) populations and the development of a rational strategy and of appropriate means to fulfil those objectives most quickly. Of course this begs further questions about how to choose goals, measure needs, and define what is rational and what is appropriate. If social policy is interpreted as the rationale for what a nation is doing in pursuing its social objectives, then social planning can be interpreted as action to confirm, review, or change those objectives and methods of pursuing them. Planning is generally, if not always, a process of detachment from the commitments to the present – which can be extraordinarily timid, substantial, or bold.

Planning as practised historically and contemporarily in fact provides some very restricted examples. Social planning in national terms has been predominantly public-expenditure planning. The private sector is left out of account and the problem has been one of attempting to contain the costs to the taxpayer of public services. Even the planning of individual public services, in this limited sense, has not been co-ordinated (see for example Townsend 1980; Walker 1982, 1984 (esp. Chap. 6); and Social Services Committee, House of Commons 1980, 1981, 1982). The nearest precedents I can find for social planning on a relatively comprehensive scale are to be found in the national plan of 1964 (Department of Economic Affairs 1965), the social contract espoused by Harold Wilson when Prime Minister in 1974–75, and the Joint Approach to Social Policy, JASP (Central Policy Review Staff (CPRS) 1975). None of these expressions of national planning went very far. For example, the experimental seventeen-page statement on a *Joint Framework for Social Policies* (CPRS 1975) argued for a 'new and more coherent framework for the making and execution of social policies'. On the positive side the review acknowledged the 'division of welfare'. Thus, 'some problems of poverty are largely conditioned by regional or employment policies'. It called attention to interrelationships between income maintenance programmes and taxation policy. It asked for a study of 'the relationship in the medium term between the level of social security benefits and tax thresholds over a period of continuing inflation' (CPRS 1975: 9). Among other things it proposed regular meetings of ministers (instead of, or as well as, the occasional subcommittee of Cabinet meeting under the chairmanship of Treasury ministers) and improvements in monitoring, for example, the distributional impact of government policies on population sub-groups. However, the proposals were locked into the cautious expectations of government. Thus, 'it does not seem sensible for the moment to try to tackle areas such as the existing distribution of income and wealth' (CPRS 1975: 3), and far from seeking to assign the job of monitoring social conditions at least in part to independent groups outside government, the setting up of a group of senior statisticians in the Central Statistical Office was proposed. The document is valuable for students of social policy because it shows how poorly policy is co-ordinated and how feeble have been the attempts to introduce coherent forms of social planning.

The document can only be understood in relation to the CPRS's role as a minor gadfly within government for less than a decade. Before being abolished by the Thatcher government the CPRS had no executive powers, a wide-ranging brief, but few staff; the unit was designed more to keep the Treasury, the Foreign Office, and other departments on their toes than to promulgate major reforms. Heads of major departments of state have been known to argue in dismissive tones that no attention needed to be paid to this 'superficial' document. A more realistic analysis of power to shape planning would assign considerable power to the Treasury and top civil servants in the major departments, with little *effective* power being wielded by ministers themselves (Blackstone 1983; also Heclo and Wildavsky 1974). The ideology of liberal-pluralism is deeply entrenched in the organization and administration of departments of state and in the values and practices of senior civil servants (Kellner and Crowther-Hunt 1980).

Social planning in Britain therefore has to be recognized as limited. It is limited because it is subordinated or secondary to economic planning or entirely divorced from such planning. Social planning is also restricted in scope, in that co-ordination between departments of state, public and private sectors, central and local government, statutory and voluntary agencies is not given much priority, either scientifically or in terms of commitment, energy, and resources from those in administration. Most planning has taken rather specialized forms. Thus there are long histories of town and country or urban planning, new towns, manpower planning, regional planning, green belts, the environment, university expansion, population prediction, slum clearance programmes, reorganization of schools, and housing schemes. Over the last two decades it would be possible to single out a large number of major specialized plans: the hospital and community care plans of the early 1960s; the Seebohm Committee's report of 1968; the Department of Health and Social Security (DHSS) planning guidelines of 1972 (DHSS 1972(a,b)), the priorities programme of 1976 (DHSS 1976a), the reversion to three-year planning in 1977 (DHSS 1979); the White Papers on mental handicap and mental illness; the Robbins, Newsom, and Plowden reports on education; the Bains, Mallaby, and Maud reports on local government and the evolution of corporate planning (for this element see for example Greenwood and Stewart 1974); and particularly the large number of publications on public-expenditure programming, beginning with the Plowden Committee's report of 1961 and continuing into the mid-1980s with such documents as the consultative paper *The Next Ten Years: Public Expenditure and Taxation into the 1990s* (Treasury 1984). Each of the specialized areas of planning – public expenditure, local authority, urban, education, health, housing, social security, personal social services, and others – has its own history, jargon, and literature. There has been little or no work to establish points of comparison and difference in their evolution, with the exception of some recent developments in joint funding between, for example, health and personal social services (Booth 1979). The histories of existing forms of planning can with profit be analysed. Another, consequential, step would be to elucidate meaning. In the table I have listed many of the meanings often assigned to the concept of social planning. Such a list can be used to illustrate biases and distortions of many institutionalized forms of planning. In particular it seems to me important to understand how the horizons of those in planning units come to be restricted by rule, convention, and practice.

Most important of all is the analysis of institutions which undertake so-called planning. Planners look to schools, training programmes and professions for the expertise upon which they depend. They are expected to conform with terms of reference or specifications laid down by an agency, local council or central government. They work to limited assignments in the terms chosen by the organization. They are allowed to consider alternative forms of organization, or alternative sequences in particular programmes. Rarely are they allowed to consider alternative objectives, or alternative conceptions of need. Planning is essentially subordinate. Planning can be subservient to existing values or agencies, with planners having freedom to vary perhaps only one or two of the assumptions or variables among the set with which they are presented.

But planning within a carefully devised framework is not the only source of control or limitation. Planners are restricted by the professional perspective into which they are trained; the social values which, as privileged members of their society, they may accept unquestioningly; and the mystifying techniques for which they may claim too much. Moreover, claims may be made for novelty which prove to be unjustified. Old ideas may be dressed up in new terminology. Practice may be regurgitated as plans. There is the process of modification between announcement and implementation. Many 'plans' are distorted by the subjective interpretations and emphases of government and officials, concessions to interest groups, and rationing of resources imposed by competing interests. Planning as practised has to be related to the unequal distribution of power and resources. It is not 'disinterested'.

Table 2   *The concept of 'planning'*

Possible contributory ideas	*Illustrations of action to fulfil ideas*	
1. *Determination and definitions of goals or objectives*	(i)	Identification of avowed and implicit goals of an organization
	(ii)	identification of preferences and options
	(iii)	definition of perceived and possible alternative goals
	(iv)	identification of priorities that are perceived and others which might be acceptable in actions leading to goals
	(v)	allocation of resources between competing goals
2. *Documentation*	(i)	structure of organization
	(ii)	services
	(iii)	staffing
	(iv)	clients
	(v)	costs
	(vi)	positional statements
3. *Measurement*	(i)	performance, consumption, input, and output measures
	(ii)	need and demand measures
	(iii)	measures of available resources
4. *Prediction*	(i)	extrapolating trends
	(ii)	forecasting future conditions or states
	(iii)	classifying likely evolutionary stages
5. *Control*	(i)	system management
	(ii)	communication of decisions

Table 2 – *cont.*

Possible contributory ideas	*Illustrations of action to fulfil ideas*
	(iii) supervision and job specification
	(iv) management information
6. *Rationalization*	(i) analysis of the economic distribution of effort, resources, manpower
	(ii) definition of efficient structures
	(iii) identification of duplication, poor coverage, imbalance
7. *Programming*	(i) designing practicable stages of development
	(ii) anticipating the timing of emerging problems of development
8. *Evaluation*	(i) policies
	(ii) policy instruments and staff
9. *Innovation, experimentation*	(i) description and analysis of possible new technology, procedures, services
	(ii) introduction and monitoring of experimental service
10. *Professionalization*	(i) introduction of specialists
	(ii) expansion of personnel with specialized training and skills
	(iii) development of in-service training
11. *Co-ordination and consultation*	(i) analysis of relationships with parallel and overlapping organizations
	(ii) analysis of joint and not only single policies and procedures
	(iii) forms of consultation favourable to development
12. *Participation*	(i) identification of scope and activity of different staff and public in the work of an organization
	(ii) review of defined responsibilities
	(iii) review of lines of accountability

This can be appreciated by comparing the planning and research units of local authorities, central departments, and universities. Each of them has restrictions on its freedom for manoeuvre. It is doubtful whether they are planning units in any objective sense of the word rather than instruments of social policy. Their detachment or impartiality is of dubious validity, if only because of the influences on them of the research foundations, professions, universities, or employing departments to which in some measure they owe allegiance.

Ideologies are embodied in methods and not only organizations and professional personnel. A government's presentation of its record will depend in part on the choice of statistics to portray achievements, developments, and problems. Values about what is and what is not relevant will be applied to statistical information and research units and will play an important role in the sponsorship of external research. The more restricted the definition of planning, the more exaggerated are the claims for certain techniques – like output budgeting, Planning Programming Budgeting System (PPBS), cost-benefit analysis, and path analysis. Measures of phenomena which are politically sensitive, like unemployment, poverty, and local authority spending – are subject to government influence and, in some cases, blatant political manipulation. Technical concepts – like 'replacement ratios' – serve the interests of the ideology which lies behind them. In the case of replacement ratios the ratio of income in unemployment to income at work is believed by neo-classical economists in general as well as by monetarists in particular to be a significant indicator for theories of the cause of unemployment. Ideology permeates the methodologies of planning no less than organizations and professional personnel.

APPROACHES TO NATIONAL PLANNING

I have argued that developments in social planning can only be understood historically in terms of ideology and structural constraint. The edicts of liberal-pluralism have conditioned the meaning, institutional form, and practices of social planning in Britain. Social planning has been largely divorced from economic planning and has been parcelled up into predominantly unconnected fragments in the public sector. Even in these fragments planning has been treated as an annexe of administration. At the national level public expenditure control has been made out to be a sufficient form of national planning.

If these arguments are correct then there is a huge battle to be won at the different ideological, structural, and policy levels. Conditions have to be created for the alignment of social and economic policies as well as their radicalization. And comprehensive planning is about changing not just policies but structures. While remaining sensitive to the criticisms of socialists like the Webbs who have in this century advocated central and in many respects élitist versions of planning, major changes in national structures will have to be made to achieve a coherent policy and strategy. Thus social departments of state will need to be reorganized, given wider functions and greater status, and placed in an office of social planning under the Prime Minister. The three principal ministers after the Prime Minister would be those for Social Planning, the Exchequer, and Foreign Affairs. Subcommittees of Cabinet would be rearranged accordingly. The election of a Labour government would also justify the large-scale appointment of advisers and specialists to such an office. A social development council would be created with direct responsibility to the Prime Minister but a duty to consult the public. This would be a semi-independent body with the remit to review and report on developments in social conditions, devise methods of resolving the problems of selecting social priorities, formulate long-term strategies and programmes for fulfilling government objectives, and collect and represent minority opinion. Through the work of such a body the competing claims of education, health, housing, welfare, and other services would be more intelligently compared and perhaps better decided. At least conflicts of aim and problems of political inconsistency would have to be confronted. The council would have the specific responsibility of examining the respective priorities of spending departments and also the wider balance of priorities among public and private social services, employment programmes, and fiscal and incomes policies.

Of course these suggestions provide no more than the barest sketch of the strategy that might be adopted. No single piece of machinery can solve deep-seated problems, but machinery must reflect purpose and ideology. There are precedents which deserve close discussion. For example, some innovations within public expenditure planning, like Programme Analysis and Review (PAR) and the short-lived Central Policy Review Staff, offer models for analysis (see Blackstone 1983; Glennerster 1975, 1981; and especially Walker 1984). Some of the more imaginative proposals for changes in structure made by royal commissions and government committees in the last twenty years also help to provide an informed agenda for debate. Thus, the Fulton Commission made very reasoned recommendations for reforms of the Civil Service (Fulton Report 1968). The working group on inequalities in health under the chairmanship of Sir Douglas Black recommended a set of proposals to achieve a more positive health policy, including a health development council (with the kind of responsibilities I have suggested for a social development council) 'with an independent membership to play a key advisory and planning role in relation to a collaborative national policy to reduce inequalities in health' (Black Report 1981: 347–48).

But 'who is to plan the planners?' This is the title of the final chapter of Barbara Wootton's book, *Freedom under Planning*. As she carefully argues, planning need not be 'the death-warrant of all private enterprise; and it is certainly not the passport of political dictatorship.' Earlier generations

were liable to elevate the importance of central planning. The problems for
socialist governments of the corruptibility of politicians, accountability of
elected leaders, and the imperious and illiberal tendencies of bureaucracies
and professional associations were underestimated. Today more socialists
are aware of these problems. There have been moves to bring the
Parliamentary Labour Party closer to the democratic processes of the
Labour movement. There have been flurries of concern over reselection of
Members of Parliament. The recommendations of the Committee of
Inquiry on Industrial Democracy (Bullock Report 1977) were rejected, but
are bound to haunt future elected Labour administrations. There has been
a flowering of interest in the potentialities of Labour local government –
especially as a result of the successes of the Greater London Council, the
Strathclyde and Sheffield City Councils, the Merseyside Council, and
others (see for example Boddy and Fudge 1984). There has been active
discussion of the decentralization and democratization of public services
(for example, Cripps *et al.* 1981). Ultimately democracy must become
participative more than representative. A cautious example of this argument was provided in the Skeffington Report (1969). Centralized planning
can be perceived as suiting only representative government in a highly
stratified society. Values about inequality are built into notions of planning no less than management. Assumptions are too readily made that
particular skills and tasks can only be performed by highly selected
groups. Bureaucratic and professional structures, however, have to be
rethought and reorganized in a society which is designed to be less
stratified. The paternalistic presuppositions of ruling establishments have
to be shed. In a revealing study of slum clearance in Sunderland in the
1960s, Norman Dennis (1971) exposed the pretensions of land-use planning and showed how local populations themselves were in many ways
better equipped to understand housing needs and developments. In one
vivid illustration officials designated houses as slums by observing them
from a moving vehicle. Community involvement in planning is necessary
if the more precious constructive elements of community structure are not
to be lost.

Comprehensive planning also implies comprehensive education. An
example can be found in the paradox of professionalism. In post-war
societies the percentage of employed workers who are professionals has
been increasing rapidly. However, unexamined professionalization may
be creating difficult problems. More professionals are expected to act for,
or act on behalf of, the increasing number of retired and unemployed
people. There is also a kind of imperialism about the expansion of certain
professions. Beyond a certain point their expansion may be questioned.
Thus, there is lively public interest in the attainment of individual health.
At bottom a choice needs to be made between the further training of

different kinds of professional to whom families can run for advice and treatment about every aspect of their health, or better universal education and communication through the media to equip families to deal with their health themselves. One option cannot be selected to the exclusion of the other. But that means that both have to be carefully explored. One of our national problems at present is that we do not attempt to find what limits should be set to professionalization – any more than patronage.

Over forty years ago Barbara Wootton understood the delicate balance which had to be sought.

> 'Success or failure [of the fusion of freedom with planning] turns on the behaviour of the actual men and women who have the responsibility of planning: on the measure in which positions of power are filled by men and women who care for the freedom of others and (what is not less important) in whom this love of liberty is not subsequently stifled by the habit of authority . . . some of the most important bulwarks of freedom, moreover, must always be built at the circumference of any large-scale plan; and our conception of what constitutes useful civic activity in a modern democracy must be revised so as to give proper place to the duty of manning those bulwarks . . . every extension of Government activity, and particularly every excursion of Government into economic planning, needs, in consequence, a corresponding growth of small local organs to control officials to co-operate in the execution of centralised plans, to discover and adjust local and personal grievances, to report on results, and to offer suggestions for future improvement . . . the last and greatest defence of freedom under planning lies in the quality and attitude of the people . . . the official on one side of the counter is not the same flesh and blood as the client on the other, and language must and will express this difference. It is not the distinction between "us" and "them" that matters, but the nature of the relationship between the two parties. That relationship must be founded on a sense of partnership and not of fear.'

These precepts of Barbara Wootton, written in the 1940s, are of lively relevance to Britain in the 1980s.

REFERENCES

Beveridge, W. H. (1942) *Social Insurance and Allied Services*, Cmnd 6404. London: HMSO.

Black Report (1981) *Inequalities in Health: Report of a Research Working Group*. London: DHSS.

Blackstone, T. (1983) Planning Social Priorities – Nationally. In H. Glennerster (ed.) *The Future of the Welfare State*. London: Heinemann.

Boddy, M. and Fudge, C. (eds) (1984) *Local Socialism? Labour Councils and New Left Alternatives*. London: Macmillan.

Booth, T. A. (1982) Economics and the Poverty of Social Planning. *Public Administration* 60 (Summer): 197–214.

—— (ed.) (1979) *Planning for Welfare*. Oxford: Basil Blackwell/Martin Robertson.

Bosanquet, N. (1983) *After the New Right*. London: Heinemann.

Bullock Report (1977) *Report of the Committee of Inquiry on Industrial Democracy*, Cmnd 6706. London: HMSO.

Central Policy Review Staff (CPRS) (1975) *A Joint Framework for Social Policies*. London: HMSO.

Cripps, F. *et al.* (1981) *Manifesto: A Radical Strategy for Britain's Future*. London: Pan.

Dearlove, J. (1979) *The Reorganisation of British Local Government*. Cambridge: Cambridge University Press.

Dennis, N. (1971) *People and Planning – The Sociology of Housing in Sunderland*. London: Faber and Faber.

Department of Economic Affairs (DEA) (1965) *The National Plan*, Cmnd 2764. London: HMSO.

Department of Health and Social Security (DHSS) (1972a) *Planning Programming Budgeting System for the Health and Personal Social Services*. London: DHSS.

—— (1972b) *Management Arrangements for the Reorganised NHS*. London: HMSO.

—— (1976a) *Priorities for Health and Personal Social Services in England*. London, HMSO.

—— (1976b) *Sharing Resources for Health in England*. London: HMSO.

—— (1979) *Local Authority Personal Social Services: Summary of Planning Returns 1977–78 to 1980–81*. London: DHSS.

Desai, M. (1981) *Testing Monetarism*. London: Pinter.

Ellman, M. (1979) *Socialist Planning*. Cambridge: Cambridge University Press.

Fulton Report (1969) *The Civil Service. Vol. 1: Report of the Committee 1966–68*, Cmnd 3638. London: HMSO.

Glennerster, H. (1975) *Social Service Budgets and Social Policy*. London: George Allen & Unwin.

—— (1981) From Containment to Conflict? Social Planning in the Seventies. *Journal of Social Policy* 10 (1).

Glennerster, H., Korman, N., and Marslen-Wilson, F. (1983) *Planning for Priority Groups*. Oxford: Martin Robertson.

Goldthorpe, J. H. (1962) The Development of Social Policy in England, 1800–1914. *Transactions of the Fifth World Congress of Sociology* 4:41–56.

Gough, I. (1979) *The Political Economy of the Welfare State*. London: Macmillan.

Greenwood, R. and Stewart, J. D. (1974) *Corporate Planning in Local Government*. London: Charles Knight.

Hayek, F. A. (1944) *The Road to Serfdom*. London: Routledge.

Heclo, H. and Wildavsky, A. (1974) *The Private Government of Public Money*. London: Macmillan.

Joseph, K. and Sumption, J. (1979) *Equality*. London: Murray.

Kellner, P. and Crowther-Hunt, N. (1980) *The Civil Servants. An Inquiry into Britain's Ruling Class*. London: MacDonald.

Mishra, R. (1981) *Society and Social Policy* (2nd edn). London: Macmillan.

Plowden Report (1961) *Control of Public Expenditure*, Cmnd 1432. London: HMSO.

Self, P. (1974) Is Comprehensive Planning Possible and Rational? *Policy and Politics* 2 (3): 193–203.

Skeffington Report (1969) *People and Planning. Report of the Committee on Participation in Planning*. London: HMSO.

Social Services Committee, House of Commons (1980) *The Government's White Papers on Public Expenditure: The Social Services*, Session 1979–80, Vol. 1, HC 702–1. London: HMSO.

—— (1981) *Public Expenditure on the Social Services*, Session 1980–81, Vol. 1, HC 324-1. London: HMSO.

—— (1982) *Public Expenditure on the Social Services*, Session 1981–82, Vol. 1, HC 306-1. London: HMSO.

Townsend, P. (1972) Social Planning and the Control of Priorities. In P. Townsend and N. Bosanquet (eds) *Labour and Inequality*. London: Fabian Society.

—— (1975) *Sociology and Social Policy*. London: Allen Lane.

—— (1980) Social Planning and the Treasury. In N. Bosanquet and P. Townsend (eds) *Labour and Equality*. London: Heinemann.

—— (1983) A Theory of Poverty and the Role of Social Policy. In M. Loney *et al.* (eds) *Social Welfare and Social Policy*. Milton Keynes: Open University Press.

—— (1984) The Development of an Anti-Poverty Strategy. In J. Brown (ed.) *Anti-Poverty Policy in the European Community*. London: Policy Studies Institute.

Treasury (1984) *The Next Ten Years: Public Expenditure and Taxation into the 1990s*, Cmnd 9189. London: HMSO.

Walker, A. (1984) *Social Planning: A Strategy for Socialist Welfare*. Oxford: Blackwell.

—— (ed.) (1982) *Public Expenditure and Social Policy*. London: Heinemann.

Webb, S. and Webb, B. (1935) *Soviet Communism: A New Civilisation?*

(special limited edition printed by the author, for subscribing members of trade unions). London.

Wilensky, H. (1975) *The Welfare State and Equality*. London: University of California Press.

Winkler, J. (1976) Corporatism. *Archives European Sociologie* XVII: 100–36.

Wootton, B. (1934) *Plan or No Plan*. London: Gollancz.

—— (1942) *End Social Inequality*. London: Kegan Paul.

—— (1945) *Freedom Under Planning*. Chapel Hill: University of North Carolina Press.

—— (1950) *Testament for Social Science*. London: Allen & Unwin.

—— (1955) *The Social Foundation of Wage Policy*. London: Allen & Unwin.

—— (1959) *Social Science and Social Pathology*. London: Allen & Unwin.

—— (1971) *Contemporary Britain*. London: Allen & Unwin.

—— (1974) *Incomes Policy: An Inquest and a Proposal*. London: Davis-Poynter.

Wright, M. (1979) Planning and Controlling Public Expenditure. In T. A. Booth (ed.) *Planning for Welfare*. Oxford: Basil Blackwell/Martin Robertson.

3

'AN ORGANIZING FEMALE WITH A BRIEFCASE'

Meryl Aldridge

INTRODUCTION

'As befits good feminists, we were married by the only woman Registrar in the country', wrote Barbara Wootton (1967: 86) about her second marriage at Fulham Register Office in 1935.

In the BBC TV series 'Women of Our Century', broadcast in 1984, she said she would not want to use the word 'feminist' of herself because it is a 'word badly abused'. Yet in the intervening years feminism had become a major movement in British political and cultural life. At times the debates have been introverted and arid but the outcome has been a refinement of theoretical understanding and a vast increase in empirical material on the standing of women in this and other societies. Barbara Wootton's autobiography contains a chapter called simply 'Woman', containing an agenda for social change of depressingly contemporary relevance nearly twenty years later. In the earlier section of the book where she outlines her life history, indignation at the restrictions on women's lives both in the public and the private sphere leaps off the page, the anger only partly tempered by irony and ridicule. With such a strong sense of being a woman, why the implicit rejection of the women's movement? The key seems to be in Barbara Wootton's fierce, obsessive independence, forged in childhood and confirmed by subsequent experience both of achievement and of pain. Barbara Wootton rejects affiliation to movements which might involve compromising one's own beliefs. 'Flat out' against violence, she does not wish to be called a pacifist (Clwyd 1984). Having worked for the labour movement she did not wish to become an MP because of the 'loss of personal and intellectual freedom' involved – especially for ministers (BBC TV 1984). As an academic researcher and

writer in economics and criminology, Barbara Wootton works in territory both theoretically sophisticated and riven with disputes of tribal
intensity, yet she rejects theorizing in a way that at times seems disingenuous but again detaches her from movements which might try to claim
her.

A WOMAN'S LIFE

Both Barbara Wootton's parents were academics and had high expectations of their daughter and her two elder brothers. Barbara Wootton
writes with warmth of her father, who died when she was 10. Despite his
intellectual demands he was neither 'remote' nor 'austere' although very
absorbed in his work so that her memories of him are 'shadowy' (Wootton
1967: 18). The strong influence in her childhood seems to have been her
mother, a powerful patrician and conservative woman whom Barbara
Wootton calls a 'slave driver intellectually'; 'I did not like my mother very
much' (BBC TV 1984). Her mother intensified her control by not
allowing Barbara Wootton to go to school despite her fervent pleas – and
prayers in the privacy of the lavatory – until her early teens (Wootton 1967:
21ff). Her education was at home with her mother and private tutors,
covering history, classics, literature, languages, and dance but little maths
and no science. Despite her mother's otherwise traditional political and
social attitudes she was an ardent supporter of women's suffrage. Barbara
Wootton writes that she and her brothers were treated in most respects
equally. They seem to have been both intellectually and emotionally very
close to each other and one gets a strong sense that from this Barbara
Wootton developed her expectation of competing on equal terms with
men. 'It is said that once, when as a child I was asked what I intended to do
with my grown-up-life, I answered that I should be "an organizing female
with a brief-case"' (Wootton 1967: 278). Yet in no sense did she wish to
take the 'honorary man' route of adopting pseudo-masculine demeanour.
Barbara Wootton is vividly aware of her own femaleness, not merely of
being one of the class 'woman': 'I greatly enjoyed my brothers and made
slaves of them whenever I could' (1967: 23). 'I learned to flirt in my cradle'
(Caldecott 1984: 129). In September, 1916 Arthur, the younger of her two
brothers, was reported missing. Eventually he had to be presumed dead;
her second major loss.

   Much of Barbara Wootton's parenting came from her beloved nanny
who came to the Wootton household after the birth of Neil, the eldest
child. Barbara Wootton writes of her deep attachment to 'the Pie' (1967:
25ff) but adds that misbehaviour and thoughtlessness were punished by
withdrawal. This, and the fear of the Pie's leaving, produced what Barbara
Wootton herself calls an experience of 'traumatic rejection'. Coupled

with her array of fears – of fire, of the dark, of dogs, 'that rude boys would call out after me' (1967: 22) – and her obsessive nature, make it hardly surprising that Barbara Wootton did not enjoy her childhood (BBC TV 1984). But the greatest loss which was to confirm her in a 'realistic sense of the impermanence of earthly relationships' (Wootton 1967: 51) was the death in action of her husband Jack Wootton. They had been married for five weeks in 1917 but had been together less than forty-eight hours before he was called back to the front. Barbara Wootton writes movingly of the emotional scars that these early experiences left on her. To the observer they suggest another source, together with the demands made on her in childhood and her intellectual ability, of her evident belief in autonomy, and the possibility of mastering circumstances by effort, self-discipline, and self-sufficiency. She strongly deprecates self-pity and refuge in explanations about one's deprived early life, though she does not lack compassion for the deprived. 'We would do better . . . to encourage children from the earliest possible age, however wretched their backgrounds, to believe that they are, or at least soon will be, masters of their fates' (Wootton 1967: 52).

Barbara Wootton's academic career started in 1915 when she took up a classics scholarship at Girton. The choice of subject was her mother's; she eventually acquired an *aegrotat* degree. The following year she studied economics, her chosen subject, and gained a First with Distinction. But she did not graduate, being a woman. A year later she returned to Girton to be Director of Studies in Economics. Again, women could be heard but not seen: during the first year, her lectures on the Economics Tripos had to be published under the name of a male colleague. As a woman, she was not a member of the university and could not therefore be officially recognized as lecturing. Much as she evidently enjoyed Cambridge life she soon became involved in the Labour Party and in extra-mural work in London. In 1922 she took up a post at the then Trades Union Congress (TUC) Labour Party Joint Research Department. It was during that time, Barbara Wootton writes, that she was 'cured for ever' (1967: 62) of any desire to be a political candidate. Her autobiography is elliptical as to the reason. In the television interview (BBC TV 1984) she was more forthright about the lack of integrity entailed in the daily barter of political life. Her time at the research department also produced further demonstrations of the inequities and absurdities of a 'woman's place'. When, in 1924 she became the only woman member of a Departmental Committee on the National Debt she was 'persecuted by the press literally night and day' (Wootton 1967: 65) questioning her about her recreations and love life. 'Secrets of Debt Enquiry woman: Does she ever play?' (Wootton 1967: 65) is a headline which still illustrates most of feminists' complaints about media coverage of women sixty years later!

At the age of 28, Barbara Wootton was appointed a Justice of the Peace, for which eligibility for both sexes was 21 years of age. In practice, however, most women appointed since they had become eligible in 1919 were of 'relatively mature years' (Wootton 1967: 67). Until the law was changed two years later, Barbara Wootton found herself in the utterly absurd position of being on the bench but unable to vote, for which the age for women was then 30.

Even in the structures of the labour movement, while men and women enjoyed equal pay 'it was plain to see that the men occupied all the higher posts and the women all the lower ones' (Wootton 1967: 69). This coupled with the anonymity of briefing 'public men' led to Barbara Wootton's moving on. In 1926 she became Principal of Morley College for Working Men and Women in South London. In the event she only stayed there two years but during that time she was invited in her own right to a League of Nations World Economic Conference in Geneva, together with a Dutch and an Austrian woman. Unlike their home governments, 'the British Government simply ignored my existence' (Wootton 1967: 74). Her expenses were paid by various women's organizations until the government changed its attitude, literally an hour or two before she was due to leave Geneva.

Shortly after her return from Geneva she became Director of Studies in the University of London's extra-mural department, a post she was to hold for seventeen years. As well as other work, this involved spending August at summer schools and it was at one of these that Barbara Wootton met her second husband, George Wright. For a second time she had to endure press persecution because of gender rather than achievement. George was a mature student temporarily driving a taxi so they became 'cabby marries don' (much more titillating than 'don marries secretary'). Barbara Wootton was 'besieged' in her flat; George had to 'spend the time riding round London on a bus' (Wootton 1967: 85) to avoid the waiting press. George subsequently became an adult education lecturer and organizer, worked at Labour Party HQ, and became a London County Council alderman. Nevertheless 'when I was one of the first women admitted to the House of Lords and George had not been near a taxi except as a passenger for nearly twenty years, I was pestered with requests for us both to be photographed outside the House, standing "beside the taxi"' (Wootton 1967: 86).

Conventional patriarchal attitudes did, however, occasionally yield dividends. Throughout their marriage Barbara Wootton was principal breadwinner but when she went to the United States on a lecturing tour in the late 1930s all the questions about earnings for tax purposes were addressed to George. He was able truthfully to say he had earned nothing; she remained demurely silent, waiting to be asked. But the question did

not come, so the money was repatriated and spent on a fridge. Barbara
Wootton adds, wryly, that the lectures had been in honour of the
American feminist Anna Howard Shaw (1967: 93).

In 1958, shortly after her retirement, Barbara Wootton became one of
the first four women life peers in the House of Lords. She writes that 'their
Lordships' House has proved to be one of the (in my experience not very
numerous) places where male and female alike are treated on merits' (1967:
133). Not so their spouses, however. Husbands of knights and life peers,
unlike wives, do not acquire a title. Apparently there are no special
facilities provided for them, while there is a gallery and retiring room for
those wives of peers who wish to listen to debates. Nor do husbands of the
ennobled take part in the ballot for seats for the state opening of Parliament. Barbara Wootton writes (1967: 131ff) of the most difficult problem
when women were admitted to the Lords in their own right: lavatories,
not only for themselves but for the awkward phenomenon of husbands.
Her amusing passage on this has an iconic quality: lavatory facilities have
so often been used as the ultimate – and allegedly most intractable – reason
for excluding women from spheres as far apart as august clubs and
building sites.

WOMEN'S PLACE: BARBARA WOOTTON'S AGENDA

The second part of Barbara Wootton's autobiography starts – significantly
– with a chapter simply called 'Woman' in which she ranges with
controlled indignation across a series of issues from attitudes and speech
usages to those aspects of taxation and social policy which demean
women. Her concerns are of continuing relevance. Data that she must
have collected specifically to make her points are now routinely published
by the Equal Opportunities Commission (EOC). What is now called
'gender-free language' is a very current controversy. Issues of caring,
benefits, and taxation are prominent among the concerns of government
and researchers.

Barbara Wootton starts with the simple assertion that women have far
to go to become 'equal partners with men' (1967: 147). While acknowledging that by 1967 many spheres were formally open to women, she notes
the small number of women actually to be found in senior positions in the
public sector and the professions, let alone at board level in private
enterprise. She adds with evident chagrin that where women figure
among the 'great and good' it is often because of their husband's position
rather than their own achievement. In the mid-1960s, it appears, it was
possible for *Times* leaders to attribute this to women's lack of willingness
to take responsibility (Wootton 1967: 149) and for employers to be openly
discriminatory not only in making appointments but in declaring their

bias in advance. Such practices are now illegal and/or driven into private procedures and assertions. The habit of talking about the 'right man for the job' (Wootton 1967: 151) is still current in universities, for example, although the phrase is now uttered with an element of self-conscious aggression rather than bland lack of awareness.

Barbara Wootton writes with scarcely less vehemence about the 'patronising archness' (1967: 151) of Percy Thrower's attitude to women horticulturalists in a contemporary television series. Apparently he not only referred to what his wife often said, but to the women horticulturalists as 'very nice ladies too' (1967: 152). It is perhaps as well that Barbara Wootton is spared the Nottingham local radio angling correspondent and his 'voice from the kitchen'.

Barbara Wootton continues on the difficulties of dining and drinking alone (still current) and of being the subject of 'exaggerated praise or applause' (1967: 152) while being ignored in discussion or debate. Returning to university life, Barbara Wootton would find women students still complaining that men expect to dominate classes and seminars. Now, at least, the issue is brought out into the open and attempts are sometimes made to understand and alter this pattern of behaviour.

Perhaps most powerfully, Barbara Wootton draws a parallel between what are now known as racism and sexism (1967: 152), pointing out that at the time she was writing, racist attitudes were 'alas! . . . far from extinct . . . [but] offend against the canons of civilized behaviour' (1967: 153), while sexist attitudes and jokes did not. It would appear that only limited progress has been made. Calling a woman the equal of a man is still seen as high praise while a number of successful comics make a good living from jokes about 'the wife' and 'the mother-in-law'.

Much of the above Barbara Wootton attributes to 'prejudice, greed and fear of competition' (1967: 155) but she goes on to discuss what would now be called structural inequalities which she attributes to women's bearing and nursing of children and their consequent withdrawal from the workplace and public life. But, as she eloquently points out (1967: 155), the expectation is also that daughters rather than sons will care for aged parents – and, one might add, the handicapped or chronically sick. In few households are domestic responsibilities actually fully shared, although at the time of writing Barbara Wootton had grounds for optimism in the new phenomenon of men taking a greater part in child care and shopping. Given the shortening proportion of their lives that women now spend bearing and caring for infants, Barbara Wootton hoped for 'bold and imaginative training schemes' (1967: 157) enabling both society and individual women to make use of this new stage of the family cycle. With this growing equality in the labour market surely the absurdities of unequal pay and the assumptions about dependency in the taxation and benefit systems would finally be confronted and resolved (Wootton 1967: 158ff)?

WOMAN'S PLACE: WHERE ARE WE NOW?

Barbara Wootton's has been a public life. In that respect her experience is remote from most men's, let alone that of ordinary women. It explains, however, her attention to the under-representation of women in influential positions. Concern with this as an indication of women's equality has become a matter of public debate, to the extent that the *Annual Report* of the EOC contains a number of sections on the occupational, political, and public representation of women. The 1985 EOC news-sheet *Equality Now!* has published an account of research commissioned to explore the channels through which ministerial appointments are made. The general conclusion is that so many of the nominating bodies – the Confederation of British Industry (CBI), TUC, local authorities and professional associations – are themselves male-dominated that the outcome is inevitable: 'the only groups outside nursing which can be relied upon, unprompted, to field a good proportion of women nominees are voluntary organisations.' The article continues that the 'EOC Chairman' has written to ministers asking them to take action to modify the position. An accompanying table shows women as a proportion of ministerial appointments in 1983: they range from 29.9 per cent at the Scottish Office through 22.8 per cent at the Department of Health and Social Security (DHSS), and 11.2 per cent at Education and Science, to the Treasury, at the bottom with 3.2 per cent, thus nicely bearing out Barbara Wootton's observation about women not being found where the money is.

The *Annual Report 1983* (EOC 1984: 95) also shows that the number of women MPs has fallen. In 1945 there were twenty-four, almost exclusively representing Labour. The peak figure of twenty-eight was reached at the 1964 election where a majority of the women returned were Labour. By 1983, however, the figure declined to twenty-three, of whom a slight majority were Conservative. The pattern of local political representation is similarly bleak. In May, 1982, women accounted for 20.3 per cent of members for the London boroughs; 18.8 per cent of members for non-metropolitan districts; and only 12.1 per cent of representatives of Scottish regions (and 6.4 per cent for the Scottish islands where presumably time and distance are major problems).

Barbara Wootton also showed an interest in women's role in the BBC. There is little to encourage her. She wrote (1967: 148) that women had 'eight out of more than 180 senior posts'. By October, 1984, the figure (BBC 1985: 197) was four in seventy-eight: the Deputy Secretary, the Chief Assistant to the Director General, the Controller of Educational

Broadcasting, and the Head of Education Broadcasting Services.

Nor have universities, another of Barbara Wootton's areas of interest, shown themselves to be in the vanguard. In the session 1983–84 women constituted 14.8 per cent of all 'full-time academic staff': 2.3 per cent of professors, 6.6 per cent of senior lecturers/readers, 16.6 per cent of lecturers, and 34 per cent of 'others' (UGC 1984). The distribution varies according to discipline: 'language and literature' has the greatest proportion of women staff at 22.2 per cent; 'engineering and technology' the least with 4 per cent (including 0.2 per cent of professors, that is: one). The EOC has compiled a statistical paper on women in universities: it confirms their general under-representation, and clustering in the arts, in more junior posts, in support functions, in part-time appointments, and in posts without permanent funding (EOC 1982b).

This distribution is reflected in women's membership of 'selected' professional institutions in 1983 (EOC 1984: 96). The Hotel, Catering and Institution Management Association has the largest female membership, 47.1 per cent of all members; 23.4 per cent of members of the British Medical Association are women; 14.2 per cent of members of the Law Society (solicitors) (at January, 1982); 5.6 per cent of the Institute of Chartered Accountants; and 2.4 per cent of the British Institute of Management. At the bottom of the table comes the Institute of Production Engineers, 0.5 per cent of whose members are women.

One might expect that if women were to hold senior positions anywhere it would be in the caring professions. From time to time articles appear on this in the social work press. One of the more recent (Popplestone 1980) shows, however, that women are again over-represented in the most junior posts in local-authority social services, the major employer. Indeed in 1976 (the DHSS seems not to publish figures by gender currently) the progression was linear: 9 per cent of directors, 29 per cent of area directors, and 83 per cent of social-work assistants were women. Unfortunately Popplestone had to rely on the limited source of a postal survey of members of a professional association for qualitative data but her conclusions are interesting nevertheless. They were, broadly, that seniority meant taking on management roles and that women did not put themselves forward owing to a combination of factors including their domestic responsibilities, a notion that managing as opposed to 'caring' is unfeminine, and the widespread belief that those appointing – male managers and councillors – would not see women as having the right qualities. And this in a profession where not only the work-force but the majority of the clients are women.

The explanation, of course, lies in the typical domestic responsibilities of women which determine the structure of opportunity for all women whether a particular individual's experience is typical or not. As Barbara

Wootton herself fully acknowledges, 'caring' is women's work and is not limited to the needs of infant children. If members of the household or close kin need care through handicap, chronic sickness, or ageing, then the first line of support is expected to be the family and that in practice means a female whether spouse, child, or sibling. Even the new 'post-child-care' phase of women's lives, identified by Wootton, may be filled by the care of parents. The material and emotional costs of caring have attracted considerable research attention recently, resulting in a number of major publications (EOC 1982a; Finch and Groves 1983; Nissel and Bonnerjea 1982). As a result of demographic trends and policies of so-called 'community care', most attention has been focused on the needs of the elderly but there have also been studies of the care of handicapped children and adults. (See, for example, the chapters by Oliver and Baldwin, and Glendinning in Finch and Groves 1983.) All reflect the same everyday reality: women most often are the carers; they receive little support from other members of the family, still less from neighbours; the commitment is open-ended and demoralizing; the structures of the labour market, taxation, and the welfare state are built on the assumption that they will 'naturally' be carers.

Nissel and Bonnerjea concentrate on a sample of twenty-two households where married couples tended aged parents. In half the cases the husband was described as 'distant or neutral' (1982: 4) in his response to the situation. Another third were 'helpful or very helpful' yet 'none of the husbands in the sample contributed substantial direct care' (1982: 40). Children were not expected to help except by putting up with the tensions and inconveniences caused. The authors report dramatic effects on the carers' marriage, family life, social activities – or lack of them – and sense of self-worth. In nine of the twenty-two households the woman had given up work while four of the seven still working had needed time off. Nissel and Bonnerjea report a tendency for those in work to switch to less skilled and part-time work in the 'secondary labour market' (1982: 55) with the resulting loss of earnings, prospects, and future pensions and benefits status. The theme of the actual cost of care is also explored by Rimmer in Finch and Groves (1983). Apart from current and prospective financial costs, some of Nissel and Bonnerjea's respondents felt a loss of self – through weariness, isolation, loss of time to themselves, and a lack of the intellectual stimulation and social contact of work and leisure – amounting to a '"broken" self-image' (1982: 44). Perhaps most tellingly, the authors comment that few of the respondents felt that they had a right to any of these lost opportunities. 'Many said that they would love not to have to respond to other people all the time and do as they pleased. . . . But this was never seen as a right. It was simply dreaming' (Nissel and Bonnerjea 1982: 44). Extending 'caring' into 'tending', and acknowledging it as a duty whatever one's class, potential, or needs, is accepted as part of a woman's destiny.

The embodiment of this set of assumed qualities in social welfare legislation is demonstrated vividly by Groves and Finch's (1983) analysis of the setting up and administration of the Invalid Care Allowance. Initially conceived as a kind of consolation for single women who gave up employment to care for close relatives, it has been extended to all men, whether married or not, and to non-relatives. At the time of their writing, married or cohabiting women were still excluded from claiming, although this has since been challenged. 'There now exists the interesting anomaly that a woman can claim ICA if she cares for a lover who happens to be female, but not for one who happens to be male. We wonder whether it was the intention of the Department of Health and Social Security to encourage this particular model of family life', write Groves and Finch (1983: 158) with a deadpan wit worthy of Barbara Wootton herself. But what the DHSS was encouraging is the perpetuation of the fundamental assumption that for a married woman, working outside the home is an optional secondary activity and that by the act of marriage she becomes financially dependent on her husband. That in many cases a woman might wish to claim ICA to care for a husband now dependent on her is a reversal apparently incapable of incorporation into legislation.

Invalid Care Allowance is, of course, in no sense different from other benefits in its definitions of dependency. Indignation over married women's tax position, which is virtually unchanged since Wootton acerbically described it (1967: 159), has now reached the ears of government. The 1985 Budget speech contained the following recantation: 'The present structure of personal income tax is far from satisfactory. . . . It denies to partners in a marriage the privacy and independence which they have a right to expect' (*The Times*, 20 March, 1985). New legislation was promised for the 'end of the decade'.

A key component of women's continued economic disadvantage is the notion of the 'family wage': the intersection of patriarchal attitudes and material interests. Barbara Wootton wrote with approval (1967: 158) of Eleanor Rathbone's long campaign against this justification for all men being paid more than all women, so that vast sums of money were spent on non-existent wives and children, while households containing dependants but no male wage-earner were under-provided. Typically, Barbara Wootton wrote more in sorrow than in anger: surely once the empirical falsehood of this was finally grasped, then attitudes would change, and taxation and benefits policy would be modified? She does not – alas! – acknowledge the vested interest of individuals or groups, still less develop an analysis at the systemic level. Historically, as Land (1980) writes in a seminal article, the wage was indeed for 'the family' which, under pre-industrial and early industrial forms of production, was indivisible. Hakim (1980) has demonstrated that only in the latter part of the nineteenth century were individual members of a household attributed with an occupation. Not until the 1881 census was 'housewife' equated officially with not having an economic function – and only then with an apologetic footnote. Land argues that trade-union interests were formed in the last years of the nineteenth century. The labour aristocracy, men possessed of the new skills in manufacturing, were able to command wages sufficient for their wives not to have to work outside the home. Given the nature of women's (and children's) employment opportunities in factories and other people's homes at that time, this could be seen as an advance. As many writers have pointed out, only recently has 'home-making' ceased to be very much a job in itself (see, for example, Hamilton 1978).

Others have interpreted the stance of working men as embracing a model of the bourgeois family foisted on them by capital with the twin aim or outcome (which one takes it to be depends on one's ideological and methodological inclination) of creating a work-force too dependent on one (high) wage to be militant while simultaneously allowing women to specialize in the domestic support of men and children, i.e. the reproduction of the labour force. Whatever the motive force, Land records that when the social realities of low pay and families without male bread-winners led to the acceptance of family allowances (Eleanor Rathbone's goal), the labour movement and employers both wished that the allowance to be set at a marginal, not an economic, level despite arguments by some groups that direct payments to women for children would increase health and living standards dramatically and at minimum cost. Many of the same conflicting interpretations emerged in the 1970s when men's tax allowances for dependent children were replaced by a benefit paid to mothers and when equal pay legislation was under discussion.

Barbara Wootton takes the argument for equal pay, coupled with an equitable system of dependency allowances, to be self-evident, noting that in 'the Civil Service and other public services this claim is now conceded' (1967: 157). Legislation on equal pay and against discrimination on grounds of sex followed in the mid-1970s, but forces more powerful than individual aptitudes and effort are at work. While the average gross hourly earnings for women rose from 63.1 per cent of men's in 1970 to 75.5 per cent in 1977, by 1983 they had fallen back to 74.2 per cent (EOC 1984: 89). This measure does not, of course, reflect the shorter hours that women work. The great increase in women's paid employment which has characterized the last three decades has been among married women with children. Many of these work part-time. In 1982 Rimmer and Popay wrote 'one in five of the employed labour force works part-time. . . . 90

per cent of part-time workers are women, of whom nine out of ten are married . . . over 40 per cent of women workers work part-time' (1982: 21). By December, 1984, 44 per cent of the labour force was women of whom 46 per cent worked part-time (Department of Employment 1985: S11).

Not only are women's wages depressed by limited hours, but they are 'ghettoized' into restricted sectors of the labour market: some types of manufacturing and the services, both characterized by low pay, low skills, and weak unionization. In 1983 women constituted 41 per cent of the labour force and were 'over-represented' in textiles, footwear, clothing, and leather, hotels and catering, retailing and distribution, banking, finance, and insurance, professional and scientific services, and 'miscellaneous services' (EOC 1984: 81).

New technology has, in some cases, replaced skilled 'male' jobs with semi-skilled 'women's work' but not at high rates of pay and specifically not in geographical areas with a strong union tradition (Massey and Meegan 1982). That same technology may in due course extinguish those jobs and routine clerical and retail jobs too.

During the last decade unemployment has superseded all other public concerns about the work-force. Some feminists have argued that women constitute a 'reserve army of labour' and will axiomatically suffer more than men at a time of rising unemployment. Others have countered that sectoral shifts and technological change qualify this model, although both implicitly agree that there is no sign of women displacing men in highly paid work. Walby (1985) examines how women become unemployed at the level of the firm and concludes, from her sample in the north-west of England in 1981–82, that there was little sign of direct discrimination. On the other hand, women's domestic commitments indirectly made them more vulnerable to redundancy. 'Last in, first out' practices fell more often on women because of their greater turnover, as did 'part-timers first'. Again, alternative jobs might be offered but not taken up because of lack of mobility or non-viability when travel was set against low pay.

'"Men must work and women must weep", we used to say: today, plainly women must do both', Barbara Wootton wrote in her autobiography (1967: 55). In recent years there has been an increasing volume of research interest in precisely how men and women organize their households: the 'domestic division of labour'. The evidence indicates that domestic work and the responsibility for managing the home and its finances still fall disproportionately on women. Having reviewed the literature on budgeting systems, J. Pahl (1983) concludes that power in the household, that is the ability to take major allocative and strategic decisions, is closely associated with share of total income. Thus the male partner will more often make the decisions seen as very important (like moving house). Women control the 'less important' but time-consuming decisions over, for example, day-to-day and week-to-week expenditure on food and clothes. This division of power and responsibility is underlined by Morris (1984) in her study of men made redundant by British Steel. Whether re-employed or unemployed, nearly all had less to spend than formerly. The worse off the family, the more likely was the woman to have control of the budget, including trying to find personal spending money for the man to participate in the local male culture. Women, unless they were earning, seemed to have little concept of personal spending money for themselves but accepted that a social life for their husband was a necessary part of his masculinity.

In 1981 R. E. Pahl and colleagues undertook a major study of household organization on the Isle of Sheppey in Kent. 'Clearly', they conclude, 'it is overwhelmingly obvious that women do most of the work in the household' (Pahl 1984: 270ff). This pattern did not vary significantly with class, although there was a strong link with stage in the life cycle. Women with young children were, unsurprisingly, doing more domestic work in absolute and relative terms than their partners, as were women who worked part-time. But women who worked full-time were also doing more than their 'share' of household tasks, and wives of unemployed men seemed to be doing more domestic work than women of the same employment status whose partners were in employment. Only at retirement did there seem to be a trend towards equalization of domestic responsibilities.

Clearly, then, domestic work is still women's work, whatever their class and even when they have declining child-care responsibilities and are themselves employed. The explanation lies not in individual attitudes and talents as Wootton seems to imply, but at a more collective level. The resurgence of the women's movement has produced a vigorous debate on the nature of the forces which perpetuate this inequality. For Marxist feminists the domestic division of labour is integral to capitalism although there are profound differences on precisely how to make sense of this theoretically, given that domestic work is not exchanged in the market-place and thus cannot directly contribute to the surplus value extracted from labour by capital. The debates over teminology and process have been both arcane and fierce (see, for example, Beechey 1978; Bruegel 1979; Delphy 1984; Kaluzynska 1980). Yet the central assertion holds and is indeed essentially the same analysis as that of the conservative social theorist, Talcott Parsons. As the major American functionalist, his position, refined but never fundamentally altered, is that women's specialization in home-making and child-rearing is necessary to the continued expansion of modern (i.e. western capitalist) economies (see, for example, Parsons in Anshen 1959). Women's role is to make the labour force geographically mobile, flexible in outlook, emotionally stable, and physically cared for. Contrary to the assertions of some of his critics, Parsons understood that this could mean emotional costs and loss of opportunity to women both individually and as a class, but in his perspective the axiomatic interest of the whole society in a stable social system and an expanding economy had to take precedence over the interests of subgroups.

Some feminists have rejected explaining women's place by the imperatives of economic or social structures, and prefer to place emphasis on the realm of ideas (Delphy 1984; Hamilton 1978). For them women's subordination springs from the cultural traditions of patriarchy in which religion has played an important part. Explaining women's place in this way does not, however, imply the individualist solution that since it exists only in ideas then if enough people change their mind, all will be resolved into a new era of equality. Patriarchy, by definition, serves the interests of men collectively so there is powerful resistance to change not only in the attitudes of many (but not all) men but in institutions and structures. Change, it fellows, can only be brought about at the same level. While contemporary feminists argue vehemently as to the historical origin and current mechanics of women's social subordination, there is no dispute about the means of change: it must come through change in structures as well as in attitudes. It may be brought about in some instances by persons in key positions of power. Even then wider support is necessary. But change in social arrangements comes more often through collective action. (Of course there is a paradox here: an individual's power in fact comes from the structural position he or she occupies; collective action will not occur without changes in the outlook of individuals.)

'Sociology is a lot of waffle', asserted Barbara Wootton in her 1984 television interview (Clwyd 1984) but the mere description of social processes does not explain them, and without an understanding of cause, finding the lever of social change is at best haphazard. All of Barbara Wootton's writing is vivid, direct, witty, and full of insights but her rejection of theory sometimes limits its potential in the long term. To draw a parallel: in *Social Science and Social Pathology* (1959) she adopted what was even then coming to be called a transactional view of deviance. If she had been more willing to enter that kind of debate – shorn of arcane definitions and unnecessary neologisms – it would have been profitable for all parties. Theorists would have had to engage with the wealth of her experience and empirical material; Barbara Wootton would have had to state more clearly her epistemology of deviance, thus clarifying its moral and legislative implications, compared with other explanations.

It is terribly easy to criticize with hindsight. Barbara Wootton did her research work in the heyday of the British empirical tradition of social research. Her working life spanned the whole historical period during which the Welfare State was conceived and created, its structures based firmly within the paradigm of equality of opportunity. The 1960s was a decade notable for libertarian reforms when socialists, too, had great hopes for social change through changes in attitude. So Barbara Wootton's sense that one's life successes are achieved through individual struggle must have seemed to be confirmed by historical experience. Constitutionally averse to being part of a mass, she was able to produce social change by her own campaigning. That some of her influence came about through 'a series of accidents happening to me rather than a pattern of my own making' (1967: 278) does not belittle her drive, ability, and sense of duty. Some of those 'accidents' were sad and painful yet, by freeing her from, for example, conventional domestic responsibilities, they perversely enabled her to achieve exceptionally. When asked about the clash of women's responsibilites at home and at work, Barbara Wootton has said, rather harshly, that women must choose (BBC TV 1984). But women choose within a socially constructed set of circumstances and without the benefit of hindsight. They are not, or think they are not, choosing between children and a successful professional career ending in a life peerage. They choose very young – and, most importantly, men do not have to 'choose' in this way.

'Others broke open the door and I walked through', says Barbara Wootton (1967: 279). On the contrary, she helped hold the door open for succeeding generations; we follow. She must excuse us if we want to catch her by the arm and argue with her over the means by which all women may follow if they wish.

REFERENCES

Anshen, R. V. (1959) *The Family: Its Functions and Destiny*. New York: Harper & Row.

BBC (1985) *Annual Report and Handbook 1985*. London: BBC Publications.

BBC TV (1984) 'Women of Our century' (television broadcast).

Beechey, V. (1978) Women and Production: A Critical Analysis of Some Sociological Theories of Women's Work. In A. Kuhn and A. M. Wolpe (eds) *Feminism and Materialism*. London: Routledge & Kegan Paul.

Bruegel, I. (1979) Women as a Reserve Army of Labour: A Note on Recent British Experience. *Feminist Review* 3.

Burns, R. (1983) Financial Management and the Allocation of Resources within Households: a research review. *EOC Research Bulletin* 8, winter 1983–84: 17–36.

Caldecott, L. (ed.) (1984) *Women of Our Century*. London: BBC Ariel Books.

Clwyd, A. (1984) Women of Our Century IV: Barbara Wootton. *Listener*, 26 July, 1984.

Delphy, C. (1984) *Close to Home*. London: Hutchinson.

Department of Employment (1985) *Employment Gazette*. London: HMSO.

EOC (1982a) *Caring for the Handicapped Elderly: Community Care Policies and Women's Lives (Research Report)*. Manchester: EOC.

—— (1982b) *Women in Universities: A Statistical Description*. Manchester: EOC.

—— (1984) *Annual Report 1983*. Manchester: EOC.

—— (1985) Women Miss Out because of Old-Boy Network. *Equality Now!* 5, spring.

Finch, J. and Groves, D. (eds) (1983) *A Labour of Love*. London: Routledge & Kegan Paul.

Groves, D. and Finch, J. (1983) Natural Selection: Perspectives on Entitlement to the Invalid Care Allowance. In J. Finch and D. Groves (eds) *A Labour of Love*. London: Routledge & Kegan Paul.

Hakim, C. (1980) Census Reports as Documentary Evidence: The Census Commentaries 1801–1951. *Sociological Review* 28(3): 551–80.

Hamilton, R. (1978) *The Liberation of Women*. London: Allen & Unwin.

Kaluzynska, E. (1980) Wiping the Floor with Theory – a Survey of Writings on Housework. *Feminist Review* 6: 27–54.

Kuhn, A. and Wolpe, A. M. (eds) (1978) *Feminism and Materialism*. London: Routledge & Kegan Paul.

Land, H. (1980) The Family Wage. *Feminist Review* 6: 55–77.

Massey, D. and Meegan, R. (1982) *The Anatomy of Job Loss*. London: Methuen.

Morris, L. (1984) Redundancy and Patterns of Household Finance. *Sociological Review* 32(8): 492–523.

Nissel, M. and Bonnerjea, L. (1982) *Family Care of the Handicapped Elderly: Who Pays?* London: Policy Studies Institute.

Pahl, J. (1983) The Allocation of Money and the Structuring of Inequality within Marriage. *Sociological Review* 31(2): 237–62.

Pahl, R. E. (1984) *Divisions of Labour*. Oxford: Basil Blackwell.

Parsons, T. (1959) The Social Structure of the Family. In R. V. Anshen (ed.) *The Family: Its Functions and Destiny*. New York: Harper & Row.

Popplestone, R. (1980) Top jobs for Women: Are the Cards Stacked against Them? *Social Work Today* 12(4): 12–15.

Rimmer, L. (1983) The Economics of Work and Caring. In J. Finch and D. Groves (eds) *A Labour of Love*. London: Routledge & Kegan Paul.

Rimmer, L. and Popay, J. (1982) *Employment Trends and the Family*. London: Study Commission on the Family.

University Grants Committee (1984) University Statistics 1983–84 Vol.
   1. *University Statistical Record*. London: HMSO.
Walby, S. (1985) Gender Relations and Job Loss: A Case-Study Approach.
   EOC Research Bulletin 9: 62–74.
Wootton, B. (1959) *Social Science and Social Pathology*. London: Allen &
   Unwin.
—— (1967) *In a World I Never Made*. London: Allen & Unwin.

4

IS ECONOMICS STILL LAMENTABLE?

David Whynes

I

At the age of 17, Barbara Wootton, or Barbara Adam as she then was, found herself facing a dilemma. It was time to select a course of study at the University of Cambridge and the parental example clearly implied a classical training. The date, however, was 1914, the beginning of the war that reshaped both Europe and Barbara Adam's academic inclinations. As she subsequently explained in her autobiography, she had become appalled by

> 'the prospect of spending the next few years in perfecting my knowledge of dead civilisations while the only living civilisation I knew was crashing about my ears. One night, therefore, when mother came up to my room to bid me goodnight, as she always did, I plucked up courage . . . to suggest that at college I should read, not classics, but economics – or at least history. Economics, I secretly thought, perhaps held the key to some of the injustices and miseries of the world by which I was greatly troubled.'   (Wootton 1967: 39)

The suggested compromise was classics followed by economics and the 'First with Distinction' in the latter subject enabled Barbara Wootton to obtain, in her early twenties, the post of Director of Studies in Economics at Girton College, Cambridge.

After such an auspicious beginning to a career it is perhaps a little sad to relate that economics failed to live up to Barbara Wootton's high expectations of it. Although she continued to occupy herself with economic matters even after leaving Cambridge – she was, for example, an invited delegate at the first League of Nations World Economic Conference in 1927 – she began to experience a disillusionment with the methods of formal economic theory. Eventually, in 1938, this dissatisfaction manifested itself as a book entitled *Lament for Economics*:

> 'In this I gave expression to my growing dismay, not only at the inability of the economists to solve the grievous economic problems of the world, but also at their ostrich-like habit of wrapping themselves up in abstractions as though those problems either did not exist, or at least were no concern of theirs. . . . *Lament for Economics* no doubt marked the beginning of the end of my career as an economist, a title to which I would not now aspire.'   (Wootton 1967: 87–8)

Lament for Economics is written in an easy and frequently amusing manner but it is by no stretch of the imagination a gentle book. The opening 'Indictment' is disarmingly frank: economics is charged with being useless and this uselessness is held to arise from a combination of factors. Economics is said to communicate nothing to the layman by virtue of the unintelligibility of its language. It has proved itself, moreover, to be incapable of generating unequivocal policy recommendations. More seriously, economic theory is useless because it is unrealistic: 'economists feed on their own tails by busying themselves with the analysis of imaginary worlds which they have themselves invented' (Wootton 1938: 35). Even when some concrete result is obtained it is likely to embody ideological bias because the explicit market/equilibrium orientation of economic theory tends to dispose it towards capitalistic solutions. All such themes are developed more fully in specific chapters of the book which concludes with 'Towards a New Foundation', recommendations for the development of a more fruitful economics discipline.

In the year following publication the *Lament* was widely reviewed in both the professional and the popular press. The reaction was mixed; in general, the further away from the economics profession the reviewers were, the more favourable were their assessments! The reviewer of the London School of Economics *Economica*, for example, felt that the book was attempting (unjustly) to ascribe the acknowledged errors of a few to the profession as a whole. Lindley Fraser, writing a long review for Cambridge's *Economic Journal*, clearly did not accept Barbara Wootton's accusations as either justifiable or provable whilst, at the other end of the spectrum, the *Saturday Review* applauded the author's denunciation of the 'misty world of abstractions in which [the professional economist] apparently delights' (for all, see Fraser 1938: 208). *The Economist* was generally favourably disposed towards the arguments of the *Lament*, adding that the Woottonian image of economics was not unfamiliar.

Such a mixed contemporary reaction to a book critical of the 1930s economic orthodoxy comes as no great surprise to the reader of the 1980s. What is perhaps surprising is how fresh the Woottonian image of economics remains half a century after its original expression. Many of her observations appear quite 'modern' and this is because there now exists a further generation of economists who make broadly similar criticisms of aspects of the current economics mainstream. The orthodox image remains as deeply ingrained; Peter Donaldson, for example, announced that his *Economics of the Real World* was written for those 'who may have been put off by various aspects of the subject; its jargon and mystique, its unreality and lack of concern with people and their problems' (Donaldson 1973: 7). More recently, the convener of a conference on economic method attended by many distinguished practitioners concluded that the findings could be summarized in a single sentence: 'The main thing that is wrong with economics is its disrespect for fact' (Wiles and Routh 1984: 293). Elaborating somewhat, he referred to economists' persistence in believing in 'worn-out paradigms', the use of 'convenient half-truths' in place of evidence, an interest in 'puzzles not problems', and ideological bias. All of these are Woottonian themes from the *Lament*.

The present essay concerns itself with the apparent permanence of Barbara Wootton's image of economics, for the persistence of the same criticisms over half a century clearly requires explanation. Rather than reappraising the image in its entirety (which would necessitate the writing of a modern *Lament*), we shall select themes from the overall argument in order to see how economic theory, and economists' assessment of such theory, has changed. By so doing we can perhaps gain an insight into the significance of the modern form of criticism. The following section of the paper deals with the issue of unreality at the methodological level and Section III discusses changes in the nature of economic theory since the 1930s. Barbara Wootton's explanation for the dominance of 'useless' theory is next restated in a more modern form and the essay concludes with an assessment of the prospects for the development of a 'useful' economics.

II

Although Barbara Wootton's attack upon economic method was the culmination of her growing dissatisfaction with what she saw as the impotence of the discipline, the writing of the book itself had been prompted by the publication, some years earlier, of Lionel Robbins's *Essay on the Nature and Significance of Economic Science*. Robbins had set himself the task of both clarifying the subject matter of economics and delimiting the conditions under which economics could be of value in practical concerns. 'As a result of the theoretical developments of the last sixty years', he affirmed that there was 'no longer any ground for serious differences of opinion on these matters' (Robbins 1935: xiv). Events were to prove otherwise.

With the benefit of hindsight we can now see that Robbins was the last in a line of classical methodologists stretching back into the nineteenth century: there were echoes of Ricardo and Mill in Robbins's approach. Broadly speaking, the members of this line held that, within the sprawling corpus of the economics discipline, there existed a kernel of 'economic science', a set of logically deduced propositions or laws based upon a priori postulates about human behaviour. Amongst such propositions would be, for example, the existence of preference orderings and maximizing behaviour: 'we do not need controlled experiments to establish their validity: they are so much the stuff of our everyday experience that they only have to be stated to be recognised as obvious' (Robbins 1935: 79). These postulates, and the theories derived from them, were seen as ahistorical with the result that relating them to reality would test not their validity (how could it, if the postulates were 'obviously' true and the logic sound?) but rather their applicability in a particular historical context. One looked at reality, therefore, to see if it agreed with the theory, rather than the other way round.

Robbins's (self-)confident claim to the effect that the methodological controversy was at an end, and the series of ideas which were to disprove it, were actually developed simultaneously. In 1934, Karl Popper published his *Logik der Forschung* which offered a completely fresh view of the relation between theory and reality. Popper himself succinctly summarized his position some fifty years later in his autobiography: 'universal theories are not deducible from singular statements. But they may be refuted by singular statements, since they may clash with descriptions of observable fact' (Popper 1976: 86). Popper came to appreciate that a scientific methodology akin to the one advocated by Robbins in the context of economics was unable to supply any answer to this question: under what conditions would we admit a theory to be untenable? This was because the recognition of a correspondence between theory and reality could be counted as a 'verification' whereas any non-correspondence could be explained away in terms of the inapplicability of the theory in the specific circumstances. Accordingly, theories were, in principle, untestable; there was no way of distinguishing a 'good' theory from a 'bad' one, and there was therefore little to prevent anyone holding any theory in perpetuity. The Popperian methodology of 'falsification', on the other hand, could not legitimacy any particular theory at any particular time but it could certainly invalidate a theory which was shown to be consistently out of line with reality.

Applications of the Popper approach in economics were not long in arriving, Hutchison's *Significance and Basic Postulates of Economic Theory* (published in the same year as Barbara Wootton's *Lament*) and Samuelson's seminal *Foundations of Economic Analysis* (1948) being examples. As both defined the economist's task as the derivation of 'operationally meaningful theorems' (Samuelson's phrase, i.e. hypotheses admitting to the possibility of refutation by recourse to evidence), the Woottonian charge of lack of realism in economics would accordingly appear to have been answered from within the discipline itself. Economics was on the road to reality. Moreover, one could be forgiven for presuming that the very first thing that the new falsificationists would purge would be the patently counter-factual assumptions upon which certain parts of classical economic science appeared to rest, assumptions such as the existence of competitive markets which cleared instantly and effortlessly and of individuals who could precisely estimate marginal costs and benefits within the wink of an eye. That this did not happen was largely due to Milton Friedman's essay, 'The Methodology of Positive Economics' (in Friedman 1953).

As Blaug (1980) demonstrates in his excellent discussion of the essay and of the subsequent controversy resulting from it, the issue was of importance as much for what economists *think* was said as for what actually was said. Stated baldly, Friedman appeared to be arguing along two lines: (i) the relative qualities of rival economic theories are functions of their relative abilities to predict the course of events in the real world; (ii) the realism, or otherwise, of the assumptions of any theory is not necessarily relevant to the qualitative appraisal of that theory.

Interestingly enough, few economists disagreed with these propositions as such; rather, a debate ensued over how far one ought to go in the directions suggested. In one sense, the debate was about the relationship of the Friedman position to that of the Popperian methodology. A stringent interpretation of Popper's scientific method, for example, would require a one-for-one correspondence between any theory under test and reality at all levels, i.e. all assumptions would have to be realistic as would all logical operations based upon such assumptions, whilst the predictions would have to conform to that which actually transpired. Friedman, on some interpretations, seemed to be implying that the correspondence was only really important at the ultimate level of prediction. The realism of assumptions was believed to be 'largely' irrelevant, but how large is 'largely'? At certain points in his argument Friedman actually appeared to advocate the extreme instrumentalist methodology: because theories are *solely* instruments for prediction they need *only* predict well to be acceptable. Given the asymmetry between explanation and prediction, most economists were understandably unwilling to countenance the possibility of an economics discipline with a non-explanatory core.

In a very much 'softer' Friedman variant, however, we can legitimately question the acceptability of the stringent requirements alluded to above. Any mental construct of reality will, of necessity, be a simplification entailing a departure from that reality to a greater or a lesser extent. In this respect, it is by no means clear that economics is in any worse position than any other science. How, therefore, are we to determine whether our simplifying assumptions should be counted as realistic or otherwise? We could, of course, argue that certain assumptions (such as the famous 'entrepreneurs maximize profits') are realistic or unrealistic on a priori grounds but this is a verificationist notion and distinctly unfashionable in the post-Popper world. We are driven more and more towards the realm of testing.

Whatever else the Friedman controversy might have produced it did hasten the expulsion of many of the vestiges of apriorism from the mainstream of economics in favour of the development of 'operationally meaningful theorems'. To satisfy Friedman, theories would now have to work (to satisfy Popper, they would have to not not work). Unfortunately, we are not yet out of the woods because such a proposition begs a further question: how can we tell when a theory is not working? The simple answer would be 'when it does not fit the facts' but the facts themselves are not that simple.

Popper himself had readily appreciated in his *Logik* that all theories were capable of being 'immunized' against testing. Whilst naïve theorizing of the 'all swans are white' variety can easily be upset by the observation of a single black swan, economic and social theories are a good deal more sophisticated. To begin with, they are generally couched in probabilistic rather than inductive terms – 'all swans tend to be white' – with the result that a number of counter-examples – a number of black swans – would have to be observed before serious doubt could be entertained. How many such counter-examples, one now asks, will be deemed sufficient to refute the theory? I do not believe that there is a non-judgemental answer to this question although, to a large extent, the response will be conditioned by the relative successes of theoretical alternatives. Second, when relating economic theories to reality we do not consider reality *in toto* but rather selected data. When we ask if our theory has accurately predicted unemployment or the growth of the money supply we do not perceive these as such but as statistical measures – x million or y per cent. Such data are experimental results, as opposed to absolutes, and whoever heard of an experimenter who would not admit to the possibility of experimental error? Anyone who has worked with even the best of official statistics will be aware that they are regularly revised over time, that they can suffer from omissions and ambiguities of classification, that categories become redefined, and so on and so forth. In the case of an apparent counter-example, therefore, it might well be reality which is 'wrong', and not our theory. Third, the point made earlier about restricted applicability is equally valid in this case. We do not expect theories to be universally applicable and it is quite reasonable to specify circumstances under which we accept the theory ought to work, i.e. the conditions under which testing would be accepted as legitimate. Reality is, of course, complex and ever-changing, certainly as far as the economy is concerned. Might it not be conceivable, therefore, that any counter-example which reality happens to generate occurs because one or more of the applicability conditions under which the theory was intended to operate were violated? 'Other things were meant to be equal' and perhaps they were not.

At this stage of the argument it is possible to understand how the criticism of unreality in economics might persist in spite of the general acceptance of a methodology which is supposed to embody empirical testing as an important (in some cases, the only) criterion for theoretical acceptability. Just like his methodological antecedent, the 'immunized falsificationist' can also, if he so wishes, avoid any encounter with reality although the line of reasoning will naturally be different. Whilst the pre-Robbins apriorist would dismiss counter-examples with the reply: 'I know the theory to be true but the current empirical circumstances are not appropriate for its application', the modern falsificationist can state: 'I shall continue to hold my theory as provisionally true because the available empirical evidence does not, in my judgement, refute it.' We are accordingly brought to a debate over the interpretation of 'facts': on this score, you might tell me that I am being stubborn, blind, or even dishonest to continue to hold my particular theory, but I shall simply reply that I set very high scientific standards and I take a lot of convincing! A more concrete reason for being sceptical about evidence will emerge shortly.

III

Let us, for the moment, leave aside issues of realism in economic method and turn to another point made by Robbins's *Essay* which featured in Barbara Wootton's *Lament*. This concerned the content of the core of economic science. Wootton's critique of the usefulness of economics was concerned not so much with the accepted content of the core itself but rather with its relation to policy matters. The core was seen to be unreal (in the sense identified above) and also of diminished value owing to the reluctance of economists to include normative prescription within the framework of analysis. The central charge was therefore that economics was simply not constructed as a policy science although it was noted that, more recently, Keynes had been casting doubt upon the integrity of certain fundamental theoretical propositions. Were the

Lament to be rewritten today I am certain far more would now be made of the very substantial cracks which appeared in the once-solid core of economics.

It is most unlikely that anyone writing before the Second World War could have forecast the profundity of the influence which Keynesian ideas were to exert on economic thinking. Throughout the 1930s, Keynes produced a series of attacks (the 1936 *General Theory of Employment, Interest and Money* being the most famous) upon the classical orthodoxy at both a theoretical and an applied level. In reality, it is not certain that a truly homogenous orthodoxy ever existed outside Keynes's imagination although there was a broad agreement on the centrality of value theory as the model of behaviour. Taking the individual as the unit, the rational pursuit of self-interest, it was held, would lead to a series of exchanges between holders of resources whereby each would give up less-preferred commodities in return for more-preferred ones. Changes in demand and supply conditions would result in variations in the exchange prices which, if free to move, would ultimately re-equilibrate.

Keynes noted that even the most casual contact with the real economy attested to some theoretical weaknesses in this position. Was it not possible, for example, that there might exist resources which no one particularly wanted? In such a case conditions of permanent excess supply might prevail even at zero price. Correspondingly, conditions of excess demand were possible. Second, what possible function could money have in this type of system other than as a unit of account and a facilitator of exchange? Existing institutions such as stock markets and commercial banks seemed to suggest rather more importance than that implied by value theory. Third, what happens in our economy when market forces are impeded, for example by the existence of imperfect competition? Fourth, could we not discover circumstances in which the supposed harmony of interests is disturbed, that is cases where a strategy pursued by an individual to better his own lot actually causes the position of others to deteriorate?

Orthodoxy might well have immunized itself against such objections had it not been for the denial of value theory at the most fundamental level. The Keynesian rejection occurred on a priori grounds and was focused on the information or certainty assumption made about those engaging in exchange. To be said to be acting rationally, in the sense in which the orthodox theorists used the idea, I should have to know in advance the consequences of my potential actions so that I could weigh up the benefits and costs, and select the best option. Which, however, is the more plausible a priori assumption, that everyone has perfect information about all economic matters concerning themselves both now and in the future, or that individuals obtain varying degrees of information by observing the environment and then operate on the basis of expectations about the future conditioned by that information?

The Keynesian assault upon rational determinacy had to be taken seriously. Keynes was not alone; there was growing enthusiasm for Keynesian-type ideas amongst sections of the international economic community. Moreover, the chronic western depression of the 1920s and the 1930s was a cause for concern for even the most insular of the orthodoxy. As is regularly the case with potential scientific revolutions, the initial response to Keynesian ideas was accommodation. The grand 'neo-classical synthesis' of Paul Samuelson and John Hicks structured the *General Theory* as a macro-equilibrium analysis, counterpoised with the existing micro-equilibrium value theory. Whilst the market mechanism prevailed at the micro-level, governments were to regulate the macro-level (Dean 1981).

Times of material prosperity not being conducive to radical revisions of accepted economic truths, the 1950s and 1960s appeared, at least as far as the public was concerned, to be the period of the Keynesian consensus. Beneath the surface, this was not so. Certain economists were unwilling to accept the implications of the Keynesian critique of the classical model, and argued that it was in some places misleading and, in others, incorrect. Such economists (for example, the members of the Chicago School) accordingly began developing refinements to the existing structure of pre-Keynesian theory which, they believed, could accommodate the more serious of Keynes's objections. Even amongst the self-avowed Keynesians, however, there existed no unanimity. One group of 'fundamentalists' (including Robinson in the UK and Weintraub in the USA) objected to Keynes's emasculation at the hands of the neo-classicists who tended to play down the volatility of expectations and the supply-side causes of inflation. A further group of 'theoreticians' (such as Arrow, Debreu and Hahn) explored in detail some of the contradictions which the neo-classical synthesis believed itself to have resolved. The consequence of introducing Keynesian-type factors (such as uncertainty, differential market information and market power, the possibility of exchange costs, and ambiguous attitudes towards the future) into equilibrium models was, to say the least, untidy. In a number of circumstances it proved impossible to demonstrate the existence of an equilibrium, a significant result in view of the centrality of the concept in traditional thinking.

With mainstream economics clearly on the defensive as a result of the Keynesian revolution, the time was right for existing 'unorthodox' economic approaches to re-enter the lists with more vigour, and their positions have subsequently been reinforced with the eventual disillusionment about the 'Keynesian consensus' during the 1970s. Marxian economics, for instance, has steadily grown in stature throughout the twentieth century with the result that many western universities now teach courses in the subject (if only to demonstrate how broad-minded they are). Institutionalism developed in the USA at the beginning of this century and proceeded to relapse into a mid-century doldrums. 'Nothing exists today that could be described as an institutionalist movement in economics', said Blaug (1968: 681) but Elliott (1984) and the membership of the Evolutionary Economics' Association in the USA would nowadays disagree. Most recently the 'Austrian' economics of Mises and Hayek has become distinctly more fashionable.

During the past fifty years, therefore, a considerable amount of uncertainty has been introduced into economics (in both senses). In consequence, the modern criticism of economists, couched in terms of their manifest inability to produce agreed policy recommendations, is directed squarely at the less-than-robust theoretical core. Economists are no longer persons holding self-evident truths in common; economists are Austrians, monetarists, institutionalists, Keynesians, neo-Keynesians, Marxists, neo-Marxists, crypto-Marxist Keynesians, and all other permutations. As I intimated above, this was far less true of the pre-Robbins era when profession and public alike had confidence in the strength of the theoretical armoury (even if the latter doubted its utility).

IV

In the preceding sections we examined two of the symptoms observed by Barbara Wootton of the uselessness of economics and we discovered that critics could still interpret the discipline as unrealistic and equivocal in spite of changes in methodology and theoretical content. Let us move now from symptoms to causes. In the concluding pages of the *Lament* Barbara Wootton advances three possible reasons for the limited relevance of economics, the first being plain ignorance. Despite their extensive researches there remains much that economists do not know and such ignorance naturally limits their ability to develop policy recommendations. As Wootton recognizes, this is a general problem facing all scientific disciplines and we shall not develop the argument here. Ignorance is endemic in all areas of study and the solution is a 'more vigorous search for illuminating knowledge' (Wootton 1938: 309). As we saw above, economists are probably less ignorant, in absolute terms, than they were half a century ago but nowadays most are more aware of their remaining ignorance.

Wootton's second reason relates the quality of economics to the manner in which it is produced. Economic ideas, she notes, are developed in academic institutions established on the 'ancient Greek prejudice against any kind of knowledge that could possibly turn out to have any practical usefulness' (1938: 310). Academics value ideas as ends in themselves, rather than for their ability to solve real-world problems.

Using more recent work we can actually give this critique a sharper edge, by developing a behavioural model of research. The elements of this model are, first, Popper's observations about the immunization of theoretical structures (see p. 60 above), second, Kuhn's work on the sociology of science (Kuhn 1970), written as a rejoinder to Popper, and, third, post-Weberian bureaucracy theory (as summarized, for example, in Jackson 1982). The point at issue is the distinction between – to use Popper's terminology – 'great science' (a body of knowledge of value to mankind) and 'big science' (a body of knowledge of value to the growing 'academic industry').

With specialization and economic development, we might argue, academic research has become professionalized and bureaucratized. Agencies which, at one time or another, were set up as a *means* to obtain some goal have become *ends* in themselves as far as the individuals employed within them are concerned. Given this, researchers have become career bureaucrats with typically bureaucratic objectives, for example job satisfaction, security in employment, rising living standards over time, promotion, recognition by peers, and so forth. These objectives are secured by means of the approval of fellow researchers and superiors within the field of study (Katouzian 1980).

What implications does a bureaucratic model have for the nature of academic research? To begin with, the profession is faced with the problem of assessing the merits of particular pieces of research because it is merit, ostensibly, which is the criterion for the academic's success within the organization. Research *per se* is unfortunately somewhat intangible. Quality must remain a subjective notion determined, in the absence of any external pressure for accountability, by the valuations of the peer group. Further, it is unlikely that such external pressure could exist in academic matters. Specialists, not unreasonably, are disinclined to respect qualitative criteria advanced by non-specialists. In order to make sensible pronouncements about the quality of research work one needs to know something about the subject. Accordingly, one implicitly becomes a member of that scientific fraternity and, most likely, comes to share the values of that fraternity.

This being the case, there is no necessary correspondence between the profession's view of meritorious research and that of the public. If, for instance, the profession as a whole prefers to solve 'puzzles rather than problems' then this is the appropriate line of attack for bureaucrats who hope to advance their positions. The manner in which the professional norm becomes established is a complicated procedure and one related to the nature of the specific abilities of the fraternity, in particular the acknowledged leadership. In a community where Smith and Jones are the accepted academic models success must be to an extent contingent upon one's ability to follow in Smith and Jones's intellectual footsteps. As a corollary, we should conclude that most research has a conservative tinge; whilst respectful criticism is certainly acceptable, the consistent exposure of the ineptitude of one's 'superiors' is a most uncertain means of securing advancement.

This model additionally provides a basis for understanding two empirical observations, the first being the proliferation of research literature over the past half-century. Our model places academic bureaucrats in a competitive game (in the game theory sense) in which an individual's success is determined by his/her research record relative to those of other academics. Research being intangible, we should rewrite 'research record' as 'publication record'. Quality being difficult to assess, let us add a quantitative dimension and rewrite this as 'number of publications of a quality deemed reasonable'. Seen in this light, the academic press becomes the arena for competition between researchers; in the absence of collusion, game theory suggests that the arena will have to get ever larger as academics escalate their publication rates in order to out-compete one another.

Our second observation involves a reference back to Section II of this essay. There I suggested that the falsificationist methodology could legitimately permit researchers to hold on to theories in the face of many counter-examples. At the time, however, no reason was given as to why they should wish to do so. The model above provides one. The abandonment of a theory could impose substantial costs on the profession because it could lower academics' competitiveness: first, it narrows the scope for academic competition (discussions about refuted theories being ruled out of court) and, second, it disadvantages those whose expertise, or competitive potential, is based upon that theory. Moreover, if this theory happens to be the one on which Smith and Jones built their reputations. . . .

The institutional and sociological determinants of the character of research are actually only part of the story. Whilst the research undertaken certainly serves the function of assisting academics in the securing of private goals within the academic organization, there seems little doubt that psychological factors must also be involved. Unlike the members of most other bureaucracies, such as the Civil Service or the armed forces, professional academics largely determine the subject of their own occupations. They themselves create and refine the theories, models, and approaches with which they operate. We must therefore conclude that economists do the sort of economics which they do because that is the sort of economics that they like doing. In this respect, useful economics, from the economists' point of view, is economics which is interesting.

Although it may appear paradoxical, the 'uselessness' of certain forms of economic theorizing stems from its need to be interesting, because

interesting economics, to many academics, has to have similar characteristics to chess. It should exist as a formalized and challenging problem,
offering great scope for development but with the promise of the reward
of mastery given the input of sufficient time and effort. The challenge
must, therefore, be difficult, but not too difficult. Perhaps the more
precise parallel with the evolution of formalized economics is the medieval
tournament, the pastime of the men of leisure of long ago. Arising directly
from a real-world phenomenon – war – it was soon left behind by
developments in military technology and strategy. There remained only a
ritualized caricature which evolved its own independent procedure for the
benefit of the *cognoscenti*. Indeed, there is more than a touch of the Sir
Lancelots in contemporary academics who are seen rushing to champion
their beliefs in purely scholastic debates.

We finally turn to Barbara Wootton's third factor explaining the
restricted utility of economics: 'unless there is common agreement . . . as
to the aims of policy . . . research must lack the coherence which is
necessary to make it fruitful' (1938: 313). Again, here is an observation
appearing pertinent today. The past few decades have witnessed many
ideological shifts in western economies. Successive governments have had
widely differing attitudes to the proper conduct of economic affairs and an
uncertain climate for research has been created. At the most tangible level,
the political complexion of a government tends to determine the type of
research which it is prepared to fund, and also the type of economic advice
to which it is prepared to listen. Further, a given political climate can
influence research orientation and this will ultimately feed back into the
norms of the profession itself. In the 1960s, for example, the 'Keynesian
consensus' at the public level encouraged the extension of research into
public-sector problems and a fair number of economists of that generation
established themselves on the basis of their research into allocation problems under conditions of market failure. The political climate of the past
decade, however, especially in the UK and the USA, has been decidedly
less interventionist, with the result that the modern 'career academecrat'
would be better advised to work in the areas of monetarism, finance, and
private-sector economics. In such a way, it will be appreciated, research
areas do eventually come to ape reality to a limited extent, although not
necessarily for the most laudable of reasons. Such is the power of the
Invisible Hand.

V

My previous remarks might lead the reader to conclude that I do indeed
view the current state of economics as lamentable. Removing my tongue
from my cheek, let me say that this is not so, for my argument has been

overstated. Although I should argue that, in the above, a substantial kernel of truth exists, all is not confusion. To begin with, not all academics could be characterized by the rigid 'academecrat' model. Even if they could, the hypothesis should not be confined in application to economics alone: if it is relevant at all then it is relevant to every academic discipline to a greater or lesser extent. Should one deem the state of economics lamentable on these grounds, then there is no reason to feel unduly optimistic about any other subject area. In common with economics, other social disciplines have passed through periods when 'high theory' – for example, Talcott Parsons's sociological theory of action and David Easton's systems theory in political science – was very much in vogue. Modern particle physics at present appears to be operating with concepts even further divorced from real existence than those of even the most cloistered economist. Moreover, all such 'high theory' has also been subjected to the criticisms of unreality and non-operationalism. I accept that this point in no way condones the economist's 'lamentable' behaviour but it does protect him or her from condemnation in isolation.

More substantively, I believe that the record of certain elements of recent economic theory can actually be stoutly defended on the grounds of utility. Interestingly enough, the particularly fruitful developments have actually occurred along lines suggested by Barbara Wootton in the *Lament* (pp. 267–68), although I doubt whether the economists' imitation was conscious. Let us consider some examples.

Barbara Wootton's first exhortation to economists was to develop 'realistic applications' of theory. We have already examined instances of 'unreal' theory but recent years have witnessed the refinement of some powerful analytical (as opposed to purely theoretical) techniques. At the broadest level, econometrics, input-output analysis, and mathematical programming have come to play a significant role in policy formulation, indeed a far more substantial role than was considered possible by the received wisdom of the 1930s and 1940s. The simultaneous advances in mathematical and statistical method on the one hand, and of data recording on the other, have led to a state of affairs where sophisticated simulation models of entire economies (as well as of sectors within them) are regularly employed by policy-makers. Such models are inevitably far from perfect, both in their predictive and their explanatory powers, yet the perennially buoyant demand for forecasts suggests that decision-makers generally find them of more use than the alternatives. At a much more specific level, I should argue that human capital theory (developed from the late 1950s onwards) has, again irrespective of its weaknesses, contributed much to our understanding of real-world labour markets, the demand for education, the nature of recruitment, and so on.

'Studies of existing social situations and trends' (the second recommendation) have produced important developments. Barbara Wootton had, in an earlier chapter of the *Lament*, criticized economics for its pro-market orientation, although, in a sense, one might have considered that the position was not unreasonable in view of the prevailing economic structure during the earlier part of this century. By the 1950s, however, we observe the substantial displacement of market mechanisms in two respects – first, by the evolving planned economies of the east and, second, by the expanded government sectors of capitalist economies. The observation of such realities, and of their implicit institutional structures, provided the foundation for a new subdiscipline of theory, non-market economics. It is a branch which has yielded useful applications. At the macro-level, the development of planning theory has eased economic management problems in certain western economies (notably in Scandinavia) and such theory naturally remains of central importance in the eastern bloc. Manifestations at the 'grass-roots' level include designs for income maintenance schemes, analysis of the implications of different methods of taxation, and the establishment of efficiency criteria in public services.

Social choice theory has been perhaps the most direct response to Barbara Wootton's third aspiration for the subject – 'enquiries into the nature of social ends in modern communities, and the means of formulating these'. In some respects, this development is a corollary of the second; as government activity within western economies assumed greater importance it became less and less plausible to assume that governments were either irrelevant or exogenous. The application of economic models in the traditional subject area of political science is producing intriguing results; an example is the model used in Section IV of the present paper. Individuals within organizations are seen to view their functions, objectives, and costs differently from those outside and, in consequence, what appears desirable from one point of view might seem less so from the other.

Barbara Wootton's final recommendations may be realizable less in any one area and more in an approach. She advocated work upon the broader issues involved in the attainment of social ends, as well as the adoption of a more overt and positive commitment to 'social betterment'. In recent years there has been a growing awareness on the part of many social analysts that such interdisciplinary and directed investigation can provide insights in areas where formalized analysis has proved itself sterile. Generally termed 'modern political economy', this holistic orientation remains in its infancy and there is, as yet, no established doctrine to parallel the conventional economics corpus. Rather, work currently proceeds in several directions, being founded upon the ideas of various groups of theorists (Whynes 1984).

Lament for Economics was written by someone who was frustrated by the ossification of a formal academic discipline. Since that time, enormous changes have taken place within the subject such that, to modern eyes, 'economics stripped of the contributions of the last fifty years looks primitive, clumsy, almost unusable' (Heilbroner 1980). There has indeed been a 'new age', although perhaps one more 'Hellenistic' than 'Periclean' (Heilbroner 1980: 6). At present, therefore, economists have cause to feel optimistic about their studies. Uncertainty being endemic, however, it is difficult to see where the future of economic theory lies. Should ossification again threaten we must hope that a future Barbara Wootton will appear to chastise us.

REFERENCES

Blaug, M. (1968) *Economic Theory in Retrospect* (2nd edn). London: Heinemann.

—— (1980) *The Methodology of Economics*. Cambridge: Cambridge University Press.

Dean, J. W. (1981) The Dissolution of the Keynesian Consensus. In D. Bell and I. Kristol (eds) *The Crisis in Economic Theory*. New York: Basic Books.

Donaldson, P. (1973) *The Economics of the Real World*. Harmondsworth: Penguin Books.

Elliott, J. E. (1984) The Institutionalist School of Political Economy. In D. K. Whynes *What Is Political Economy?* Oxford: Blackwell.

Fraser, L. M. (1938) Economists and Their Critics. *Economic Journal* 48: 196–210.

Friedman, M. (1953) *Essays in Positive Economics*. Chicago: University Press.

Heilbroner, R. L. (1980) Modern Economics as a Chapter in the History of Economic Thought. In *Political Economy at the New School*. New York: New School for Social Research.

Jackson, P. M. (1982) *The Political Economy of Bureaucracy*. Deddington: Philip Allan.

Katouzian, H. (1980) *Ideology and Method in Economics*. London: Macmillan.

Kuhn, T. S. (1970) *The Structure of Scientific Revolutions* (2nd edn). Chicago: University Press. (First published 1962.)

Popper, K. (1934) *Logik der Forschung*. Vienna: Springer.

—— (1976) *Unended Quest*. Glasgow: Fontana/Collins.

Robbins, L. (1935) *An Essay on the Nature and Significance of Economic Science* (2nd edn). London: Macmillan. (First published 1932.)

Whynes, D. K. (ed.) (1984) *What is Political Economy?*. Oxford: Blackwell.

Wiles, P. and Routh, G. (eds) (1984) *Economics in Disarray*. Oxford: Blackwell.

Wootton, B. (1938) *Lament for Economics*. London: Allen & Unwin.

—— (1967) *In a World I Never Made*. London: Allen & Unwin.

5
TOWARDS A RATIONAL
INCOMES POLICY
Joan Mitchell

Thirty years ago, Barbara Wootton ended *The Social Foundations of Wage Policy* with an account of some of the requirements of a viable incomes policy. Twenty years ago, the first systematic attempt began to apply an incomes policy, on lines not dissimilar to Professor Wootton's suggestions. Ten years ago saw the beginning of the era of the Social Contract. Now, as we do honour to her, we are without a formal incomes policy, but are even more in need of progress 'towards a rational incomes policy'. During the past two decades the idea of incomes policy has sometimes been neglected and unfashionable, sometimes eagerly cultivated and fashionable. But the original analysis and the conclusions drawn from it have become neither out of date nor irrelevant. That in itself is a truly formidable achievement in a complex and politically sensitive subject.

In 1955, the subject of wage policy could hardly have been less well regarded, or even less regarded, especially by the great majority of politicians. How could there be a wage policy worth the name in a market economy? Or, if there was, it would be another name for wage restraint. Yet at the same time, the logic of reality was forcing tentative steps to be taken towards such a policy, incoherent though it then was. During the 1950s two significant trends were developing.

Governments, sympathetic though they then were to market philosophies, were having to set up commissions to settle pay and conditions of work for workers in the public sector, including highly paid professionals like the doctors and dentists; and commissions set up to inquire into public-sector professions in general, like the Civil Service (1955) and the police (1960), had to make recommendations about pay and settling pay disputes. Inflation was a chronic threat to successful economic management, while increases in earnings continually exceeded increases in output. A White Paper, *Incomes Policy: the Next Step*, appeared in 1962, its publication being very largely explained by the second sort of pressure, macro-economic policy difficulties, though clearly having implications for the sectoral problems of governments as employers. This particular White Paper scarcely dealt with the problems adequately, and was almost totally ineffective, if only because it had the opposition of unions. But it signified that the subject was on the political agenda.

The principles on which pay is to be settled for separate negotiating groups of professions, trades, skills, or occupations are relevant not only to public-sector groups, where market pressures manifestly do not entirely operate, but to others, where they overtly do but where arbitration or administrative inquiry is the method of reaching a settlement. As well as arbitration tribunals to settle disputes, there are the wages councils and boards set up specifically for workers not sufficiently protected from market forces to get socially tolerable pay and conditions. Arbitrators can only be dispute-settlers; and wages councils can only be copiers of trends perpetually set by others without some guiding principles about what pay ought to be. There is merit in both these procedures; but their success is entirely dependent on the viability of settlements made elsewhere. If those other leading settlements are inflationary, the processes of arbitration and wage-council bargaining will reinforce the inflationary pressures. Arbitration is only too likely to be inflationary on its own account as well, as a dispute-settling award in a leading sector is often copied elsewhere. An incomes policy, meaning principles or figures on which individual micro-level settlements can be made to avoid or damp down inflationary tendencies, has been needed and intermittently sought ever since.

How to settle public-sector pay without either disproportionate strife or plainly inflationary additions to public expenditure is the other main problem increasingly prominent in governments' preoccupations with incomes, and a large part of the reasons for their failure to live up to their own targets or intentions. Governments are in a particularly exposed position in dealing with either public servants, for whom they are the employer; or local-authority staffs, where they plainly determine the money available for the employing authorities to dispense; or public-corporation employees, especially where public money is needed to support current activities.

An agency somewhat removed from government proper was prominent in the discussions which put incomes policy into the centre of economic policy. This agency, the National Economic Development Council (NEDC), only began work after the first tentative Incomes Policy White Paper had appeared. But its first task was to study what determines economic growth, which it duly did in the early 1960s, culminating in the publication of *Conditions Favourable to Faster Growth* in 1963. The NEDC's great strength politically was that it was 'tripartite', that is trade union leaders and industrialists took part in discussions with government ministers. This meant that at least some of these trade union leaders became convinced that an incomes policy to control inflation was required in the context of faster economic growth, of which they were passionate advocates; and that the terms of an incomes policy in that context were not necessarily anti-labour or anti-egalitarian. However, with an increasingly weak government, it was not possible for the NEDC itself to say much publicly about incomes policy. The purposeful discussions were taking place between union leaders and the Labour Party leadership, against the background of an economic policy for faster growth through economic planning, modernizing industry through science and technology, and protecting the poorest through better pensions, housing, and food subsidies. The consequence was that a new Labour government in 1964 introduced an incomes policy of unprecedented detail and with unprecedented support, the first major attempt to deal with the twin problems of macro incomes restraint and acceptable micro settlements.

By this time, it was taken for granted that incomes policy would only be acceptable with some reciprocal control on other factor rewards, and with some protection of real incomes. Rent controls already existed, and interest rates were low; profits were the remaining flow to be curtailed in line with employment incomes. Profits were already curbed if not controlled by taxation, but this was thought to be too slow and indirect a check to be a satisfactory complement to incomes policy. Hence the acceptable compromise was to be prices policy. In any case, prices policy was desirable, especially to trade union leaders, so that incomes policy could be compatible with the maintenance of real incomes. Moreover, the previous government had clearly made a serious political mistake in trying to introduce an element of incomes policy without constraint on prices.

The prices and incomes policy of the new government was published in the White Paper of 1965. It was plain that macro-economic policy was the main determinant. Inflation was to be eliminated by constraining incomes growth to that of expected productivity. Optimism ruled. Output per head was expected to rise by some 3½ per cent a year for the five years to 1970, though not so much in 1965. Nevertheless the 'norm' – the expected general increase in incomes – was to be 3 to 3½ per cent. Thereafter the White Paper laid out guidelines for micro-level income determination. Individual wage agreements would provide for shorter hours and longer holidays, continuing trends already well established. There would be exceptional increases justified by major changes in working practices, to effect a desirable redistribution of labour, to maintain 'a reasonable standard of living', and to restore pay rates which had 'fallen seriously out of line' with rewards for similar work elsewhere. But generally speaking 'less weight than hitherto' should be given to comparisons with pay elsewhere (especially in other sectors). It was clearly expected that relativities would change smoothly, where efficiency or equity dictated.

The design of the policy paid due regard to considerations of market pressures and of equity. Pay has a key micro role as incentive to workers to take up more demanding or more versatile work, and to induce shifts between firms or industries as demand patterns change. At the same time, the low paid, and those with a particular grievance in comparison with analogous groups, would be able to restore their welfare somewhat within the rules of the policy. To provide a guarantee of fairness and ensure the participation of interested parties, a politically balanced and independent body, the National Board for Prices and Incomes (NBPI), would examine cases against the general criteria.

All this was not at all far removed from the remedies Barbara Wootton had formulated ten years before. At least an attempt was being made to articulate guiding principles for 'fair' and 'reasonable' pay bargains whose previous absence had so provoked both her interest and disapproval. Cumulative inflation through leap-frogging pay settlements should be generally avoided (though the politically necessary concession to restore those 'seriously out of line' allowed a bit of jumping if not leaping). Facilitating desirable changes in the distribution of labour was allowed for; and the social and political desirability of greater equality was at least recognized in special treatment for the low paid. Finally the 'impartial commission' able to 'explore the steps necessary to carry into effect a wage policy' was being set up, and given the principles without which it would have had 'a task beyond its capacity' (Wootton 1955: 166–68).

The White Paper generally concerned itself both with the 'size of the whole cake' and 'its division into appropriate slices', and the government had firmly tackled both the technical and political problems of 'calculating the divisible total'. Professor Wootton foresaw only too well what opposition there is in practice to egalitarianism, not least among trade unions; and in spite of her own deep attachment to the idea, she recognized the force of economic considerations especially concerning structural changes, which often dictate departures from egalitarian policies. Her minimum demand was for a mechanism whereby a specific case had to be made; and this had now been established, in principle at any rate.

The 1965 version of incomes policy lasted until 1970 – for as long as the Wilson administration remained in office, and for as long as the policy had been intended to last. But its history was more turbulent than so bald a summary suggests. The Wilson government had lost its enthusiasm for the policy by 1967 or 1968 as it did not appear to be giving quick results. The policy was then abruptly abandoned when a new government came to office (under the leadership of Mr Heath) partly because of opposition to both incomes policy and the NBPI on the grounds that they interfered with free collective bargaining (leap-frogging and all) and with the free play of market forces, as seen in labour markets by industrial negotiations. It also finished under the cloud of failure, as inflation and strife over pay persisted and now showed every sign of increasing.

There were many at that time, on both the political left and right, who concluded that the Wootton remedy for economic management problems had been proved wrong, and that the country could now get on with their several chosen policies, having been rescued from mistaken side-tracks. Certainly, the 1965 version of incomes policy had not worked out as expected in practice. But the particular sources of difficulty reflect not so much the policy as such, but rather particular forms and circumstances.

First, for all its attempts to match macro and micro criteria consistently, just how serious their incompatibility was had not been fully appreciated. Professor Wootton herself had devoted some space to the tension between pay negotiators' (especially unions') passionate devotion to differentials, relativities, and redistribution of income at the micro level, and general pay constraint at the macro level. The NBPI had done its best to square the circle in a number of cases it reviewed, by finding and recommending such changes in productivity and working practices as to facilitate desired pay increases, which at the same time could restore or prevent rewards seriously out of line with appropriate analogues, and induce extra output or reduced input without parallel cost and price increases. These cases were not to be counted as failures. But there were too few cases to make an impact on national trends in so short a time, and the demonstrative effect on similar cases not reviewed was nullified by too many cobbled-up 'productivity deals' that did not in fact deliver extra output or reduced unit cost commensurate with the extra pay.

Secondly, the incomes policy and the NBPI were convenient vehicles for the government to use for drastic changes in macro policy, the micro criteria making it acceptable politically. In 1966, rather than devalue the pound (a policy with its own problems of implementation) in order to improve the balance of payments and counter speculation, the government chose to deflate, using the incomes policy for severe restraint of incomes, which meant reductions of real income for many. Thereafter, though the restraint was gradually lifted according to government policy, the perpetual struggle to defend or expand real incomes at the micro level rendered the national incomes policy norms and targets less and less effective.

Thirdly, inflationary though comparisons between sectors might be, there was little else by which many public-sector jobs could be judged. Exactly what is to be compared is an important and sometimes difficult question, whose answer can often improve the macro impact of an acceptable settlement; but comparability there has to be.

But the political problems of the policy should not conceal entirely the progress that had been made before 1970, which went very much on the lines foreseen by Professor Wootton. She had complained, quite justi-fiably, about the excessive secrecy surrounding pay questions. A consider-able part of the 'Curiosities of British Wage Structure' (Wootton 1955: 28–38) itemizes the paucity of official figures, the difficulty of sup-plementing them, and the utter confusion introduced by the absence of information about fringe benefits and by the widespread habit of express-ing increases in pay over varying and sometimes unspecified periods of the past. The NBPI found all of that completely inhibited its casework. But its members and staff were sufficiently determined and powerful at least to remedy some difficulties. Having got the distinction between pay and quoted wage or salary rates firmly in the public (i.e. political) conscious-ness, by its instigation the New Earnings Survey was initiated covering pay and its constituents more systematically and more frequently than before. At last the facts for a viable policy – or even view – of incomes were available.

The next episode of (prices and) incomes policy in the UK began in 1972, in spite of the then government's earlier protestations. Apart from corroborating Professor Wootton's conviction that there must be such a policy for effective economic management in relatively prosperous times, the policy itself owed little either to ideas she had originally helped to formulate, or to the preceding attempt. The Counter-inflation Act, 1973, owed most to the policy introduced in the United States in 1971, again in spite of the Republican-led government's vehement opposition to administrative controls. Increases in incomes were controlled by a Code, having statutory force through the Act under which it was promul-gated.

In 1971 and 1972, the government seemed less and less able to control inflation. The problem was that in spite of falling production and a then alarming increase of unemployment to over one million, the rise in retail prices did not falter. The 1972 Budget allowed aggregate demand to rise again, partly through increasing public expenditure, partly by stimulating a consumer boom. Inflation speeded up in the summer and autumn, fed by lax credit policy at home and relaxed exchange policies internationally, and by deficiencies in supply on some world markets for food and raw materials. But wage costs were also pressing. The government felt it needed a fourth means of control, along with fixed control of aggregate demand, monetary policy, and allowing sterling to float free of officially fixed rates. This fourth means was a demonstrably tight prices and incomes policy, to steer the economy back to higher output and employment, balance of payments equilibrium, faster growth, and more stable prices. Hence, a quickly designed incomes policy.

Stage one of the new policy was actually a freeze, to last for six months. Stage two, for the following year, was set out in the Pay Code, and consisted of a limited cash increase (£2.50 a week), carefully not called a norm, plus a few extra increases. There was, predictably, uproar in the trade unions over the new policy, mainly for its alleged unfairness. But there were in fact more concessions to income redistribution than before. The £2.50 was a much higher proportionate increase for the lower paid than for the higher paid, and the policy was made still more progressive at higher salary levels by an absolute limit of £250 a year. Moreover, instalments due to women to bring their rates nearer equality with men (to be achieved by the end of 1975, in accordance with the Equal Pay Act of 1970) were outside the Pay Code limits, and women were overwhelmingly the largest group of the low paid.

There was widespread criticism of the inflexibility of the stage two rules, because the uniform cash increase reduced differentials. Skilled and supervisory workers' unions were frustrated by the policy, and hence by the government, rather than by employers. Employers were unable to reward skill or responsibility enough to retain their staffs. However, in the private sector, where government writs, statutory or not, are not observed quite so meticulously or literally as they are in the public sector, promotions, regrading, and a selection of 'perks' (especially company cars) were soon found to ease the constraints somewhat.

The government endeavoured to make stage three rather more acceptable by allowing pay negotiators to choose either £3.25 a week or 7 per cent on basic rates; this meant that a significant number of the low paid got considerably more than a 7 per cent increase. In addition, there was another 1 per cent of pay bills allowed for 'flexibility', i.e. for regrading, or restoring particularly sensitive differentials. At the last moment a further modest increase was found for 'unsocial hours', specifically, it was said, to allow a somewhat higher increase to be paid to miners, who were already taking industrial action.

However, the most significant innovation of this incomes policy episode was the introduction of so-called 'threshold agreements'. The intention was to counteract the inflationary effect of expectations. It was thought that an important element in wage inflation was the trade unions' effort to protect their members' real income by demanding pay increases at least equivalent to *expected* inflation, rather than just inflation as *experienced* in the immediate past or present. As inflation had been and was still accelerating, this made an acceleration of pay increases inevitable; and as productivity could hardly go on accelerating at the same pace, nor could increases in consumption be accommodated continually, constraint of costs, and increased resources for investment or earning more overseas, required the expectations to be punctured. The Pay Code increase had been based on official forecasts of a 7 per cent increase in prices during the year. If the Retail Price Index rose more than that, pay could be increased *automatically* (with a threshold agreement) by 40p a week for every 1 per cent extra. This was in effect virtual indexation of pay increases, and all unions hastened to get threshold agreements included in their various conditions of work.

The intention was that once unions and their members knew that real incomes would at least be protected, further increases could be negotiated in closer relation to productivity or improved labour management practices, and the general effect would be counter-inflationary. But the viability of the policy depended crucially on the official forecasts being realistic. In fact, they were not only wrong, but wildly optimistic, since the introduction of the policy roughly coincided with the first OPEC oil price crisis, as well as with further world inflation of food and other commodity prices. The early months of stage three coincided with the impact on the UK of these international influences. The first threshold increase in the pay bill was triggered in April, 1974; it was followed by such rapid further increases that several extra payments became due *per month*. Furthermore, it was doubtful whether many recipients really knew what the payments were for. It was perhaps not surprising that union pay negotiators showed no sign at all of changing the basis of their still-increasing claims. If anything, their expectations were more inflationary than before.

Unfortunately (for the policy) the government had now changed again, to a Labour administration dedicated, under strong union pressure, to free collective bargaining 'with moderation'. Inflation, home-produced, was added to the growing influences from overseas. For once, public-sector unions and workers were able to lead the process, taking the opportunity to restore relativities eroded by the Counter-inflation Act. This was partly just because the public sector more precisely and immediately applies government rules, whatever they are. Usually, this means government constraints. For once, it meant government largess, though nothing more than even-handedness was the intention. Furthermore, a number of special settlements had been made by the in-coming government, to put an end to damaging disputes with public-sector workers. There was the miners' settlement (of around 20 per cent extra) to end the strike which had led to the general election. There were unusually large settlements for nurses and teachers, after special inquiries, backed by more generous settlements in normal public-sector negotiations than had been possible for the previous four or five years. In the nature of things, public-sector workers can never lead in actual pay increases for long, given reasonable prosperity: it is too easy for private-sector workers or their employers to catch up or keep up, by pay supplements, fringe benefits, promotions, and regrading, if not by more direct increases in pay rates.

Fortunately (for the policy) the uncontrolled 'moderation' lasted little over a year before several of the trade union leaders (notably Hugh Scanlon of the engineers, and Jack Jones of the transport workers, two of the largest and most influential unions) became thoroughly alarmed at the prospect of inflation, plainly home-generated, continuing to accelerate beyond the 25 to 30 per cent rate it had reached. Another hastily arranged incomes policy began in summer, 1975.

This time it was much cruder in administrative or political terms, far cruder than Professor Wootton had ever envisaged. Yet at the same time, it met one of the conditions she had clearly foreseen: it was acceptable to enough of the unions, and sufficiently tolerated by employers, to over-come the continual underlying pressure to maintain differentials and relativities. Resort was had again to a cash increase for all, of £6 a week (for those earning up to £8,500 a year, then a high wage income). For the low paid, including many women workers, this was the most generous increase they had ever had, and probably a good bit more than they would have got by normal negotiation. For skilled workers in high-paying industries (including some in the public sector), it was trivial but was acceptable politically, especially after a bout of practically unrestrained increases. This, phase one of a 'Social Contract', as it was known, was followed by another universal increase, but this time in much the same form as the stage two increase, a (smaller) cash increase or a percentage increase. This again was tolerated, especially as 1976 ended with the currency very weak, an atmosphere of financial crisis, and an emergency loan, with stringent conditions, from the International Monetary Fund (IMF). Phase three went back to a straight percentage increase – the norm of earlier days – and was accepted, though with union negotiators clearly more restive, as 'anomalies' and special cases accrued; in other words, uncomfortable differentials and relativities increasingly needed adjust-ment. Nevertheless, the policy still held, and had a major part in mitigating home-generated inflation. The index showed declining increases, down to between 10 and 20 per cent in 1977, and to single figures in 1978. But there were still difficult macro adjustments to make, requiring constraint in consumption. The fiscal arithmetic showed that little extra pay could be accommodated generally. The government tried to get another agreement on a 5 per cent increase. Union agreement was not forthcoming; and a spate of strikes and other industrial action started and continued through to 1978, concerning mostly lower-paid public-sector workers.

The government's response was to go back to an independent com-mittee of inquiry, limited this time to public-sector cases. This was the

Standing Commission on Pay (the Clegg Commission) set up in 1979, months before another general election. All the difficult public-sector pay negotiations, almost all already in dispute or very near it, were referred to the Commission. Relativities were investigated, with the help of the Pay Research Unit, the comparability-seeking unit for Civil Service pay, and the Office of Manpower Economics, originally a rump of the pay inquiry part of the NBPI staff, then providing secretarial and other back-up services for the four independent review bodies serving public-sector workers indefinitely (for doctors and dentists; the armed forces; 'top people's' salaries: judges, nationalized industries' chairmen and boards, Members of Parliament, and so on; and the police). Local-authority manual workers and National Health Service (NHS) ancillary workers were two large negotiating groups among the first bunch of references who had to be investigated by the NBPI, and who had not had a major review since 1966. Nurses and teachers were other groups with difficult pay problems which erupted every few years. (A major pay adjustment follows, succeeded inevitably by enough change of duties and gradual attenuation of relativities to create another intolerable situation.) Both nurses and teachers had had major inquiries, followed by pay settlements based on comparability in 1974–75; and before that nurses' pay had been adjusted on the recommendation of the NBPI, after investigation, in 1968.

Since some major cases were referred to the Commission, and since public-sector workers anyway negotiate in large groups which include an unusually large number of separate occupations, the results of the comparisons, meticulous though they were, involved large sums of money. An appreciable boost to public expenditure followed. Some pay increases were directly inflationary; for instance, extra pay for local-authority workers might lead to increased rates which are included in the retail price index. Some increases were thought to be inflationary indirectly, since they were financed from government revenue; for instance, increases in nurses' and teachers' salaries are financed from extra taxation or from extra borrowing, both of which the in-coming government (the first Thatcher administration) was convinced soon led to higher prices.

In its first eighteen months or so, the government was nevertheless happy to send various difficult public-sector pay problems to the Clegg Commission. Disputes and difficult negotiations have to be resolved somehow, and a standing commission is a convenient emollient in a situation of political conflict. But as inflation climbed again to over 20 per cent a year, under the impact of another elevation of oil prices, the government grew more determined to constrain public expenditure even at the expense of comparability in the settlement of public-sector pay claims; the Clegg Commission was blamed for the inflation which followed its recommended settlements and was wound up. Nevertheless:

'The relevance of comparability to public sector pay is one of the central issues of British industrial relations. For more than twenty years public policy on the subject has swung backwards and forwards. Another swing away from comparability is already gathering momentum; but it is likely that pressure for comparability will sooner or later mount again to the point where the government of the day will find it irresistible, as governments have in the past.'   (Clegg 1980: 32)

So said the Clegg Commission in its *General Report* (its final report). The rest of its report set out what it had achieved, the methods it used, the difficulties still remaining, and the possible ways to develop usefully on work already done.

After the Clegg Commission and the end of formal attempts to settle either public-sector pay or any other in a systematic way, with a place for the national interest at the negotiating table, there started another period of sporadic breakdowns in relations between public-sector employees and their employers. Government pay rules, of whatever kind, apply directly and literally to government employees. Excepting only pay freezes, any incomes policy is subject to enough flexibility, especially after permissible techniques have been learned, for public-sector workers to be left behind again in terms of relative incomes.

The third decade after Professor Wootton's pioneering work was thus occupied by the two most recent attempts at wage policy, the one cruder than she had forecast, the other more confined in scope though not in the sophistication of its methods. Once more, dominant opinion, led by the government, its supporters, and ideologues, held that incomes policy does not 'work': that is, it either fails entirely to produce the intended result, or any result is short-lived.

Discussing the practical success or failure of the various episodes of incomes policy is never easy, since the results which are put down as partial successes or failures are most often not specified. Governments have mainly had objectives of economic management in mind. In macro terms, only the Social Contract crude version of 1975–78 was accompanied by a clear declaration of pay increases and labour costs. It is said that this was offset, or partly offset, by consequential rebounding pay increases in the next few years, as eroded differentials and relativities were restored. But in 1978–80, as so often, there were so many other changes in the various determinants of prices and incomes that the relationship remains dubious. The Counter-inflation Act Code of 1973–74 was so overwhelmed by the effects of the threshold agreements that no conclusions follow. The NBPI episode of the 1960s was being operated in such differing circumstances, ending at a time of even greater turbulence, that general effects of a rather tentative policy are not likely to be apparent.

We are left with Professor Wootton's original arguments more or less intact. It is still true, as it was in 1955, that: 'the contemporary wage and salary structure of this country [is] the accumulated deposit laid down by a rich mixture of economic and social forces' (Wootton 1955: 161). But it is still true also that: 'No longer the private concern of the worker and his employer alone, every wage bargain is now a matter of threefold concern; at least a watching brief. . . must be assigned to the representatives of the general public' (Wootton 1955: 161).

In 1974, after experience of the two more elaborate and structured incomes policies of 1965–70 (with the norm and NBPI) and 1972–74 (with the C-I Act and the Pay Code), Professor Wootton herself drew some conclusions from the history of these two periods, looking towards more effective solutions to the problem. Her interest is still in longer-term adjustment and in social change by means of incomes policy. Her personal preference is for much greater equality of disposable incomes, by whatever means.

In her 'inquest' into the two main attempts at incomes policy Professor Wootton concentrated on the differences between the functions and activities of the boards, the NBPI and the Pay Board. The most striking difference of all was the lack of discretion left to the Pay Board, whereas the NBPI had been left with wide discretion. The Pay Board had only to apply a detailed code, which itself had the force of law. It could not have the last word in contentious cases, since the law courts must be the final arbiters of interpretations of the law. The NBPI worked with specific terms of reference, taking explicitly into account far wider considerations concerning fairness and acceptability than the Pay Code; and could (and did) grace its interpretations with recommendations for pay increases, as well as general comment on the application of the current rules. The NBPI dealt with prices and profits as well as incomes; the Pay Board dealt only with pay, everything else being dealt with by separate codes (if at all), with a separate Price Commission on the sidelines.

The NBPI had shown, if demonstration were needed, that most pay negotiations for significant groups of workers have important economic ramifications, as well as raising keenly felt questions of equity. Its terms of reference were always wide enough, even in the days of severe restraint, for some consideration to be given to these. Squaring circles, combining equity with economic efficiency, was the constant preoccupation of the NBPI at work. In contrast, some provisions for meeting special cases, partly based in equity, partly in efficiency, were added to the Pay Code; but its primary purpose was still the counter-inflationary constraint of all incomes, according to the macro economic management arithmetic.

Professor Wootton concludes:

'any long-term policy must avoid excessive rigidity on the one hand, and undue laxity on the other . . . the rules under which the NBPI operated offered plenty of loopholes; but after experience of the tightly drawn Codes . . . a garment disfigured by holes is to be preferred to a strait-jacket – provided only that the holes are not too large, or in unsuitable places.'   (Wootton 1974: 83)

The analysis was intended as the prelude to a proposal for a longer-lasting incomes policy, without the weaknesses appearing in earlier attempts. That proposal was for a new tax, instead of either broad, basically voluntary rules, plus interpretation by a board, or narrowly defined statutory rules requiring separate administration.

In the decade since then, a fiscally based incomes policy has been Liberal Party policy, then more hesitantly, Social Democratic Party policy. In so far as the politicians have produced specific proposals, they have some major differences from the Wootton scheme. So it remains to discuss some of the general problems arising from using taxation, and then some of the possibilities of, or possible obstacles to, the specific proposals.

The general concept of using taxation is to allow bargaining over pay to proceed in the normal way; but to prevent the macro effects, namely the increase in the national pay bill, from being inflationary, all increases, or increases over the odds, are made subject to taxation. The rates of tax would have to be high, if not as high as 100 per cent. Any scheme to use taxation for control purposes starts with one major advantage and one major disadvantage. The advantage is that public awareness of taxation is very high; there is a familiar mechanism for applying it; and there is no doubt that it is universally compulsory. To a large degree, individuals and companies are law-abiding. Taxation is embodied in the law, so the policy would be quickly observed at least in the letter. Moreover, the majority of companies and many individuals rely on accountants to apply tax law for them; being professionals, accountants quickly and accurately apply whatever the law is to their clients.

However, taxation for whatever purpose is unpopular. Who ever liked paying taxes? Moreover, almost all taxation is imposed to collect revenue, some of it for purposes widely accepted or applauded by the taxpayers. It is unusual, to say the least, to have a tax whose overt purpose is to stop the taxpayers doing something which would render them liable to tax. It is unusual to use the tax system for purposes quite so near punishment. It is a curiosity of politics in the 1980s that politicians contemplate putting their heads into that noose, especially with well-advised special-interest groups ready to spell out exactly what is happening to the relatively poor, or other deserving cases.

Beyond these essentially political questions, we have to distinguish between Professor Wootton's income gains tax, which would be imposed on the recipients of income, and inflation tax proposals, whereby the employers, mostly companies, would be subject to the tax. Supplements to income tax, or to corporation tax, raise rather different issues, for or against them.

In favour of a Wootton income tax-based scheme is that it is the most direct way of dealing with excessive pay increases. Because it is individually based, with assessment of individual circumstances, it is best fitted to take account of either special cases or graduation according to income or other related levels. It is a relatively promising way of combining general restraint with more equal distribution. This is indeed one of the major attractions for Professor Wootton, who is as anxious as ever to bring about a major shift towards equalization.

Against levying incomes policy taxes on individuals rather than companies it can be said that this underplays the significance of pay in the micro workings of the economy. Pay is connected with productive functions, often very closely. Some increases in pay are directly related to extra output, through overtime, piece-work, or productivity supplements and bonuses. Some increases result from incremental scales, or promotion to grades carrying more responsibility. Individuals may obtain increases by moving to a new and better job. And there are the wholly or partly self-employed developing and expanding their business. Professor Wootton of course recognized all these, and concluded that tax inspectors could deal with them, given rules on the lines of the then current Pay Codes, in the same way as they deal with business expenses. But there would be a great many more such cases to deal with, and one might doubt the competence of inland revenue staff to assess worthwhile and worthless productivity schemes without in any way decrying their ability to deal with business expenses under present arrangements. The position of employers who positively want to use pay increases of some sort as incentives to more or different production would be complicated and weakened by the interference, as they would undoubtedly see it, of tax inspectors (with the Chancellor of the Exchequer behind them). Union negotiators would also find themselves considerably inhibited in getting alterations in pay structures, if not straight increases. No doubt, one response would be similar to what was happening under the Pay Code: attention would be diverted to fringe benefits, to more and more perks in kind as a means of reward. It is not clear that this development is in any way desirable, nor does it help more rational distribution. There would be some truly formidable problems to overcome.

A counter-inflation tax on companies would have the advantage of being more direct, in that it is companies (and other enterprises) who hire the labour and set the pay. It is also more direct than taxing individuals in that pay bills, rather than individual pay rates, could be taxed, and this is after all the macro purpose. There would then be an incentive for the employer to employ less labour, as well as to restrain increases in pay rates, and to spread a modest permitted pay bill increase more generously among fewer recipients. It looks like a laudable incentive to efficiency. However, it perhaps takes too little account of the complexities of technological advance. There are firms which can and do shed labour with no particular effort as a result of technological improvements. There are other firms, especially new or developing ones, who cannot do any such thing but who need to attract skilled labour by offering more money more quickly than is offered elsewhere.

Of course, rules can be laid down about permitted exceptions to any general policy; and this could apply to taxation also. But the more special cases are allowed to match the micro complexities, the less the macro desiderata of simplicity, economy, and above all public comprehension can be met.

The proposals for tax-based incomes policy grew immediately out of dissatisfaction with the obvious defects of the Pay Code of the Counter-inflation Act. But since it was laid to rest many years ago, and we have had more episodes of different policies, and an unhappy period of non-policy to add to the history, there is another recurring problem to be put back into prominence among the aims of incomes policies: the question of public-sector pay.

All incomes policies practised so far have disadvantaged large numbers of public-service employees because the rules of constraint have been applied to them more rigorously than to others. Consequently strife follows, the settlement of which is only too likely to be inflationary or destabilizing. Policies which do not recognize this are surely doomed to failure. On the face of it, taxation would get over this. After all, public servants and private-sector employees alike pay taxes. However, policies do not start from either perfect neutrality or from some ideal distribution. There are always anomalies somewhere, usually major, intolerable ones. Special arrangements, commissions, and so on can be provided. But they are bound to be of major significance for the national economy and for the feasibility of a national incomes policy of which they are part.

Public-sector pay was not a particularly sensitive issue when the 1965 policy was introduced, though it had already helped to hasten the collapse of the 1962 attempt at moderation. However, some negotiating groups of public-service workers (being also some of the largest negotiating groups in the country) were referred to the NBPI within the first few months of its existence: first, industrial civil servants; then manual workers in local authorities, the NHS, and the gas and electricity industries. This in itself was a good example of an 'accumulated deposit' laid down by economic forces then past. Before the Second World War, already twenty-five years past, most of these had been local-authority employees, and had naturally negotiated pay and conditions together, with due attention to proper differentials and relativities. But for already nearly twenty years, though these were still all public-sector workers, they were now employed by different authorities, with different aims and conditions. Their pay in relation to methods of work and their employers' needs was more important than relativities to one another. At the same time, some of them were very badly paid; so general constraint in the national interest was hardly appropriate without qualification or concession. The NBPI did its best to ignore comparability and turned to productivity instead.

Other elements of public-sector pay had overwhelmed the previous attempt to get pay restraint. The government had at first proposed to decide nurses' pay according to its policy rules rather than to the justice of the nurses' case in relation to other people's pay, but it had had to give way to public support for nurses and grant them more than the initial proposal. By the middle of 1967, nurses' pay had once more got sufficiently out of line with other groups to create another surge of discontent. Their case was referred to the NBPI. Once more, the Board tried to reduce the significance of comparability, and find reasons, mostly internal to the nursing profession, for enough of an increase to quell the unrest.

It was not possible to give special attention to particular groups under the Pay Code, particularly where comparability was concerned. But nurses' pay was once more given a major review and made less 'anomalous' in 1974, but as the result of an *ad hoc* inquiry (the Halsbury Committee). Local-authority and NHS manual workers were laboriously realigning their pay by various locally negotiated productivity deals. By the end of the Social Contract, phase three, local-authority workers were once more so dissatisfied with their relativities that they played a prominent part in the unrest of the winter of 1978–79. The Clegg Commission had local-authority workers and NHS workers among its first cases. This time comparability was specifically applied, but in a more sophisticated and less inflationary way than the over-generalized comparisons of political rhetoric. The nurses were referred soon afterwards for another thoroughgoing review. School and college teachers were another Clegg case. They had previously had a special review (by the Houghton Committee) and settlement in 1974, after conflict. Since Clegg, as we have noted, there has been no overt incomes policy. By 1984, however, both nurses and teachers again felt that their pay had fallen so far behind as to warrant serious agitation. The nurses actually got another standing review body set up, broadly analogous to that of the doctors, police, and armed forces. This of course is an incomes policy of sorts – without any very clear general principles. In summer, 1985, the outcome of the teachers' case is awaited with interest. Meantime, non-industrial civil servants have a new regime for settling pay (after the Megaw inquiry) which takes a sort of comparability into account, along with other managerial-type considerations.

It has emerged more and more clearly that there must be an incomes policy of some kind for large groups of public-service workers, and that it must concern itself with comparability in some sense, perhaps in addition to other principles. It is also clear that the outcome of the policy is likely to be acceptable for longer, and arguably less inflationary, if it relates to some general aims or limits, rather than if the review committees are left, as Professor Wootton and her colleagues on arbitration tribunals were, with 'a sensation as of a great void opening; for one cannot decide whether the salary of a particular post should or should not be increased, or how great the increase should be unless one has some principles from which to start' (Wootton 1955: 10).

Even in the context of arbitration, which is a short-term fire-fighting sort of activity, the lack of longer-term principles or guidelines worried economist Wootton. The best of arbitration can only settle disputes which have arisen in particular circumstances, with specific ground rules normally adopted by the parties. In pay negotiations, history has often had a lot to do with those rules. But conditions of work, job content, and required skills change more, and more rapidly, than is often realized – until serious pay disputes arise. Providing a new basis for negotiation, making disputes less likely in the new circumstances, these are often more important than thinking of a number to satisfy the parties for another few months. Providing the new basis, taking the national interest into account, is something which is not, and probably could not be, done by arbitration.

A relatively impartial and independent but expert adviser can often smooth the difficult process. Consultants are more and more often so employed. But inserting a national interest can only be done by a body with some sort of national responsibility, as government-created agencies have by means of their constitution and terms of reference, for which ministers are accountable. The national interest may subsist primarily in avoiding inflation, and hence in keeping increases in the total pay bill within limits; or it may also include elements of redistribution in favour of the low paid or the victims of anomalous pay structures; or there may also be acute shortages of recruits to particular occupations which pay can help to correct.

An incomes policy which does not take account of such issues, or which does so only awkwardly, or at great cost, is not likely to benefit either the national economy or the workers very much. The tax system is not well adapted for such purposes; it has its own horrible complexities; and the existence of well-entrenched evasion techniques does not bode well for any addition to the tax system. The arbitration system is not particularly suitable either, though it might well be a valuable adjunct to a feasible policy. Above all, an incomes policy which does not immediately specify how public versus private sector changes can be rationalized ought not to be regarded as a practical starter.

Be that as it may, we must still pay attention to Professor Wootton's conclusions:

> 'It is just not true that what people are paid concerns only those who make the payment and those who receive it . . . the alternative to an incomes policy is universal respect for the commandment: Thou shalt do what it would be a good thing for everybody else to do.'
>
> (Wootton 1974)

REFERENCES

Clegg Commission (Standing Commission on Pay Comparability) (1980) *General Report* (Cmnd 7995). London: HMSO.

Halsbury Committee (1974) *Report of an Enquiry into the Pay and Conditions of Service of Nurses and Midwives*. London: DHSS.

NEDC (1963) *Conditions Favourable to Faster Growth*. London: NEDC.

White Paper (1962) *Incomes Policy: The Next Step*. London: HMSO.

—— (1965) *Prices and Incomes* (Cmnd 3639). London: HMSO.

Wootton, Barbara (1955) *The Social Foundations of Wage Policy*. London: Allen & Unwin.

—— (1974) *Incomes Policy*. London: Davis-Poynter.

6
EQUALITY
IN HARD TIMES
Raymond Plant

Barbara Wootton has been a life-long socialist and, in this essay, I shall be examining aspects of the intellectual cogency of the socialist belief in equality. This belief has become increasingly unfashionable and its upholders increasingly defensive since the 1970s with the ascendancy of the neo-liberal, free-market views of the political right, views associated with writers such as Hayek (1960) and Friedman (1962). In her early work on planning Barbara Wootton devoted a good deal of time to the analysis of earlier Hayekian themes. I now propose to focus upon some of the later ones. These are issues concerned specifically with the relationship between equality on the one hand and economic growth and efficiency on the other.[1]

GROWTH AND EFFICIENCY

Fundamental to socialist thinking about equality since the end of the Second World War is the belief that economic growth is central to the achievement of greater equality. This argument was put most elegantly by Tony Crosland in his Fabian pamphlet, *Social Democracy in Europe*:

> 'The achievement of greater equality without intolerable social stress and a probable curtailment of liberty depends heavily upon economic growth. The better off have been able to accept with reasonable equanimity a decline in their relative standard of living because growth has enabled them (almost) to maintain their absolute standard of living despite redistribution.'
>
> (Crosland 1975)

The fiscal dividend of growth has enabled the position of the worst-off to be improved without making the better-off very much worse off. Granted the existence of electoral politics, how then can the egalitarian argue for greater equality in a situation of very low or zero economic growth? In such a situation the egalitarian strategy seems to be a zero sum game in which, in order for the worst-off members of society to benefit by a significant amount, a large number of electors will have to be made worse off.

There are of course things which can be done in a period of slow growth, as Crosland (1974) recognized in his later writing. These would include paying attention to non-material inequalities, such as inequalities of power, and concentrating limited resources upon those most in need. Concentrating resources where they are most needed is obviously a rational policy in hard times but we ought to be able to say more than this. One of the problems with the egalitarian vision is that it poses as a rather profligate one, concentrating on distribution and leaving the problem of production to be solved by other means. Even so, it is central to the egalitarian view that it is a production philosophy as much as a policy for distribution; in this sense, a more egalitarian society ought to be a more productive one. I shall consider this important point at a later stage of the argument and concentrate here on one or two ways in which growth and equality are linked.

It is often argued that the unemployment of the past decade is not likely to be solved by greater economic growth and it is this fact which makes the current unemployment more soul-destroying than that of the 1930s. In earlier periods of depression the unemployed could look forward to an economic upturn which would not be a sort to displace their particular skills but would, rather, create an increased demand for such skills and thereby increase employment opportunities. However, it is now argued that any future economic upturn will not lead to dramatically increased employment prospects. New industries which might benefit from economic recovery are not likely to be labour-intensive, based as they will be on information technology, computers, robotics, and the rest. If this is a correct prognosis (although I see no way at all in which we can decide this question at the moment), what are the consequences for socialist values and equality? Of course, modern neo-liberals and conservatives will argue that it is not the role of government to organize the distribution of work opportunities if these are as restricted as some pessimistic forecasts predict. Those who fail to find a job in the shrunken job market suffer from bad luck and that is all there is to it. There exists no 'right to work' and no duty on the part of the state to secure work opportunities to satisfy this 'right'. Another strategy is to argue that we need to change our attitude to work and concentrate on leisure-orientated activities in which the out-of-work will be able to find a meaningful life without stigma. This proposal is all very well but suffers from two crucial drawbacks. First, the stigma of unemployment is not likely to disappear for a generation or more, and the long-term unemployed will accordingly suffer a good deal of frustration at not being able to meet society's expectations of them in the interim. Second, a leisure society is going to require generous levels of unemployment benefit and investment in social capital to provide the facilities for the large number of leisured citizens. The consequences for public expenditure are obvious.

It would appear that socialist values, particularly distributive/collective ones, are the most relevant here. *If* there are a very large number of unemployed in the future, and *if* jobs are going to be scarce, then the question of why some people have markedly different life chances to others will be posed most acutely. Unless those in work are to be regarded as beneficiaries of the neo-liberal 'luck of the draw' mechanism, which is perhaps not all that likely, there is going to be a demand for work opportunities and the differences in income which these opportunities represent to be shared fairly. Work sharing and income/salary sharing may become important items on the political agenda, items which can only be tackled through some coherent and consensual egalitarian values for work sharing so that those employed can be seen as consuming a 'scarce resource' in a fair and legitimate manner. Of course, any work-sharing scheme is going to involve many hard choices because if it includes income sharing, and a situation of low growth would seem to require this, then some people's incomes are going to have to be lowered in order to improve those of others. Such a strategy could only work in a society with a far more equitable overall distribution of resources, particularly income and wealth.

The practical difficulties involved in facing up to these issues are immense in a parliamentary system. On the one hand, if we, as a society, link people's integrity, standing, and personal qualities generally with their being in work, and yet decline to recognize a right to at least a share in a job for all who want one, then our society is deeply unjust. It defines a norm of human fulfilment but is indifferent to whether three or four million people and their families have the means to fulfil it. On the other hand, the unemployed are in the minority: if a political party believes in establishing a right to job sharing when jobs are in short supply, then it will have to convince the majority to vote for policies which may make them worse off. In this kind of future scenario we cannot appeal to growth to act as the solvent of distributional dilemmas; rather, growth in 'high-tech' industries could well be the cause of the dilemma. The only possibility in these circumstances would seem to be to concentrate on the propagation of socialist values such as equality, solidarity, and community. Unfortunately there is no magic wand which can be waved to solve the distributional dilemma without making many people worse off.

As has been made clear, scarcity exacerbates the problems of distributional politics. While Gross National Product (GNP) is growing and individuals and groups are getting more, there will be less concern about fair shares. However, if GNP is static, shrinking, or growing at a low rate, the question of relative shares is much more likely to become accentuated. This problem has been raised in a very broad perspective by Fred Hirsch in his *Social Limits to Growth* (1977).

One of the principal claims to legitimacy of the market order follows from its asserted ability to increase wealth more efficiently than socialism and, through the 'echelon advance' or 'trickle-down' mechanism, to benefit the worst-off more effectively. In the absence of a more overtly distributive morality this promise seems crucial to the acceptability of markets. Hirsch, however, argues that this argument is as seriously flawed as the egalitarian redistribution argument favoured by Crosland because each strategy presupposes that all goods can either be distributed more widely (neo-liberal) or more equally (Crosland) at the same levels of quality and value. In Hirsch's view this is false. Certainly some goods, such as electric fires or washing machines, can be distributed more widely or more equally without their qualities or values being changed, but there are particular sorts of goods – Hirsch calls them 'positional goods' – which cannot be more widely distributed without their economic value being altered. The value of some sorts of goods depends on the fact that only a limited number of people are consuming them.

An example will help to explain this. The paradigm case might be a person standing on tiptoe in order to see a procession better. This is a positional activity in the sense that its value declines as more people take part in it. Tourism, and access to secluded beaches or cottages, are also positional goods in this sense. Were these the only examples of positional goods, we could contemplate them with equanimity because they seem marginal and unimportant. However, for Hirsch, education is also a positional good – it is an instrumental good, one having a marketable value as opposed to being a means of non-material self-fulfilment, and this value depends to a great extent upon scarcity. Therefore, it cannot be distributed more equally without its value to those who consume it being changed. Individuals are not able to consume today the *same* educational goods which were reserved for the rich a few generations ago (as in the trickle-down theory) because the good has declined in value as the number of consumers has increased.

Education was a major weapon in the Croslandite armoury for increasing equality and lessening social resentment although the Hirsch analysis indicates some problems here. Far from increasing equality and lessening tensions the more equal distribution of education has led to the growth of 'credentialism', with more and higher qualifications being demanded for jobs which, in previous generations, may not have required qualifications at all. It would, of course, be comforting to think that the demand for qualifications was the result of the growing complexity of the jobs concerned but this is clearly not always the case. Credentialism is a function of the paper chase and not the cause of it. In so far as this is true it follows that a good deal of working-class demand for education is defensive in nature, an attempt to secure access to the same jobs which in previous generations might not have needed publicly certified levels of educational attainment. As the American economist Lester Thurow has written:

> 'As the supply of educated labour increases individuals find that they must improve their education to defend their current income position. If they don't they will find their current jobs no longer open to them. Education becomes a good investment not because it would raise people's incomes above what they would have been if no one had increased his education, but rather because it raises their income above what it will be if others acquire an education and they do not.'
>
> (Thurow 1977)

In this sense education acts as a screening device for recruitment to unequal positions, rather than as a Croslandite engine for equality.

The idea of positional goods, and the social limits to growth which they imply, pose two sorts of question to political theory. For the Hayekian neo-liberal there is the problem of the legitimacy of the market order. The neo-liberal claims that we can dispense with raising distributional questions about the market because, if left unconstrained, the trickle-down effect will make all (including the poorest) better off. Even if this is true of material goods which can be consumed without positional advantage resulting, it is not true for positional goods including education and recreation. If we all become richer in material terms then it is likely that attention will focus on the consumption of positional goods, where the trickle-down promise of neo-liberalism is an illusion. The failure to deliver the illusory promise might well cause frustration and resentment and, in turning his back on distributional questions, the neo-liberal has no theory about who should legitimately consume positional goods. That they are legitimately consumed by those whose market position enables them to consume them is about all the neo-liberal can say. This, however, is not going to be sufficient.[2] The failure of the promise is more likely to give rise to demands that opportunities for the consumption of these goods be seen as fair and legitimate, and this makes socialist values which focus on distribution far more relevant than market principles.

Second, the positional goods argument underlies what might be called the oblique approach to greater equality favoured in the 1950s and 1960s. This involved looking for greater equality through expenditure on health, education, and welfare rather than acting directly on inequalities of income. In so far as these goods are positional in character there is a flaw in the strategy. The particular scarcity engendered by positionality makes the whole business of scarcity more acute than the egalitarians of this period realized, and this is particularly so if the positionality of goods like education is combined with the projected shortage of work opportunities discussed earlier.

Hirsch concentrates his argument on the social rather than the physical limits to growth. However, and leaving aside his strictures, even if we assume that the more doom-laden predictions relating to the depletion of natural resources are exaggerated and that in the sphere of material goods we can look forward to some incremental advances, it is doubtful that growth can play the role assigned to it by Crosland in the quotation cited on p. 92. His strategy could be called a 'hidden hand' approach, in that it does not stress a direct attack on inequalities in the spheres of income and wealth but concentrates on removing the consequences of inequality by public spending in the sphere of education and welfare. However, recent evidence collected by Julian Le Grand in *The Strategy of Equality* (1982) suggests that, with inequalities of income and wealth, the better-off will still be able to make better use of welfare services than the less well-endowed, and that the impact of such services on inequality has not been particularly great. This problem becomes even more stark if we accept that goods such as education are positional, because the better-endowed will be able to make differentially better use of a service which already has a strong positional element within it. However, if we are to approach the problem of inequality in a more direct way by looking closely at policies for diminishing inequalities of income and wealth than we shall have to face the accusation that we are fostering inefficiency by disregarding incentives and concentrating our attention on distribution when the real need is for competition and efficiency. We shall therefore have to confront directly that aspect of the ideology of inequality' (Le Grand 1982) which insists that there is a substantial trade-off to be made between efficiency and equality and that in the harsh world of the 1980s we have to choose the former rather than the latter. It is this influential aspect of the ideology of inequality to which I shall now turn.

EFFICIENCY AND EQUALITY

It might be argued that at the present time it is wholly unrealistic to be concerned about equality and distribution. The fundamental problem is going to be one of production, and distribution will have to take second place. A redistributive policy treating goods and services as manna from heaven will eventually kill the goose that lays the golden eggs. Taxing the products of labour for redistributive purposes would lead to gross in-efficiencies, irrespective of any moral rights to property which may be overridden by such taxation. On this view, workers and professionals need incentives to work harder and both need to pay lower taxes. Both of these features have strong anti-egalitarian overtones: incentives *ex hypothesi* create differences between people which cannot be reconciled with equality and lower taxes will limit the possibilities of public spending for egalitarian redistribution.

It would be ridiculous for an egalitarian to dismiss arguments about production because high productivity is indeed important to the achieve-ment of distributional aims. What, therefore, can be said about the view that a substantial trade-off between efficiency and equality exists? Is this true, and how far are incentives necessarily incompatible with equality?

The first point to make is that if any such trade-offs exist then they are going to be extremely complex. Certain sorts of egalitarian strategies, for instance, can be seen as enhancing efficiency. We can take two examples here. Greater equality of opportunity in the sense of fair and open com-petition for jobs must be more efficient in matching talents to jobs than more restrictive recruitment. Fair equality of opportunity must be more efficient economically if it involves more than just the removal of legal and conventional restrictions on recruitment and if it makes positive attempts to encourage groups of people who have typically not entered a particular area of the job market to do so. A wider pool of talent coupled with fair equality of opportunity ought to be the best way of matching abilities and jobs. Similarly, positive training programmes which improve the skills and earning capacities of manual workers could be defended as a gain in both efficiency and equality. Forms of educational provision which involve spending more money on the children of unskilled manual workers could again be defended as much on grounds of encouraging the efficient use of scarce resources as on grounds of equality. We must beware of slogans in this field and of over-simplified views of the nature of the trade-off. This is not to deny that there are trade-offs to be made, but the important point is to be aware of precisely where they occur and to examine the consequences for egalitarian policies.

The fundamental point at issue here is the extent to which incentives are needed to make people work more productively and efficiently. It should perhaps be said in passing that the empirical truth of this claim is shrouded in mystery and many confident assertions have been made about the need for incentives without it being at all clear what evidence there is for this view beyond anecdote.[3] Indeed as even some conservative commentators have realized, arguments about incentives can be stood on their heads: if incomes above a certain level are taxed at a differentially higher rate then individuals will work harder to maintain their standard of living. However, it is no doubt also true that they will resent so doing and we must take this resentment seriously, just as we ask the better-endowed to take seriously the justice of the resentment of those less well-circumstanced.

Let us therefore accept as a fact (although it may not be) that incentives are necessary for higher productivity and efficiency. Perhaps the first point then to note is that if this is the ground on which the argument for inequality of income is based, it has nothing whatsoever to do with moral qualities like merit and desert. What society is being asked to pay is a rent on ability, in order to mobilize skills which otherwise would not be mobilized and without which we should be worse off. The moralizing of incentives is a nauseating and a smug business. They are not ends in themselves; they are means to ends and they are linked to justice only in the sense of the amount of economic rent necessary to generate prosperity for the welfare of the citizens. The argument about incentives is not a moral argument at all; indeed, moral considerations might well take us in the opposite direction if we were to follow them through.

What this incentive argument really asks is that we pay a differential rent to mobilize abilities for which the individual may claim only a modest responsibility. Abilities and talents are not engendered by individuals in a vacuum; rather, they are in some large part due to genetic inheritance, fortunate family background, and education, for which the individual concerned bears little or no responsibility. If I *deserve* something it must be in terms of a feature of my life for which I myself am responsible. Individuals are not the sole bearers of responsibility for their abilities; in some respect these abilities already represent a considerable investment of social capital which in turn is rewarded by more expenditure on the individual. Thus we should not be confused by the moralistic fog which sometimes envelops discussions about incentives. We are talking about a purely economic criterion, that sum of money which will get a job done without which society would be the poorer.

I do think we have to recognize and accept this notion of incentives. While it is true that some socialist societies and some socialist theories try to get away from the notion of incentives altogether they do presuppose some fundamental change in consciousness and in human attitudes which seem Utopian and unrealistic. Certainly societies which tried to do away with the rent on ability – such as China during the Great Leap Forward – were not particularly successful. On empirical grounds, therefore, there do seem to be good reasons for accepting that there is an ineliminable role for incentives in economic relations, and this fact must place a constraint on the principle of equality. The point could be put in a more theoretical way by linking incentives, efficiency, and personal liberty: were we to believe in absolute material equality (so that we fixed 100 per cent taxes on incomes above the norm and 100 per cent subsidies on incomes below it) then there would be no reason at all to move economic resources such as labour, capital, or land to areas or occupations in which the marginal value of production was higher. This must limit efficiency and innovation. If there were no incentive to respond to these technological and other changes without which society would be worse off, labour would have to be directed, which would entail considerable loss of personal freedom. Given this powerful argument, what place can the recognition of the need for incentives have in egalitarian political theory?

Apart from those incentives which could be seen as compensation for dirty, risky, or health-threatening jobs where the incentive is compensation for the 'diswelfare' experienced, it is in the nature of the case that incentives will create inequalities. We are accordingly going to be concerned with the range of legitimate inequalities, that is, with those considerations which will give the structure of differentials some legitimate role in society. No one is suggesting that there is a way in which a pay relativities board could produce a hard-and-fast scientific answer to the question of the proper rent on ability to be paid; rather, there is an onus to justify incentives and the level at which they are set. If, as I have argued, incentives as legitimated by economic rather than by moral criteria to do with desert, then of course incentives can be limited by the rent of ability criterion.

Some jobs incorporate a wide band of incentive factors which may well go beyond what is necessary to secure the rent of ability. In case I am accused of trying to sort out other people's lives, let us take the example of university professors. Here we might well consider that the rent of ability criterion has been exceeded: the job is highly paid, enjoys a high social status, and involves civilized hours of work together with a good deal of self-direction in terms of mode of working and what to work on. Are *all* these incentives necessary to mobilize the rent of ability in such cases? In this, as in many other professions and in business, incentives have arisen on an *ad hoc* basis and may have moved a good deal further than what is strictly necessary to recruit people to such posts. Of course, we could only secure an empirical answer to this question if we were to squeeze these incentives for egalitarian reasons until such time as the rent of ability clearly came into play, weakening recruitment for such positions. If the argument about incentives is genuinely related to rent of ability rather than to desert it might well be that the structure of incentives to meet the genuine social requirements mentioned earlier would look quite different from what it does today.

An egalitarian government might therefore attempt a strategy of taxing incentives on jobs over a certain upper limit. It would seem that if a government is serious about greater equality of income and the social distance between occupations it will have to tackle the financial aspects of the reward structure directly, partly because this is more clearly within the competence of government (for example, through a payroll tax) and partly for a more complex reason connected with positional goods. Some of the non-material benefits of high-status occupations, such as self-directed work, the exercise of choice over work routines, foreign travel, the exercise of authority, and so on, may all be much more closely integrated into the nature of the occupation in the sense that the job itself demands some of the features which are positional advantages. Granted that these cannot be squeezed directly without the nature of the job being altered, which it is beyond the competence of the government to do, the obvious egalitarian solution is to tax income up to the point where rent of ability considerations come into play.

In this sense a theory of legitimate inequality might be necessary for the legitimacy of markets as such. If Hirsch is right that the market cannot meet the promises held out by the trickle-down effect once we go beyond material consumer goods then I should argue that it is only a market constrained by a theory of legitimate inequality which is likely to ease the inherently frustrating competition for goods which are in socially short supply – while we may all carry a field marshal's baton in our knapsacks, and while anyone can become a field marshal, of course not *everyone* can become one. It will be important to limit as far as possible the social distance and resentment that frustrated competition for positional goods may take. As I have argued, this might be done by trying to reduce some of the extraneous material incentives which currently accrue to such positions.

Thus equality is not incompatible with efficiency. Indeed, a theory of legitimate inequality based on considerations of rent of ability may take a genuine concern for efficiency much further than do those who shout the loudest about the need for incentives. However, the egalitarian will require a justification of the range of incentives in society, to make sure that they really do reflect the claims of efficiency rather than privilege unrelated to economic function. In this way the system of rewards would come to have some principle and structure and we should no longer be involved in the terrible anarchic 'free for all' which is characteristic of British society. Only a structure of rewards based broadly on principle can provide the foundations of an incomes policy. Barbara Wootton once said that incomes policies operate in an ethical vacuum and that this is one reason why they are difficult to operate. An egalitarian vision may go some way towards filling that vacuum. In spite of the prevalence of right-wing theories, distributional dilemmas will not go away as the neo-liberals hope; despite their temporary popularity the unprincipled individualist solutions have very serious shortcomings which are not likely to be resolved without resort to a degree of coercion which the neo-liberals profess to abhor. A more equal, fairer society can be a more efficient and a more productive society because the basis of co-operation will be present. In the final section I shall try to spell out more clearly the conception of equality with which I have been operating, and the justification for it.

SOCIALISM AND EQUALITY

Although I have so far operated with an undefined conception of equality I think the final form of the concept is implicit within aspects of the argument up to this point. Now I shall say something more directly about what I take to be a defensible socialist view of equality. A theory of equality has to do several things: it obviously has to recommend a particular distributive outcome, it has to say what kinds of goods and services, benefits and burdens, are to be distributed according to this rule, and some justification of the rule has to be given. In addition, a socialist theory of equality will have to relate to other socialist values such as liberty and community. At the same time, it must take into account the circumstances of human life as we know it. There is no virtue at all in a normative political theory which recommends arrangements which are themselves unworkable. In this context we should bear in mind the arguments about incentives and positional goods which are bound to place fundamental constraints upon egalitarian theories. Having said this I shall now turn to an examination of three types of egalitarian theory: equality of opportunity; equality of result or outcome; and democratic equality, that is, a theory of legitimate inequality.

Equality of opportunity seems on the face of it to be a very persuasive conception of equality and perhaps the most consensual form which it could take in British society. It is concerned with fair recruitment procedures and can be portrayed as an important factor in increasing efficiency (because it matches recruitment to ability rather than to birth, race, or sex). However, the principle has to be subjected to a good deal of interpretation and when this is done it becomes clearer that it is, at bottom, very vague and ambiguous. Its widespread acceptance in society may well depend upon this ambiguity. On a minimalist interpretation of the principle we might say that it is concerned with the progressive removal of legal impediments to recruitment and with all children having a fair start at school. It is a procedural notion concerned with making sure that the race for position is a fair one and it is this procedural aspect of the equality of opportunity which makes it attractive to liberals. Liberals argue that more substantive forms of equality, such as equality of outcome, will involve intolerable interferences with personal freedom, whereas a procedural form of opportunity will involve few, if any, such interferences.

This easy compromise is none the less illusory. Fair equality of opportunity cannot be attained on a purely procedural basis, otherwise we shall be in the position of maintaining that there is equal opportunity for all to dine at the Ritz. There are doubtless no legal impediments to dining at the Ritz so long as one has the resources to do so. If we are concerned with an equal or a fair opportunity for the development of talent and ability then more substantial policies than the removal of procedural and legal limitations on recruitment will have to be involved. Granted that background inequalities between individuals and families are going to affect the development of talent, if we are going to equalize opportunities then we shall have to act on these background inequalities.

If we do this, however, two problems arise as far as the liberal commitment to the principle is concerned. First, if we try to compensate for background inequalities which bear on the development of talents in children, then this might threaten the personal freedom of families to live their lives in their own way. Thus we could claim that equality of opportunity and personal freedom are not so compatible as is usually supposed. Second, if a policy of seeking to compensate for background inequalities which make a difference to the development of talent is adopted seriously, then the redistributive consequences of such compensation would make the principle of equality of opportunity merge into that of the greater equality of outcome which liberals reject. Equality of opportunity is the equal opportunity to become unequal but, unless we stick to a disingenuous procedural conception of equality of opportunity, the idea of equalizing starting places in the competition will take on very substantive aspects in the sphere of compensating for unmerited inherited disadvantage and in restricting rights of bequest for the better-off. Only strategies of this sort are likely to be able to equalize opportunities but such strategies pose exactly the same problems for liberty as do the socialist conceptions of equality.

The basic socialist objection to equality of opportunity is concerned with the fact that there is no critical approach to the differing positions to which equal access is being proposed. It takes the existing structure of inequality for granted and is concerned about recruitment to it. This is not satisfactory for socialists who will want to probe the legitimacy of the differential reward structure, and fear that greater equality of access may give a greater legitimacy to a structure of rewards which could be regarded as unjust. Of course, if there is a socialist defence of differential reward structures, as I earlier suggested, then equality of opportunity for recruitment to such positions would only be consistent with general socialist values. However, this equality of access would have to embody substantive compensatory techniques for background inequalities which bear upon the fair development of talent.

The obvious alternative to equality of opportunity, given the difficulties which it involves, would be to endorse greater equalities of outcome in terms of income, wealth, and welfare. The reasons for this can be developed out of an internal critique of equality of opportunity. I have already suggested that the redistribution necessary to secure a fair development of talent would itself make inroads on the reward structure and thereby narrow differential outcomes. However, there is an important subsidiary aspect to this argument. If we seek to compensate those who do not have a fair chance to develop their talents because of circumstances beyond their control – their genetic endowment, family background, sex, or colour – there will in fact be very definite limits to the extent to which this can be done consistently with the maintenance of the family and individual freedom. After a certain point the attempt to secure a fair background for the development of talent becomes intolerably intrusive.

What do we do at this point? There are two alternatives. One is to endorse the existing differential reward structure, admit that there are limits to equality of opportunity, and argue that it is simply an unfortunate fact that some individuals will be penalized in realizing their life chances because of factors outside their control, factors which cannot be altered in a way compatible with individual freedom. The other alternative is to argue for a greater compression of the reward structure and for greater equality of outcome. If the family is to be maintained and personal liberty secured, which means that equality of opportunity must be limited, then surely it is wrong to reward as prodigiously as we do a narrow range of talent for which the individual does not bear entire responsibility and to make the costs of failure so heavy for those whose opportunities have been more modest and who similarly do not bear full responsibility for their condition.

This is the general ground for equality of outcome and it follows fairly naturally from a recognition of the defects of equality of opportunity. The obvious difficulty with it is that in endorsing a wholesale critique of an income and status hierarchy it may well embody very weak demands in terms of efficiency while, at the same time, failing to recognize the positionality of certain goods which cannot be distributed in a substantively equal manner. The obvious solution to this difficulty is to seek to develop a theory of legitimate inequality. This, I believe, is the central socialist task in the field and one which will have to involve a social consensus if it is ever to be supported electorally. In what follows I give only the broad parameters within which such a theory could be developed.

The defence of equality should be linked to the defence of liberty in order to secure a fair and equal worth of liberty. This proposition can be developed in the light of the idea that political and social freedoms and rights are credited on an equal basis to citizens although differences in social and economic circumstances mean that these liberties have differential value to individuals. As purposive creatures, liberty to pursue our own good in our own way is central to us, but this means that we cannot be indifferent to the worth of liberty to individuals and to the resources they have to pursue their conception of the good. Consequently a socialist theory of equality will be concerned with the distribution of those resources which are necessary basic goods for experiencing a life of purpose and making full use of the rights of citizenship (Plant, Lesser, and Taylor-Gooby 1980). In our society these will include health services – unless people maintain their optimum physical integrity they will not be able to act effectively – education, and welfare goods generally. These resources are also going to include income because, as Le Grand (1982) has shown, differences in income lead to marked differences in the use of other sorts of basic welfare goods. A fair distribution of the worth of liberty is therefore going to involve far greater equality of income and wealth as well as the provision of services. I suggest also that these basic resources which are necessary for a life of active citizenship should as far as possible be distributed in cash rather than kind, in order to enhance the ability to live in one's own way and avoid bureaucracy and paternalism. This linking of equality and a more equal worth of liberty demonstrates how equality can be thought of as a means to freedom.

Even so, we have to take into account the points about incentives and positional goods made earlier. It follows from these points that while I have used the terms fair worth and equal worth of liberty interchangeably, these may diverge; this marks the difference between the view which I am advocating and strict equality of result. Moves away from equality in the worth of liberty would be justified on this view if such moves would lead to a greater value of liberty, i.e. resources, both financial and welfare, for all. If incentives are needed for reasons of economic efficiency, to produce more goods without which the worst-off members of society would actually be worse off, then a theory of legitimate inequality would justify incentives on the grounds that they still secure a fair, but not an equal, worth of liberty to all members of society, including the worst-off. Similarly, positional goods such as limited educational opportunities which *ex hypothesi* cannot be distributed more equally would also be consumed legitimately if their consumption by particular individuals benefited society as a whole.

It might of course be suggested that this argument diverges too far from a genuine socialist outlook because it does not *constrain* the extent to which inequalities could exist if they were for the general good. There are, I believe, two answers to this suggestion. First, if we are concerned with individual liberty then it would be irrational to prefer a more equal distribution of goods in which the worth of liberty to many citizens would be less than it would be under some degree of inequality. Second, we might emphasize the values of community and fraternity operating here independently. There is a point, which cannot easily be specified in advance, at which the inequalities linked to efficiency to pursue a greater value of freedom will threaten a sense of community and fraternity because of the social distance which would be created between those occupying differential positions and the rest of society. However, this social distance would be lessened in some degree because my argument would presuppose common, and not private, services in the spheres of health, education, and welfare. In spite of the earning of differential rewards it is likely that this sort of provision will limit any social distance which might otherwise occur. Nevertheless, it is still true that there may come a point at which we would prefer community to efficiency if the structure of incentives required for the latter threatened to override the former.

There is no point in pretending that thinking about values can provide us with a detailed blueprint of the future. Political values and principles are always going to be ambiguous and susceptible to many interpretations. All of our values will not necessarily be reconcilable within one coherent schedule – there are trade-offs and choices to be made. Yet a moral theory is still central to socialism. Unless it is explicitly grounded in a clear moral standpoint the claim for greater equality can be misrepresented by critics as simply the product of class resentment or the 'politics of envy'. In the view developed in this essay, however, by securing a fairer value of liberty, and thus a share in the common rights of citizenship, the greater equality can be seen as an essential means both to liberty and fraternity; it is thus central to any restatement of the socialist position.

NOTES

1 The remainder of this essay consists of the final two sections of my 1984 Fabian Society pamphlet (Plant 1984), with corrections and amendments. Permission to reproduce the material is gratefully acknowledged.

2 See J. Gray, Classical Liberalism, Positional Goods and the Politicisation of Poverty, in Ellis and Kumar (1983). See also my own contribution to the same volume for the contrary view.

3 For a sceptical view of the role of personal incentives in economic growth see Denison (1974), who argues that the major factors making for growth are the size of the labour force, its educational level,

increasing human knowledge, and economies of scale. The personal qualities of entrepreneurs come a very long way down the list.

REFERENCES

Crosland, A. (1974) Socialism Now. London: Cape.

—— (1975) *Social Democracy in Europe*. London: Fabian Society, Tract 438.

Denison, E. F. (1974) *Accounting for United States Economic Growth*. Washington: Brookings Institution.

Ellis, A. and Kumar, K. (eds) (1983) *Dilemmas of Liberal Democracies: Studies in Fred Hirsch's Social Limits to Growth*. London: Tavistock.

Hayek, F. A. (1960) *The Conception of Liberty*. London: Routledge & Kegan Paul.

Hirsch, F. (1977) *Social Limits to Growth*. London: Routledge & Kegan Paul.

Le Grand, J. (1982) *The Strategy of Equality: Redistribution and the Social Services*. London: Allen & Unwin.

Plant, R. (1984) *Equality, Markets and the State*. London: Fabian Society, Tract 494.

Plant, R., Lesser, H., and Taylor-Gooby, P. (1980) *Political Philosophy and Social Welfare: Essays on the Normative Basis of Welfare Provision*. London: Routledge & Kegan Paul.

Thurow, L. (1977) Education and Economic Equality. In J. Karable and A. H. Halsey (eds) *Power and Ideology in Education*. New York: Oxford University Press.

7
POVERTY, PRIVILEGE, AND WELFARE[1]
Adrian Sinfield

'The certainties of one age
are the problem of the next.'
(Tawney 1938: 275)

In less than a generation general acceptance of the achievements of 'the Welfare State' has been replaced by almost universal concern with its crisis. The paradox of increasing poverty amid increasing welfare in many, if not most, western societies has been receiving growing attention. In the last ten or twenty years country after country has, with varying degrees of reluctance, acknowledged the persistence of poverty (see for example George and Lawson 1980; Walker, Lawson, and Townsend 1984). Since then the much higher levels of unemployment which have beset most of these countries have led, both directly and indirectly, to increasing and deepening deprivation. The problem has been made even worse by the inflationary erosion of living standards against which the poor have least protection and by the growth in the size of the most vulnerable groups, particularly the elderly and very elderly, as a result of demographic change.

At the same time, but by no means simply as a response to the recognition of increasing poverty, there is much discussion of social policy couched in terms of the future of 'the Welfare State'. In Britain political parties invite support by calls to 'roll back the frontiers of the Welfare State' or attempt to rally the faithful 'to defend the Welfare State'. Throughout most of western Europe and North America similar conflicts have grown in intensity in recent years. These have been reflected in discussions within international agencies, e.g. the OECD seminar on 'The Welfare State in Crisis', and many domestic and international conferences on the costs of financing social security or the 'Welfare State'. 'Can we afford the Welfare State?' has become a recurrent theme.

Yet the very use of the term 'Welfare State' to encapsulate the issues in these debates foreshortens the discussion in some very significant ways. As Barbara Wootton observed in 1961, many analysts have allowed themselves 'to be deluded by the myths and clichés that have grown up round the term "welfare state"' (Wootton 1961: 1). 'The facile assumption that everything that is commonly labelled as a "social service" involves a transfer from rich to poor is quite untrue' (Wootton 1962: 188). Such beliefs supported the creation and maintenance

> 'in the public eye of something akin to a stereotype or image of an all-pervasive Welfare State for the Working Classes. Such is the tyranny of stereotypes today that this ideal of a welfare society, born as a reaction against the social discrimination of the Poor Law may, paradoxically, widen rather than narrow class relationships.'   (Titmuss 1958: 37)

But this is 'a stereotype of social welfare which represents only the more visible part of the real world of welfare. The social history of our times inevitably becomes, in the process, sadly distorted' (Titmuss 1958: 53).

The importance of the social division of welfare for understanding the distortion created by a focus on 'the Welfare State' is even greater in 1985 than in 1955 when it was first set out (in Titmuss 1958, Chapter 2). Within the division at least three separate systems of 'social services' have been identified. The first is social welfare, the traditional area of social policy and administration, which I would prefer to call *public welfare* to emphasize the public provision. The second, tax or *fiscal welfare*, includes tax reliefs and allowances from the government but these are not included in the public expenditure accounts 'though providing similar benefits and expressing a similar social purpose in the recognition of dependent needs' as public welfare (Titmuss 1958: 44). The third system, *occupational welfare*, covers benefits received by employees through or as a result of employment. These include what is generally called industrial welfare for manual workers and fringe benefits or 'perks' for white-collar and executive staff.[2]

Constant discussion of public welfare alone, neglecting what has been happening in the other systems of welfare and in the wider society, has only served to reinforce dissatisfaction with 'the Welfare State'. Its costs have increased along with its acts of intervention, as critics predominantly on the political right have had no difficulty in pointing out. Yet as their opponents, mainly on the left, do not cease to stress, its activities have failed to overcome those problems of poverty, deprivation, and diswelfare that it was set up to combat. Instead of reducing poverty, 'the Welfare State' often only contains it and, in many poor people's experience, has become a new form of control or even oppression. There has been surprisingly little recognition on either side that other polices have in fact increased the demands on 'the Welfare State' while cutting back its resources. This double pressure itself has led to an increase in rationing and controlling within 'the Welfare State'.

One effect of the combination of these generally unconcerted assaults on 'the Welfare State' has been to weaken support for it. There is reduced willingness to fund existing programmes, let alone expand them or even replace them by more radical and effective strategies at greater public cost. In Britain this widespread frustration with 'the Welfare State' has encouraged arguments for 'welfare pluralism' or 'a mixed economy of welfare' with reduced state welfare and increased private, voluntary, and other effort.[3] In some respects this resembles the older cry for 'welfare capitalism' in the United States and other countries. These proposals are particularly attractive to many because they do not appear stridently political and they seem to invite policies of reasonable moderation. To both politicians in office and administrators they may be especially congenial because they require little determined action and allow a policy of welfare *laissez-faire* – 'Let a thousand welfares bloom'.

These beliefs rest on a profound misunderstanding of the social division of welfare. The different systems do not run in parallel and independently of each other so that they can be treated as categories to be studied in isolation by separate specialists of, for example, social administration, accountancy, and personnel management. It is essential to study their interaction. They may complement or supplement one another but they may also handicap, obstruct, or exclude each other, leading to conflict and inequality.

THE TRENDS OF THE LAST GENERATION

This can be seen by comparing the different trends within the social division of welfare over the last thirty or forty years. In public welfare, increases in spending very largely reflect a response to two changes: inflation and increases in the number of people coming into categories of need for which programmes of benefit or service were legislated many years ago. There has been a shift away from universal provision and towards increased reliance on means-tested selective programmes which are limited to poorer groups. Criteria for eligibility have generally become more tightly, and often harshly, defined.

In fiscal welfare the evidence is much less clear because successive British governments have been very reluctant to say how much revenue is not collected as a result of tax allowances and exemptions. They have only begun to reveal some of the 'tax expenditures' which are becoming more regularly debated in many other countries, including the United States,

‑Canada, Germany, France, and Australia (Owens 1983, 1984; OECD 1984). There is little doubt, however, that the range and variety of tax benefits have increased greatly.

The cost of some of the main direct tax allowances and reliefs, and their increase since 1978–79 when the data were first published, are shown in *Table 1*. In calculating tax expenditure, some would omit the main allowances but the fact that £4 billion of income tax was foregone in 1984–85 in recognition of the need or status of being a married man instead of a single person must make it a significant element of fiscal welfare. The total subsidy to owner-occupiers through relief on mortgate interest and exemption from capital gains tax on any profit from selling their home has now reached £6 billion, almost twice the total of public expenditure on housing.

Table 1   *Direct tax allowances and reliefs, 1978–84 (estimated cost in £ millions)*

	1978–79	1981–82	1984–85	1978–79 to 1984–85 % increase
married man's allowance	6,600	8,540	11,700	77
single person's allowance	3,200	4,640	6,750	111
wife's earned income allowance	1,800	2,390	3,100	72
husband and wife: election for				
separate taxation of wife's earnings	90	160	190	111
additional personal allowance for				
one-parent family	60	115	140	133
relief for:				
pension schemes (depending on				
methodology)	450	1,000	900–3,400	100–656
self-employed: retirement annuity	70	310	500	614
life assurance premiums	260	530	725	179
mortgage interest	1,110	2,030	3,500	220
capital gains tax exemption on				
disposal of only or main residence	1,500*	2,800*	2,500*	66

*This figure is particularly tentative and subject to a wide margin of error.
Source: *Inland Revenue Statistics.*

The value of these allowances continues to be generally very much greater for the higher paid and wealthier members of the population. Partly as a result of tax expenditures, less than half of the total recorded income is now subject to tax in the United Kingdom, 'and perhaps one-third of acutal incomes received' (Day and Pond 1982: 164). For the tax year 1984–85 it has been estimated that only 3 per cent of the 24 million taxpayers pay any tax above the standard rate of 30 per cent and the small proportion paying higher rates of tax in an allegedly progressive tax system reflects the large number of allowances and exemptions (Inland Revenue 1984: Table 1.3).

The growth of occupational welfare has been even greater from the limited indications one can find. *Table 2*, based on annual surveys of the proportion of executives receiving fringe benefits, indicates the general growth in provision since the first surveys. It excludes the basic occupational pension which is almost universal among management and does not reveal changes in the amount spent on fringe benefits. This amount has been significant – for example, the proportion receiving free life assurance exceeding three times their annual salary has practically doubled to 42 per cent in the last decade.

Table 2   *Fringe benefits other than retirement pensions, 1965–84*

Proportion of the sample of managers and executives receiving benefits in:	1965	1969	1974	1979	1984
top hat pension	n.a.	28.7	19.3	16.1	23.9
full use of company car	37.0	49.7	62.0	69.0	77.9
allowance for regular use of own car	24.0	18.7	12.3	7.3	4.4
subsidized lunches	59.0	71.2	64.2	74.4	63.2
subsidized housing	3.0	2.4	0.9	0.7	0.3
assistance with house purchase	n.a.	n.a.	4.7	5.8	8.4
life assurance	n.a.	18.8	53.1	65.1	52.0
free medical insurance	20.0	14.5	30.1	50.6	68.9
low-interest loans	n.a.	n.a.	n.a.	9.0	10.5

Source: Inbucon; and Green Hadjimatheou, and Small (1984: 38).

Although the percolation of occupational welfare, and especially the more valuable forms, down the occupation hierarchy has probably been less than some would suggest, evidence from many sources would indicate that there has been a massive increase in the extent of this form of welfare, particularly in the inflationary years of the 1970s. This is generally claimed to result from the combination of three factors: a) high inflation; b) an incomes policy that limited the highest salaries; and c) personal taxation for the higher paid which their associations and lobbies denounced as 'penal' or 'punitive'. It is less clear to me that these factors are a cause rather than an excuse – or, more precisely, an incentive and a convenient justification – for a major extension in the form and value of fringe benefits which had already been gaining momentum for many years before (see, for nearly two decades earlier, Titmuss 1958: Chapter 2; Titmuss 1962; also the annual Inbucon reports from 1965).

Any assessment of developments in these systems over time must also take account of changes in the wider society. If more and more welfare effort and resources are going to meet the needs of those in employment, the roughly tenfold increase in unemployment since the 1950s deserves particular consideration. Despite the emphasis of the main 'Welfare State' programmes on universal access to benefit, 'employmentship' is today even more firmly established over citizenship as the significant and honourable status for the receipt of welfare – and the more secure that status, the more, and the more generously, are needs likely to be met. 'The more secure are the "ins", the less secure are the "outs" (Kerr 1954: 105). Unemployment strikes disproportionately at the poorer and more marginal groups in society. If public welfare is being cut and those without work are disbarred from entitlement to the non-public welfares obtained through employment and earning, unemployment becomes in effect a double and even more severe tax (Sinfield 1981).

The unequal distribution of security and reward also helps to explain the persisting sexual division in welfare (Rose 1981). The greater and longer labour-force participation of women has not yet opened up the higher-status salaried posts with fringe benefits and other opportunities for 'efficient tax-planning'. Forty per cent of the much increased number of married women in employment have only obtained part-time jobs with little if any entitlement to occupational welfare. Many more are in low-paid, insecure work, and with higher unemployment their insecurity has increased.

WHO PAYS FOR WELFARE?

So far I have committed one of the more persistent errors of social policy analysis, examining who benefits but neglecting who pays. The full redistributive effects of any benefit system can only be understood when we have examined the other side of the accounts too. Once again the lack of comprehensive and precise data has to be stressed but the general trend can, I believe, be clearly indicated.

Public and fiscal welfare are in their different ways funded by governments raising revenue from one or other form of taxation or contribution, such as national insurance. The evidence we have shows that the burden of these costs has come to fall much more heavily on the average and below-average income recipient than on those with higher incomes. In the twenty years up to 1979 the burden of taxation doubled but most of the increase was borne by those with incomes between one-half and twice average income, not those with higher incomes (SPITIS 1983: xiv). In the years since 1979 this imbalance has undoubtedly been increased.

Who pays for occupational welfare is both less clear and less considered. Much of it is deliberately 'tax-efficient' and is set against the taxes that would otherwise be paid by the employee and employer, and so should appear within a full and proper accounting of fiscal welfare. In September,

1983, the Board of Inland Revenue conceded that 'tax expenditure' on occupational pensions might actually be £5 billion a year rather than just over £1 billion as it had previously estimated (Inland Revenue 1983). This disclosure warranted a short piece in the Business Section of *The Times* (28 September, 1983) and that is all. One can only speculate on the political and media uproar that would have followed a disclosure of a similar scale of underestimate on some 'Welfare State' expenditure for the poor.

The loss in tax revenue, however, is not the only price that the citizen pays for occupational welfare. We appear to know – indeed to ask – even less about the other ways by which companies meet the cost of giving extra rewards to their staff. How much is passed on to the purchaser of the product or service in higher prices, how much met by keeping salaries and wages lower? If inflation really did give an impetus to fringe benefits, the extent to which these tax-efficient benefits were financed by raising prices and so themselves contributed to pushing inflation even higher would seem to be a reasonable question to ask. The importance of the question is all the greater because these benefits for a few deprived society as a whole of the extra tax revenue that would have resulted from increases in pay; in consequence there were fewer resources for public welfare and other public spending. Yet I have been able to find no evidence of this question receiving any attention in Britain, or apparently anywhere.

Despite the serious inadequacies in the data on the two less visible systems of welfare, the general trend appears clear. Redistribution in social policy debates is still all too often assumed to be a process that occurs downwards from the better off to the poorer, in short 'to those in need'. But the three systems not only identify and define 'need' in very different ways, they also meet recognized need to very different extents. Redistribution in the fiscal and occupational systems is generally upwards, providing what Stanley Surrey has neatly described as 'upside-down benefits' (1973: 37). By no means all redistribution in public welfare is downwards: much spending in the public system is a transfer sideways from, for example, the healthy to the sick or across each individual's lifetime. This system, however, remains the only or the most important source of welfare for those on low and even below-average incomes.

The total effect of these trends is to produce greater inequality. These three systems are, as Titmuss predicted thirty years ago, 'simultaneously enlarging and consolidating the area of social inequality' (1958: 55). The evidence I have been able to locate for other countries seems to confirm that this is a common trend. In Australia, for example, inequalities have been reinforced by tax expenditure on fringe benefits which has been 'estimated to be approximately one-half of the Commonwealth Government's expenditure on social security and welfare' (Jamrozik *et al.* 1983: 55). In the United States, official estimates of tax expenditure made it equivalent to 'about a quarter of the Federal Budget' (Pond 1981: 51; see also Surrey 1973; and Owens 1983).

THE REINFORCEMENT OF PRIVILEGE AND STIGMA OVER TIME

The study of who pays as well as who receives provides fuller evidence of the inequalities created or reinforced by the combined impact of the different systems of welfare, but we cannot begin to grasp the complete picture until we pay more attention to that most neglected dimension in social policy analysis – the significance of time.

Council housing provides accommodation for nearly one-third of the population, but the payment of rent over many years secures nothing more – and when 'the Welfare State' is being cut, council housing may decline in quality and value with length of residence. By contrast the subsidy of tax relief on mortgage interest assists owner–occupiers over time to obtain a capital asset that may be sold or passed on. Even during the years when the home is being bought, it may provide the social and financial credit that facilitates access to other aspects of 'the good life'. It tends to enlarge freedom in many ways not available to a council tenant and yet 'in any real meaning of "cost" . . . the average owner–occupier pays less *absolutely* as well as *relatively* for his housing than the council tenant' (Townsend 1979: 511).

Ironically, the benefit which enhances status and is seen as greater proof of personal success is achieved at greater expense to other members of that society. This is even clear when the dynamic patterns of distribution and redistribution are examined over time and not just in snapshot form. The inequalities generally widen rather than diminish with time. Much occupational welfare is even more obviously the visible acknowledgement of senior status or success. Analyses of 'Welfare State' services have drawn attention to the stigma of selective means-tested services which has survived the official demise of the Poor Laws and of the bad old days when the badge of shame of public dependency could be seen visibly in the 'p' for pauper on the clothes of eighteenth-century paupers. Today occupational and fiscal welfare provide badges of honour that enhance status: the spacious home, the expensive company car, and business suit are only the more obvious examples of those equally selective systems.

A less sheltered and blinkered approach to sociology and social policy is required that will examine how some benefits raise recipients up while others literally trap them in poverty. While the receipt of public assistance cancels out or at least devalues most alternative income, receipt of other welfares can make it easier to obtain yet more resources. To examine stigma but not the badges of honour is to build into research and teaching the class-blind notion that we are all equal except for those pulled down. A less restricted structural analysis reveals that it is the support of the other welfares which enable some to manage on the basic universal provisions of public welfare when others cannot. It also helps to explain why the first group cannot understand how the others need to apply for means-tested public welfare as well. It is the latter's failure to gain entry to what Lawrence Root (1982) has called 'the employment-based enclaves of protection' that often makes them appear less deserving rather than any other personal inadequacy.

Those who have advocated the public provision of a minimum level of welfare, leaving the rest to much-valued private initiative – as William Beveridge did – have failed to take account of the class structure of modern industrial societies. Such a strategy rests upon assumptions about a classless or at least relatively equal society with equal opportunity. In western societies, and perhaps others too, the misconception is more serious because public welfare tends to lack the legitimacy of the other systems where benefits are awarded to job-holders or by concessions to taxpayers. The other systems of welfare are more likely to be regarded as right, proper, and even natural while the receipt of 'unearned' public benefits, as opposed to 'unearned' incomes, is more questionable.

THE POLITICAL AND ECONOMIC DYNAMICS OF THE DIVISION OF WELFARE

Privilege has not only been protected and perpetuated by the separate and unequal systems of welfare. New forms of status and reward have reinforced existing inequalities and created new ones. For example, the fiscal and occupational systems of welfare play an important part in maintaining and even creating desirable lifestyles. As Egon Ronay has commented, 'today the company executive plays an overwhelming part in enabling most of the better class hotels and restaurants to exist' (Barron 1977: 19). And at one major marina in the south of England one in six of the yachts belong to companies and are mostly used for entertaining rather than serious sailing. The publicly subsidized enjoyment of private welfare therefore maintains old and creates new models of the good life.

The impact of the non-public systems is increased by the fact that allocation through them is supported by widely held beliefs about the rightness or appropriateness of entitlements to certain groups rather than others. Workers earn what they receive and tend to be seen as members of and contributors to society: non-job-holders are not. Job-holding legitimates one's political role, as well. In local and national politics, more is heard about 'taxpayers' than about 'citizens' (Tussing 1974: 53).

The political implications of this dynamic of the social division of welfare deserve much more attention than they have been given. In 1978 I suggested that 'the more successful the social construction of "the welfare state" in disguising who really benefits, the less likely we are to accept the need for changes that will help to reduce inequalities' (Sinfield 1978: 148) and I quoted a comment on trends in the United States: if, with 'a selective vision that serves some interests very well, we focus on how well the poor seem to be doing, we are diverted from realising that others are doing much better' (Corwin and Miller 1972: 200, 213).

While many social scientists have criticized the imperfections of political debate and scrutiny of governments' raising and spending of public revenue on 'the Welfare State', they have tended to overlook the 'agenda-setting' that has already occurred by the exclusion from discussion of the spending on welfare in the other systems. This blinkered view might be less disturbing if there were a genuine possibility of 'welfare pluralism', but the belief that there can be is itself encouraged by tunnel vision induced by the mesmerizing language of 'the Welfare State'. The different systems of welfare are not necessarily compatible and are often in competition and direct conflict. This can be seen when one examines, first, how the social division of welfare exacerbates 'the fiscal crisis of the state' (O'Connor 1973) and, second, how growth in the other welfare systems disables public welfare.

Because of the concealed subsidies that reduce revenue, the costs of better welfare for some are being paid for by many non-recipients, most poorer than those who benefit and including some of the very poorest. When public revenue is sufficient to fund public spending and more, the result might be described Micawber-style as happiness. However, when public revenue is deprived by tax expenditure, the result may be greater happiness for the beneficiaries of fiscal welfare but greater difficulty in funding public programmes for the rest and a consequential increase in misery.

There are essentially two responses to the erosion of the tax base – and the poor have been more likely to be disadvantaged by both. Either public spending is cut, with a reduction in public welfare, or taxation is increased to raise the revenue lost in tax expenditure. With cuts there has generally been little success in carrying out promises to protect the poor and most vulnerable. When taxes have been increased, the burden has fallen disproportionately on those with average or below-average incomes. In both instances there is an incentive for those who have the ability and power to push for higher non-public benefits to replace lost public services or to avoid the higher taxes. And the vicious circle becomes a downward spiral for the poor and the other outsiders of the non-public systems of welfare.

In Britain in recent years both responses have occurred, creating what can only be described as the 'fiscal diswelfare' of the poverty trap. The number of taxpayers has doubled in forty years and now very few earners escape paying some tax. The public welfare programme, Family Income Supplement, is intended to help families dependent on the lowest earnings, yet four out of five recipients now pay tax – many pay back more in tax than they receive in benefit. The effect has been all the more serious given the rise in needs resulting directly and indirectly from the combined impact of inflation and recession.

One citizen's welfare therefore becomes another one's tax increase or reduced service, or both. In a society of unequal power, status, and resources, the result is greater protection to the privileged and greater inequality and poverty for the more vulnerable. Yet the aggrieved appear to be the better off who loudly protest against their higher taxes and condemn the profligate 'Welfare State'.

However, the issue is not simply one of distributing and redistributing scarce resources. Even when the resources are increased, the growth of the other systems of welfare can handicap or disable public welfare. Tax subsidies for owner-occupation have distorted the housing market, favouring the larger homes and the second- or third-time buyer, while opposition to subsidies for council housing has grown. Similarly, occupational pensions have tended to act as a check on any improvement of national insurance pensions and have reduced political support for increasing the value of the state retirement benefit among the more vocal middle classes who are protected by their tax-subsidized occupational pensions.

The economic, social, and political significance goes much further than this because the diversion of private funds into pensions and housing without any deliberate public debate and political decision has absorbed resources which might have done more for the British economy, and welfare more generally, if they had been invested in British industry. The operation of the different systems of welfare therefore affect the production and creation of resources as well as their distribution. This is all the more serious given, first, the declining state of the British industrial structure and, second, the fact that this diversion is encouraged by tax concessions and exemptions, whether or not this is the government's deliberate intent. Investment by the pension funds abroad and in property speculation was noted twenty-five years ago by Richard Titmuss as one aspect of 'The Irresponsible Society' (1959). Between the end of 1979 and 1984 the total value of self-administered pension funds increased from £40 billion to £125 billion, more than twice as fast as earnings or prices (Phillips and Drew, quoted in *Financial Times*, 3 June 1985). The funds are now the largest holders of quoted shares and have been described as 'the fastest growing concentration of economic power in Britain' financing 'most major property development . . . the biggest lenders to the government and major shareholders in British industry' (Dumbleton and Shutt 1979: 334). The activities of these major welfare institutions have been allowed to grow with scarcely any of the discussion of the effects on the economy to which public welfare programmes have been increasingly subjected.

The pursuit of welfare outside 'the Welfare State' is therefore not simply an issue of who individually benefits and who individually pays. The ways in which this is done have wider implications upon the economy and society, affecting us all. The question of company cars, while it may be peculiarly British, provides a particularly clear and revealing example of how limited is the conventional definition of social policy to issues concerned almost wholly with the 'Welfare State'.

THE SOCIAL DIVISION OF TRANSPORT: A CASE STUDY

The social division of transport has received little attention in Britain despite the importance of physical mobility for participation in society and access to many resources. A good, cheap, efficient public transport system is essential to any real form of community care. The reduction of public subsidies to nationalized railways and public and private bus systems when fuel costs have raised fares has limited the freedom of very many people.[4]

By contrast the most important growth in fringe benefits has been the company car. In twenty years purchases of new cars by companies have increased from below 20 per cent of all purchases of new cars to nearer 70 per cent, and at least one in eight of all cars are now owned by firms. The benefit and value of this form of occupational welfare increases with status and salary: some companies provide nine 'classes' of car. The travel subsidies from local government to elderly and disabled people, predominantly with low incomes, is below £200 million p.a.; but the revenue lost by the generous undertaxing of the car as a company 'perk' to the higher paid is variously estimated to be between £750 million and £2 billion. So this unpublished subsidy could be twice the controversial and hotly debated government allocation to British Rail.

But that is only part of the picture. The premium placed on high-status luxury cars increases fuel consumption by at least 10 per cent and makes a highly visible nonsense of public campaigns to reduce energy consumption. The inflated demand for these status conveyors has also helped to divert the British car industry from being more competitive with foreign producers, which would mean developing cheaper, smaller, and more fuel-efficient family cars. As if that were not enough, traffic studies in London have demonstrated that the single traveller in the company car, often with all fuel, servicing, and parking costs paid by the company, is a major contributor to traffic congestion, while remaining largely protected from any of the increased costs. He – for 70 per cent of women in Britain have no driving licence and are even less likely to gain a company car – holds up public transport as well as reducing its load, in both ways increasing its costs and only speeding up the introduction of a slower and poorer public service.

An OECD report in 1982 concluded that the growth of car use 'has gone hand in hand with some of the most radical socio-economic upheavals of our century' (1982: 10), leading to a marked change in our lifestyles. In Britain, where there has been no co-ordinated public transport policy but a concealed double subsidy through the non-public systems, the change has benefited some very much more than others. The advantages, therefore, to the better-off one-eighth of drivers have been achieved at a cost of lost revenue, increased expenditure, and slower, poorer services to the rest of society. Added to this is the economic impact of problems for the car industry and increased car imports.

Other countries do not, it seems, allow the particular privilege of the company car. We need to undertake more generally a comprehensive analysis of the combined operation of the different systems. The systems of welfare are not so many separate categories that run in parallel. They do not simply help some more than others. They may conflict, increasing problems for those outside some systems and affecting the production of the resources available for distribution and redistribution in society.

CONCLUSION

The differential development of the systems of welfare has played an important but relatively neglected part in the maintenance of both poverty and privilege. The operation of occupational and fiscal welfare outside 'the welfare state' is not only redistributing resources but also power and status *upwards*. It is at one and the same time increasing the problems of those left out and making it more difficult to help them. The narrow focus of debate on the stereotype of 'the Welfare State' has distracted attention from the fact that the growth of other forms of welfare has led to the widening rather than the narrowing of class disparities, just as was predicted some thirty years ago (Titmuss 1958: 37).

NOTES

1 This chapter is based on the Richard Titmuss Memorial Lecture given at the University of Jerusalem in March, 1984.
2 I would not wish to argue that these three systems comprise the full extent of the social division: David Donnison, for example, has suggested that religious or church welfare should be included in Ireland and

this may be equally valid for countries such as France, Israel, and Italy (1975; see also Field 1981).

3 For a vigorous critique, see Beresford and Croft 1984, though regrettably they largely overlook the role of occupational and fiscal welfare despite their claims to a 'radical' attack on what they see as 'the new face of Fabianism'.

4 I am grateful to Stephen Potter of the Open University for much of the material on which the next two paragraphs are based, and to Test 1984, which he co-authored.

REFERENCES

Barron, Cheryll (1977) The Five-Star Executive. *Management Today*, December: 19–33.

Beresford, Peter and Croft, Suzy (1984) Welfare Pluralism: The New Face of Fabianism. *Critical Social Policy* 9: 19–39.

Briggs, Asa (1961) The Welfare State in Historical Perspective. In Mayer N. Zald (ed.) (1965) *Social Welfare Institutions*. New York: Wiley.

Corwin, R. and Miller, S. M. (1972) Taxation and its Beneficiaries: The Manipulation of Symbols. *American Journal of Orthopsychiatry* 42(2).

Day, Lesley and Pond, Chris (1982) The Political Economy of Taxation and the Alternative Economic Strategy. *Socialist Economic Review*: 157–74.

Donnison, David (1975) *An Approach to Social Policy*. Dublin: National Economic and Social Council.

Dumbleton, Bob and Shutt, John (1979) Pensions: The Capitalist Trap. *New Statesman*, 7 September: 334–37.

Ferge, Zsuzsa (1979) *A Society in the Making: Hungarian Social and Societal Policy 1945–75*. Harmondsworth: Penguin.

Field, Frank (1981) *Inequality in Britain: Freedom, Welfare and the State*. Glasgow: Fontana.

George, Vic and Lawson, Rover (1980) *Poverty and Inequality in Common Market Countries*. London: Routledge & Kegan Paul.

Graycar, Adam (ed.) (1983) *Retreat from the Welfare State*. Sydney: Allen & Unwin.

Gregg, Pauline (1967) *The Welfare State*. London: Harrap.

Green, Francis, Hadjimatheou, George, and Small, Robin (1984) *Unequal Fringes*. London: Bedford Square Press.

Hamer, Mick (1980) The £2,000 Million Perk. *New Statesman*, 21 March: 426.

Higgins, Joan (1981) *States of Welfare: Comparative Analysis in Social Policy*. Oxford: Blackwell & Robertson.

Inbucon Management Consultants (Annual) *Survey of Executive Salaries and Fringe Benefits*. London: AIC/Inbucon.

Inland Revenue (1983) *The Cost of Tax Relief on Pension Schemes: A Consultative Document*. London: Inland Revenue.

—— (Annual) *Inland Revenue Statistics*. London: HMSO.

Jamrozik, Adam, Hoey, Marilyn, and Leeds, Marilyn (1983) Occupational Welfare: Supporting the Affluent. In Adam Graycar (ed.). *Retreat from the Welfare State*. Sydney: Allen & Unwin.

Keens, Carol and Cass, Bettina (1983) Fiscal Welfare: Some Aspects of Australian Tax Policy. In Adam Graycar (ed.) *Retreat from the Welfare State*. Sydney: Allen & Unwin.

Kerr, Clark (1954) The Balkanisation of Labour Markets. In E. W. Bakke (ed.) *Labour Mobility and Economic Opportunity*. New York: John Wiley.

O'Connor, J. (1973) *The Fiscal Crisis of the State*. New York: St Martin's Press.

OECD (1981) *The Welfare State in Crisis*. Paris: OECD.

—— (1982) *Forecasting Car Ownership and Use*. Paris: OECD.

—— (1984) *Tax Expenditures: A Review of the Issues and Country Practices*. Paris: OECD.

Owens, Jeffrey P. (1983) Tax Expenditures and Direct Expenditures as Instruments of Social Policy. In S. Cnossen (ed.) *Comparative Tax Studies*. Amsterdam: North-Holland.

—— (1984) Spending through the Tax System: A Review of the Issues. *OECD Observer* 128, May: 18–20.

Pond, Chris (1981) Tax Expenditures and Fiscal Welfare. In Cedric Sandford, Chris Pond, and Robert Walker (eds) *Taxation and Social Policy*. London: Heinemann.

Reddin, Mike (1985) *Can We Afford our Future?* Mitcham: Age Concern England.

Root, Lawrence S. (1982) *Fringe Benefits: Social Insurance in the Steel Industry*. Beverly Hills: Sage.

Rose, Hilary (1981) Re-reading Titmuss: The Sexual Division of Welfare. *Journal of Social Policy* 10(4): 477–501.

Sennett, Richard and Cobb, Jonathan (1973) *Hidden Injuries of Class*. New York: Vintage.

Sinfield, Adrian (1978) Analyses in the Social Division of Welfare. *Journal of Social Policy* 7(2): 129–56.

—— (1981) *What Unemployment Means*. Oxford: Martin Robertson.

SPITIS (1983) *The Structure of Personal Income Taxation and Income Support*. Third Report from Treasury and Civil Service Committee. Session 1982–83. House of Commons Papers 386. London: HMSO.

Surrey, S. (1973) *Pathways to Tax Reform*. Cambridge, Mass.: Harvard University Press.

Tawney, R. H. (1938) *Religion and the Rise of Capitalism*. Harmondsworth: Penguin.

Test (1984) *The Company Car Factor*. London: London Amenity and Transport Association.

Titmuss, Richard M. (1958) *Essays on 'The Welfare State'*. London: Allen & Unwin.

—— (1959) *The Irresponsible Society*. London: Fabian Society. Reprinted in paperback edition, 1962.

—— (1962) *Income Distribution and Social Change*. London: Allen & Unwin.

—— (1963) The Welfare State: Images and Realities. *Social Service Review* xxvii(1): 1–11.

Townsend, Peter (1979) *Poverty in the United Kingdom*. London: Allen Lane.

Tussing, A. Dale (1974) The Dual Welfare System. *Society*, January–February.

Walker, Robert, Lawson, Roger, and Townsend, Peter (eds) (1984) *Responses to Poverty: Lessons from Europe*. London: Heinemann.

Wootton, Barbara (1961) *Remuneration in a Welfare State*. Eleanor Rathbone Memorial Lecture. Liverpool: Liverpool University Press.

Young, Hugo and Sloman, Anne (1984) *But, Chancellor*. London: BBC.

—— (1962) *The Social Foundations of Wage Policy*. London: Allen & Unwin, 2nd edn.

8

SOCIAL WORK AND MENTAL ILLNESS: DEFINITIONS AND DOUBTS

Philip Bean

It is salutary to remember that Barbara Wootton's book *Social Science and Social Pathology* (1959) was written over twenty-five years ago; that is, well before the reorganization of the social-services departments and before the 1959 Mental Health Act came into operation. Social work and mental illness as areas of interest have moved on since then although the two chapters in Barbara Wootton's book dealing with those topics (Chapters 7 and 9) remain as fresh as ever. Here I wish to examine some aspects of those chapters and show that the problems of definition posed there are as valid now as then. Moreover, new strains have arisen in those subject areas which make definitional problems even more acute.

Consider first Chapter 9 entitled 'Contemporary Attitudes in Social Work'. This chapter must have irritated some of those trained in the social work methods of the 1950s and 1960s, especially those ardent caseworkers who saw casework as the solution to mankind's problems. It would have comforted and reassured others like myself who had been subject to that training and saw Barbara Wootton's book as providing relief and sanity. Looking back on our training, we knew at the time that casework was pretentious and occasionally ridiculous but did not always know quite how pretentious and ridiculous. Casework, that is the full-blooded version taught then in the centres of higher education, was based on principles of Freudian psychology and the world of the id, ego, and superego. It was supposed to assist clients, all of them that is, by providing insights to release them from their tortured inner worlds. No matter that the clients were being seen by the probation officer, the hospital almoner, or the moral welfare worker, these insights would somehow do the trick; the only provisos being the client's level of maturity and ability to accept them. Casework of course did nothing of the sort and from my experience left the client at best bemused and at worst bewildered.

Barbara Wootton set about the claims of caseworkers with gusto and her chapter was polemical and funny. It was, however, carefully slanted in a certain direction, for she chose definitions of casework from the more esoteric American sources which did not always apply to Britain. Even so, some did; and if not they certainly acted as a warning against importing them. She said of one definition 'it might well be thought that the social worker's best, indeed perhaps her only chance of achieving aims so intimate and so ambitious would be to marry her client' (1959: 273), and of another, 'the suggestion that the complex problems of personal unhappiness or of defiance to social standards can be resolved by a young woman with an academic training in social work is difficult to take seriously' (1959: 274). A Mrs A., married to a man who changed jobs frequently, who was often unemployed, and left her short of money, was said by the caseworker 'to have only a glimmering being largely unconscious of her real needs': Barbara Wootton thought it strange that 'anyone not imbued with the ideology of modern casework might have thought that women who are married to shiftless men are only too well aware of the fact' (1959: 278).

But casework ideology did not permit such simple truths to emerge. Claiming to be sophisticated, it none the less missed the obvious. Casework ideology emphasized the 'ego libido method of analysing case histories which would penetrate below sociological generalities discerning subconscious or preconscious motivations' (1959: 274). And if that was not a reason for missing the obvious, nothing was. As with all Freudian theories, treatment followed the manner of the case of Mrs A. cited above; that is, to use Barbara Wootton's terms, the professional caseworker claimed to understand those with whom she dealt better than they understood themselves, discerning those subconscious motivations of which they were themselves unaware (1959: 276). Worse than that, treatment emphasized The Relationship.

Oh, how we as trained caseworkers talked of The Relationship! That mystical entity was not to be confused with simple human friendship or friendliness, although as Barbara Wootton observed artificial tricks of friendliness were used to create an impression of hopeful and cheerful things if only to provide the client with an energizing force at the end of an interview and a willing hand helping to face the future (1959: 280). A social-work student seeing The Relationship in non-casework terms would be accused of naïvety at best, or at worst of being 'defended' against its truths. The Relationship had a professional and self-conscious character; it was the technique by which social workers made emotional contact, and the method by which treatment was determined. It was the key:

without it caseworkers could expect nothing; with it, all was possible. The Relationship involved a complexity of feelings which the client had to 'work through'. These moved from initial hostility to transference, that is love of the social worker, and finally to self-determination. All had to be handled with subtlety and delicacy for to misinterpret the hostility would not lead to the correct application of the transference situation. Eventually the client had to be 'weaned': that is, abrupt or lengthy changes had to be avoided in intervals between interviews lest he should feel rejected. The social worker symbolized the mother's breast as it were, and woe betide any student who did not represent that life-giving force or, worse, had the temerity to view abrupt weaning as advantageous to the client by ridding him of the social worker and those impertinent questions. If handled correctly The Relationship would move to its inevitable conclusion, that is successful treatment. Client and social worker had different parts to play, of course. The client 'after floundering in indecision or premature decision would eventually create the inescapable moment when he must take over to himself responsibility for affirming through word or action or both that that is the way it will be' (1959: 281). In contrast the social worker held 'the slower, more rhythmic movement', a process reduced by Barbara Wootton to the prosaic when she said the social worker gets on with her knitting whilst the client makes up his mind (1959: 281).

The pretentiousness of those claims invited attack and Barbara Wootton did it beautifully. No one else had, to my knowledge, produced a polemic of such quality or been so destructive of a type of training foisted on so many who entered social work for more apparent, mundane reasons. Nor has there been to my knowledge a counter-attack on Barbara Wootton. Perhaps that form of casework could not be defended, or if it could then its defenders chose to operate by way of lofty indifference – the most common defence in these times when professionals are under attack. Yet whatever the reasons casework never seemed the same again, at least not to some in whom doubts had already been sown.

Barbara Wootton's attack on social work was on a certain type of social-work training not on social work as such. And even so, casework was contrasted with nineteenth-century almsgiving and found superior in the manner in which it provided protection and escape from the inquisitorial methods of earlier times; superior too in the standards of manners and courtesy used. Moreover, Barbara Wootton said the aims of social work had not changed and could not change: that is, to provide relief for those in need. Indeed 'the majority of those who engage in social work are sensible practical people who conduct their business on a reasonably matter of fact basis. The pity is they write such nonsense about it' (1959: 279) – a view she still held thirty years later. This particular bouquet to social work is, in my view, hardly deserved for whilst casework may have lost its importance it is not altogether clear that newer forms of social work could be any more welcomed. For whilst the Freudian caseworker could be railed against for her pretentiousness, a later version appeared similarly vulnerable. The lurch to the 'politicalization' of social work where those employed by central or local government claim to be in the vanguard of the new revolution merely swaps the process of social change for individual change. It will be remembered that Barbara Wootton said of casework that the suggestion that complex problems of personal unhappiness or of defiance of social standards can be resolved by a young woman with an academic training in social work is difficult to take seriously. For 'personal unhappiness' substitute the term 'modern society' and the point is surely made.

The critique in Chapter 7 of the then current views of mental illness was less polemical but no less valuable. Briefly the aim was to show that those definitions of mental illness, and correspondingly mental health, found in the contemporary literature were inadequate. After listing over twenty-five definitions of mental health and reviewing some of the literature on mental illness, Barbara Wootton concluded that whichever way the problem was approached no solid foundation was discoverable on which to establish the major proposition that mental health and its correlate mental illness were objective, in the sense that they were more than an expression of tastes, value judgements, or cultural norms. Indeed mental health and mental illness were 'value soaked terms' (1959: 220) linked to adjustments or unhappiness.

Moreover the diagnosis of mental illness was not, according to Barbara Wootton, made on the basis of objective criteria independent of the behaviour of those who suffer from it. The symptoms themselves she said were dependent on social norms. Consequently, claims to assimilate mental and physical health were, in her view, premature – a view incidentally not shared by the Royal Commission on Mental Disorders which was then sitting and whose report formed the basis of the 1959 Mental Health Act (HMSO 1957). That Commission put forward the then more fashionable view that mental illness should be seen in like terms to physical illness in order that the associated stigma be removed. Barbara Wootton's approach to the subject was altogether more rigorous and not concerned to make statements of intent although she allowed herself the luxury of predicting a time when every mental process would have its known physical accompaniment. Even so there would, she said, remain the problem of social judgements being attached to the behaviour created by the illness and the basic problem in that sense would remain.

Barbara Wootton proposed different solutions to the problems posed in social work on the one hand, and mental health on the other. In social work they were more straightforward; in mental health they were many-sided, involving amongst other things the matter of criminal responsibility (this forms the basis of Chapter 9 in this volume, written by Professor John Smith). For social work the solution was to forget casework, let social workers be generalists as far as their agency tasks would permit, and let them learn the minutiae of that legislation which impinges more closely on their clients' lives. 'The service rendered by those who are master of all this, and much more besides and who can mobilise the facilities intelligently and efficiently to suit the requirements of particular individuals is both skilled and honourable' (1959: 296). Were social workers to do this they would, according to this viewpoint, assist in the functioning of the Welfare State and 'involve a genuine professional skill at the disposal of those who may properly be called her client' (1959: 297). And as the poor will require those services most, the social worker's traditional role will be maintained. So the link is neatly conceived, and has, it must be admitted, been achieved partially in the twenty-five years or so since Barbara Wootton's book first appeared, welfare rights being an obvious example. For mental health, however, the solutions were more complex, defying a simple change in structure or attitude.

II

What is interesting about these two chapters in *Social Science and Social Pathology* is that the subjects of criticism and the critique are but two sides of the same social science coin. On the one side there are the social theorists, or policy-makers as we can call them, eager to fashion the world in their image, and on the other, the sceptical positivists, also eager to change the world but on the basis of a social-science methodology derived from Descartes, and developed and refined by Comte and J. S. Mill. Barbara Wootton belonged and still belongs to the latter.

In the former tradition social casework programmes – and mental health programmes too for that matter – were products of an age in western culture when the solutions to mankind's problems were sought in the psyche of the individual. For if the individual was adjusted to himself he would, so the argument goes, be adjusted to others and to his environment; hence those numerous definitions of mental health which spoke of 'the adjustment of human beings to the world and to each other with a maximum of effectiveness and happiness' (1959: 211). No matter that this view helped a branch of psychiatric thinking assume dominance out of all proportion to its quality, i.e. the Freudian view. What was important to the policy-makers was to produce the policy or ideals by which people could be sustained.

It is well to remember that other branches of social science assisted the process. The sociology of the 1960s and 1970s may have been deeply antagonistic to the so-called policy view, but it was more supportive of it in the 1950s. Indeed the major sociological theory of that time, functionalism, was often nothing more than Freudian psychology with a sociological face. In addition, social policy more often than not acted as a bridge between sociology and casework. What was needed, said the major social-policy theorists of the time, for example Titmuss, was to produce more social workers trained in the art of helping and financed of course from central government funds. That this help was based more on a belief and an ideology than anything else mattered little.

Opposing this more esoteric stance was the other strand, more positivist in outlook, which saw the need to evaluate the evidence preferably though not exclusively by statistical techniques and sound research methodologies. That strand still remains at the heart of social-science thinking even if it is occasionally submerged by the more policy-orientated approach. Barbara Wootton represented that strand, stating in Chapter 3 of her book *Social Science and Social Pathology* (1959), in which she reviewed the then fashionable criminological hypothesis, that although the results were strikingly negative, the review was worth while for it induced a wholesome scepticism, showed up the major technical weaknesses, and concentrated attention on technical improvement (1959: 83). Her claim was for sound evidence, sound methodologies, and the scientific method defined some twenty-five years later as 'what you are saying [must be] borne out by facts and [you must be prepared] to establish that those facts exist and that they are relevant to what you are saying' (*Listener*, 26 July, 1984). Of course the champions of casework and mental health did not live up to that rigour though they may have been prepared to use the scientific method as and when it suited them. Their world was of less tangible matters: of the emotions, feelings, and adjustments.

The clash between these two strands lies dormant at present. Meanwhile the use of new technologies has helped the scientific method to appear more amenable, though not necessarily more considered. For this new brand of scientific positivism appears to be centred on the technology rather than on the quality of the argument. Modern social science has lost much of its fervour and clashes between opposing schools of thought are less trenchant now. The policy-makers and scientific positivists have produced an alliance, or if not then they no longer oppose each other with the same enthusiasm. The policy-makers are a little less fervent and the scientific positivists a little less certain. The result is an uneasy compromise perhaps brought about by a new climate where social science generally is under sustained attack.

It is interesting, although equally unwise, to speculate as to why Freudian psychology and the importance of the individual psyche should have been given such prominence in the 1950s. Perhaps we are still too close to that period to answer those questions but it was an extraordinary time and a unique period of history nevertheless. In the intervening years social work and mental health have changed. The formation of social-services departments after the Seebohm Report is testimony to that change whilst the exuberance attached to the 1959 Mental Health Act has been replaced by a drift back to legalism in the 1983 Act. Except in Scotland, the probation service has remained aloof. It no longer has very much to do with juvenile offenders but is more tied to the adult penal system. The drift to and the development of social-work bureaucracies, as notable in the probation service as elsewhere, is a long way from that rather freewheeling approach of the casework days. Whether these changes have produced less role confusion and less bewilderment for the clients is a matter still to be resolved.

III

Perhaps the impression has been gained that Barbara Wootton's approach is as outdated as the theories she criticized. No such impression is intended for it is my contention that we need the same rigour now as then and this can be achieved without taking on board any additional commitment to a certain model of social science. Social work and mental health practices may have moved on but in doing so have left behind a residue of unanswered questions, some of which adversely affect the recipients of those services.

There is still the problem of social-work training, as there was in the 1950s when casework was under attack. We can accept that no progress has been made towards a general theory of helping, nor could there have. The moral, social, political, and economic dimensions (to name but a few) defy that. This implies no direct criticism of social work as such, for the nature of the subject renders the development of such a theory implausible. And for all its deficiencies casework had a certain appeal; it was amongst other things appropriate to the social-work method for it emphasized the position of the individual relative to the social worker, and in doing so allowed social work to be operationalized. (In contrast sociology did nothing of the sort. And in the same way as casework was attacked, so too was sociology which was described by Barbara Wootton as a 'lot of waffle and mostly bunk' (*Listener*, 26 July, 1984).) But once casework was discredited and to some extent discarded, the same old question appeared once more: training for what? It will be remembered that Barbara Wootton's solution was for social workers to advise the poor on their statutory rights but this can only be a small part of what social workers can and ought to do. Their statutory commitments in the fields of mental health, child care, etc., require more than this. But 'training for what?' is still an appropriate question. And because the answers have been various and seem to satisfy so few, the question has, I suspect, often been shelved. Yet it seems that social work will suffer further if that question is not repeatedly asked and the answers subjected to scrutiny.

Consider the training courses themselves. There can be no other occupational group whose training courses are so heterogeneous, their disparities so apparent. There are postgraduate courses, undergraduate courses, and non-graduate courses, all offering the CQSW qualification. The standards of entry vary enormously, some requiring an upper second honours degree in social science, others GCE O level certificates. Some courses for graduates last one year, others two, some offer an MA degree with the CQSW qualifications, others not. Yet all have the seal of approval of the Central Council for the Education and Training in Social Work (CCETSW).

It is not surprising then that employing authorities are often critical of the so-called trained social worker. But their criticisms tend to be of social workers' technical knowledge, or rather lack of it. Social-services departments often complain that social workers require additional training before they are of use to their employers. One can appreciate this point of view for no one is ever really fully trained, but it implies that social work is essentially a technical exercise. Yet a social worker is, or should be, more than a technician because social work operates at the sharp end of modern society, seeing at first hand its complexities and contradictions. Barbara Wootton would not agree, yet I think she was inconsistent on this point, or perhaps she wanted the best of both worlds. She attacked casework partly because it concealed moral judgements through the language of science and medicine, yet she wanted the social worker to ignore the moral judgements involved in acquiring those 'genuine professional skills' which oil the wheels of the welfare state. Advice on the working of, say, the Mental Health Act may be all to the good but in that Act are contentious moral and ethical issues which cannot be walked around by any technical expertise.

These criticisms of social-work training – unwittingly perhaps – fit into the cost-cutting plans of central governments in the 1980s. If accepted, and there are some indications that they could be, it is possible to visualize a time when social-work training is taken out of the universities and polytechnics altogether and confined to in-service training. It would be cheaper and would no doubt appear to some as more relevant. Yet social work has always contained a restless morality, and if occasionally that borders on the ridiculous, so be it. We need to be alerted to the poverty of many people's lives and to the deeper contradictions of our society. Technicians are the last people to do that since they resemble too often the bureaucracies they inhabit. In-service training will do little to produce thinking social workers though it may make them more efficient – in the terms of their employers, of course.

If questions about in-service training begin to dominate, they will do so because social workers have handed the argument to their opponents by default. Social workers have neglected to state what they are doing in clear and concise terms, preferring to complain about what they cannot do. Of course, the social-work task is a complex one, no one denies that: on the same day a social worker may be called upon to be involved in a compulsory detention of a patient in a mental hospital, collect arrears from a parent with a child in care, and arrange for meals on wheels for the elderly. Similarly a probation officer may be involved with parole, voluntary after-care, Community Service Orders, and weekend imprisonment. Gone are the days when social workers could say they assisted the victims of society; sometimes they are the victims and sometimes they produce their own. We can recognize all this yet insist that if social workers are to operate, say, the 1983 Mental Health Act they must do it soundly, that is theoretically and practically, and not cover up inadequacies by complaining of a lack of resources, or see their defects in terms of some pseudo-political analysis. So too for child care or any other area of their work.

If rigour is to be achieved, or rather be seen as a goal worth achieving, it will be arrived at by a slow laborious process which will involve amongst other things discarding some deeply held beliefs. One of these is the belief that social workers are experts at dealing with feelings or the minutiae of social relationships – a left-over if ever there was one from the casework era. Feelings and social relationships are by their nature poor topics for analysis and to embark on such a study is to enter a minefield of uncertainties best left to linguistic philosophers. Social workers cannot readily assist the debate, at least not in the manner in which they currently describe their cases. To make claims to understand or deal with clients' feelings is to claim expertise which can never be substantiated. Social relationships at their most personal and intimate will remain for ever a mystery, and claims to be experts in this field will rightly be treated with scepticism and perhaps disdain.

The more appropriate method in my view is to start from the other end: that is to begin with the task in hand as defined by statute, or by the agency, or whatever, and move towards the minutiae of the relationships once that task is clarified. This approach will involve a study of the constituent parts of the social-work task and the methods involved. In social work those tasks vary, and as in the examples given above, defy a simple thematic view. Adoption differs from fostering, which differs from other branches of child care, and so on. So I would suggest an approach or method which does not see social work as being founded on the social relationships of the client for these will always be poorly understood. Rather, the method by which social workers analyse their task must begin at the point where intervention begins. Anything else would continue the confusion, for the assumption will persist that social work is about social relationships and little else. And the universities and polytechnics can play their part by encouraging that method of analysis in a manner unlikely to be provided by in-service training programmes. So for example, social work in mental health requires an understanding not only of the techniques of compulsory admissions, but also of medical dominance in psychiatry, mental health as a social goal, etc. I am sure that social workers say they understand this already but an examination of their practice suggests otherwise (Bean 1980).

In mental health matters things are no better now than they were twenty-five years ago; in fact it would be no hyperbole to say that if anything they are slightly worse. Inadequate definitions continue to pile on inadequate definitions, the 1983 Mental Health Act being the most recent example, and definitions or commands remain as value-soaked as before. Diagnostic categories remain imprecise – a glance at the World Health Organisation (WHO) classification of diseases will confirm that – and reliability in psychiatric diagnoses is as elusive as ever. The basic problems in mental health and its counterpart mental illness, are the same as ever – that is essentially about the internal validity of the subject matter.

Consider the question of definitions: I wish to take as an example the 1983 Mental Health Act for it forms the basis of modern thinking on mental health issues. Of course criticisms of the 1983 Act and related legislation are not criticisms of clinical psychiatric practice as such, but of those who debated and drafted the legislation. Nevertheless the debate was partly fashioned by clinical practice, and some of the evidence, such as it was, was derived from informed psychiatric thinking. What is apparent at the outset is that the clarity of legislation, and especially the clarity of definitions, have hardly increased over recent decades. Indeed on this and other matters similarities abound. Nowhere is this more clearly shown than in the basic definition on which the Act is founded.

Following earlier legislation (the 1959 Act) the 1983 Act uses the generic term 'mental disorder' defined as 'mental illness, arrested or incomplete development of mind, psychopathic disorder, or any other disorder or disability of mind' (Sec. 1(2)). Four specific forms of mental disorder are then listed: mental illness, mental impairment, severe mental impairment, and psychopathy. The first, mental illness, which concerns the bulk of mental hospital admissions, is not defined; its operational definition and usage, we are advised, are matters for clinical judgement in each case. That may be so, but when turning to the clinical side of matters, including the standard dictionary of psychiatry, we find that it is not defined there either. In other volumes definitions vary substantially from one text to another. Indeed matters are so bad that the Department of Health and Social Security (DHSS) canvassed the possibility of a closed definition of mental illness but abandoned the attempt because the lack of a definition was not thought to have caused any difficulties in practice (Hoggett 1984). Now, of course, the absence of a clinical definition may be of little consequence to psychiatrists, and it is after all for psychiatrists to agree on the nature of their subject matter, and if agreement is not forthcoming then presumably their subject matter suffers. It may also be of little consequence to the patients, that is to those who are prepared to accept and receive willingly the attentions of psychiatrists with the associated risks and dangers. But mental health legislation does more than this; definitions are required to exclude those not falling into the category and include those who do. The more so because this particular piece of legislation provides psychiatrists with compulsory powers to detain patients against their will. What we find, therefore, is that the basic premise, mental disorder, remains as cloudy and elusive as ever, and mental illness itself even more so (Bean 1986).

The second and third forms of mental disorder listed in the 1983 Act are mental impairment and severe mental impairment. The definition of mental impairment has two main components: first, a state of arrested or incomplete development of mind which includes significant impairment of intelligence and social functioning; second, there is the qualification that it must be associated with abnormally aggressive or seriously irresponsible conduct (Sec. 1(2)): the latter is inserted as a means of ensuring that mentally handicapped people are not subject to long-term compulsory powers unless the behaviour which is part of their condition justifies the use of those powers (DHSS 1983: para. 11). Severe mental impairment is defined in the same way as mental impairment except that it encompasses 'severe' instead of 'significant' impairment of intelligence and social functioning.

The differences between these two forms of impairment are by no means clear: the DHSS sees it again as a matter for clinical judgement (DHSS 1983: para. 12). Nor is there a clear distinction between 'significant' and 'slight' mental impairment (the latter condition was included under the old Mental Deficiency Acts). Clinical distinctions are normally of little importance to those not directly involved in the practice of psychiatry, but in law 'mental impairment' and 'severe mental impairment' are grounds for compulsory detention. Moreover there are differences in the grounds on which the patients can be detained or have their detention renewed if they suffer from mental impairment as opposed to its more severe form. But how does one decide whether there is 'significant' or 'severe' impairment? For example, one person with a relatively low IQ may function reasonably well, but another with a higher IQ may function less well. Which, if either, is the 'significantly' mentally impaired and which the 'severely'? Of course, no one knows nor could they, given the legal definitions listed above.

But added to this are the problems contained in the phrase 'abnormally aggressive or seriously irresponsible conduct'. The intention behind it was, on the face of it, sound: that is, to prevent mentally handicapped people from being detained unless they are a problem in a defined social sense. But what does that phrase mean? Does it relate to current conduct or conduct in the immediate or distant past? Does a single incident suffice or should there be a pattern of such behaviour? Would hurling insults count as 'aggressive' behaviour and if so would such behaviour on retributive terms be sufficient to warrant detention in a mental hospital? And finally what does 'irresponsible' mean? Spending too much money perhaps, or not being punctual, or not showing consideration for others? For whichever way the matter is approached it surely must be based on a judgement of behaviour and of behaviour that someone disapproves. And even if agreement was reached on what those terms mean, it extends only to providing a justification for compulsory detention; it provides little hope for treatment.

The fourth category is psychopathic disorder defined in the 1983 Act as a persistent disorder or disability of mind (whether or not including significant impairment of intelligence which results in abnormally aggressive or seriously irresponsible conduct on the part of the person concerned (Sec. 1(2)). There is little need to go through the arguments about psychopathy yet again; Barbara Wootton summed them up neatly when she said the psychopath is 'in fact *par excellence* and without shame or qualification the model of the circular process by which mental abnormality is inferred from anti-social behaviour while anti-social behaviour is explained by mental abnormality' (Wootton 1959: 250). It remains astonishing that in spite of the countless criticisms psychopathy still appears in legislation in England and Wales, though not in Scotland or Northern Ireland. It is not part of the WHO's Classification of Diseases, although it is referred to in definitions of personality disorder. The WHO itself has noted the inclusion of psychopathic disorders in current legislation as one of the most serious problems in the mental health system of England and Wales (Curran and Harding 1978). Nevertheless, the definition of psychopathic disorder is included in the definitions of mental impairment and severe mental impairment discussed above. And to show how wide that definition can be and how flexible the interpretation, it will be remembered that mental impairment and severe mental impairment replaced the categories of subnormality and severe subnormality contained in the 1959 Act and did so in order to exclude certain mentally handicapped persons who did not have a psychopathic component to their condition. One would have expected, therefore, that when new legislation was introduced a number of patients in the old subnormal category would have been discharged on the grounds that they did not have a psychopathic condition. At the time of writing (1985) all subnormal patients have been automatically reclassified as mentally or severely mentally impaired (Gostin 1984).

Of course many psychiatrists are fully aware of the difficulties this legislation imposes and of the criticisms levelled at modern psychiatric practice. Attempts to deal with accusations that their subject is value-soaked and not related to criteria independent of the behaviour of those who suffer from mental illness are, more often than not, based on the fond hope that a materialist basis of mental illness will be discovered. Once the underlying disease conditions are discovered, so the argument goes, inadequate definitions will evaporate and psychopathy, mental illness, etc., will be defined as succinctly as diseases in other branches of medicine. There will be no need then to talk of functional conditions in psychiatry any more than there is a need to talk of functional conditions in other branches of medicine. The subject matter will have its own internal validity and questions of reliability of diagnosis will assume less prominence. Or so it would appear.

There is, however, the awkward question of the behaviour of patients suffering from such conditions and the necessity to rank that behaviour as acceptable or not, and define the behaviour according to various gradations on that scale. For whilst it is clear that physical illnesses exist within a social context, the more so do mental illnesses. We may one day understand perfectly the underlying disease condition of, say, schizophrenia (though I doubt it); we would none the less have to evaluate the behaviour of the schizophrenics in social and moral terms. We would be no further forward than we are today with the knowledge of say, mental impairment or dementia. Those disease conditions may be understood but the behaviour associated with them involves moral evaluations. And more often than not it is the behaviour rather than the disease condition that poses the problems – of a definitional and moral nature. The manner in which mental impairment has been dealt with under the 1983 Act illustrates the enormous difficulties involved and the pitfalls which are present.

Nor would a materialist view solve that other problem in psychiatry, that is the justification for compulsory hospitalization. A high degree of internal validity or inter-rater reliability provides no reason for detaining patients against their will or treating them against their will. We do not give such powers to surgeons although they claim their specialism is valid and reliable. We give it to psychiatrists because the patients' behaviour is evaluated in moral terms and psychiatrists are seen as having a closer working relationship with that type of behaviour than anyone else. Or at least we ought to do so for that reason, although I suspect there are some psychiatrists who claim additional expertise in the behavioural field and see themselves as social and moral experts also. A purely materialist view involves a separation of the disease condition from the behavioural manifestations, but it is the behaviour that produces a danger to the patient or others and the behaviour must become the reason for the detention. A materialist view would not affect that. But we are a long way from a materialist view of psychiatry and still a long way too from being able to define the basic subject matter. Indeed if anything the 1983 Act has shown how little the subject has advanced and how elusive are those attempts to make it rigorous. Barbara Wootton's demands are as relevant now as ever.

REFERENCES

Bean, P. T. (1980) *Compulsory Admissions to Mental Hospitals*. Chichester: John Wiley & Sons.
—— (1986) *Mental Disorder and Legal Control*. Cambridge: Cambridge University Press.
Curran, W. J. and Harding, T. W. (1978) *The Law and Mental Health*. Geneva: World Health Organisation.
Gostin, L. (1984) *A Review of Secure Provision for Mental Patients* (mimeo).
Hoggett, B. (1984) *Mental Health Law*. London: Sweet & Maxwell.
Wootton, B. (1959) *Social Science and Social Pathology*. London: George Allen & Unwin.
—— (1984) *Listener*, 26 July, 1984.

PART TWO

CRIME AND THE CRIMINAL LAW

9

RESPONSIBILITY IN CRIMINAL LAW

J. C. Smith

Not the least of Lady Wootton's many achievements is that she has caused others to think furiously about matters which they had previously taken for granted. For some lawyers it is her criticisms of their cherished doctrine of *mens rea* as the basis of criminal responsibility which has caused the greatest heart-searching. As I count myself as a firm adherent of that doctrine, the invitation extended to me by the editors to write on the subject of responsibility has led me, almost inevitably, to reconsider – not for the first time – the doctrine's validity or lack of it, and its place in the criminal law today in the light of those criticisms.

In 1963 in her Hamlyn Lectures, *Crime and the Criminal Law*, described by Professor Herbert Packer as 'by far the most lucid and cogent statement of the behavioral position' (Packer 1969: 13, 2), she warmly welcomed what she then saw as the decline of the importance of *mens rea* and its replacement, though not immediately, by strict liability. Naturally this produced several replies; but they have left Lady Wootton totally unmoved. In 1981, in the second edition of *Crime and the Criminal Law*, while recognizing that things were not turning out quite as she had hoped and forecasting gloomily that 'we are in for a period in which the traditional moralistic and punitive attitude will dominate the penal process' (1981: 63), she particularly emphasized her earlier arguments against the inclusion of *mens rea* as an essential element in the definition of a crime.

THE MEANING OF 'MENS REA'

It is well to be clear what we mean by *mens rea*. It is a complex subject upon which volumes have been written and it has different shades of meaning for different writers and, indeed, for different courts and judges. The law relating to one aspect of it – the concept of recklessness – is in a state of flux at the present time and is the subject of a fascinating disagreement between some judges of the House of Lords and some of those of the lower courts. For the purpose of this essay, however, these controversies can be ignored. I shall state the general principle of the doctrine as I understand it.

It is that a person who has caused a result which the criminal law forbids should be held responsible only if he intended to cause that result or took a deliberate risk of causing it. The defendant is responsible for the result *because* he deliberately chose to cause it; or *because* he deliberately chose to take an unreasonable risk of causing it. Those who define *mens rea* in this way contrast it with liability for negligence. This is imposed when a person is held liable for the forbidden result although he did not foresee that it might occur, but a person behaving with reasonable prudence would have foreseen the risk and avoided the result. Strict liability is liability without fault. It is imposed although the person who caused the forbidden result neither intended nor foresaw it and although a person acting with reasonable prudence might similarly have failed to foresee it.

Offences may be graded according to the nature of *mens rea*. For instance, to cause serious injury intentionally is an offence punishable with life imprisonment under Section 18 of the Offences against the Person Act, 1861; to cause the same injury recklessly is an offence punishable with five years' imprisonment under the same Act; whereas to do so merely negligently is not a criminal offence at all. In all these cases, of course, the injured person may seek a remedy in damages in the civil courts. Occasionally the criminal law imposes liability for negligence – an example is manslaughter where gross negligence must be proved – that is, it must be proved that the defendant's conduct fell far short of the standard of care to be expected of a reasonable man.

The elimination of 'mens rea'

A mere defence of the place of strict liability in the present law would have left the lawyers relatively unperturbed. What was so shocking in *Crime and the Criminal Law* was the suggestion that the concept of responsibility should be allowed to 'wither away' and that strict liability might, not immediately but in due course, take over altogether. The mental state of the defendant, or his negligence, at the time of committing the offence would come into the picture only 'after what is now known as a conviction' for the purpose of determining the appropriate treatment. This treatment would presumably not be voluntary, so the defendant would become subject to the compulsory process of the law even though he was completely without fault. Until after 'conviction' it would be irrelevant whether he acted with *mens rea*, negligently, or without fault of any kind. Thus –

> 'If, however, the primary function of the courts is conceived as the prevention of forbidden acts, there is little cause to be disturbed by the multiplication of offences of strict liability. If the law says that certain things are not to be done, it is illogical to confine this prohibition to occasions on which they are done from malice aforethought; for at least the material consequences of an action, and the reasons for prohibiting it, are the same whether it is the result of sinister malicious plotting, of negligence or of sheer accident. A man is equally dead and his relatives equally bereaved whether he was stabbed or run over by a drunken motorist or by an incompetent one.' (Wootton 1981:46)

And 'if the object of the criminal law is to prevent the occurrence of socially damaging actions, it would be absurd to turn a blind eye to those which were due to carelessness, negligence or even accident' (Wootton 1981: 46).

STRICT LIABILITY: A CREATION OF THE COURTS

It would be a mistake to suppose that offences of strict liability have been thrust by Parliament on an unwilling legal profession. Nothing could be farther from the truth. The architects of strict liability are the judges. Rarely if ever does Parliament expressly declare that no *mens rea* is required for an offence. It frequently omits any reference to a mental element in the definition of offences; but that is no obstacle at all to a judge who believes that *mens rea* should be imported into it. There is abundant authority in favour of a rebuttable presumption that *mens rea* is an essential ingredient in every offence. All the judge need do is to hold that there is nothing to displace the presumption in the provision before him and it follows that *mens rea* is required. The courts have found no difficulty in implying a requirement of *mens rea* although the subsection at issue did not use the word 'knowingly' and the immediately adjacent subsection did. When an offence is construed to impose strict liability it is generally because the judge considers that this is required or desirable as a matter of policy. It is a judicial invention not a parliamentary one. As Lord Devlin has said –

> 'One is bound to come to the conclusion that Parliament likes it this way. It is usual of course to pay lip service to what is supposed to be the intention of Parliament. The fact is that Parliament has no intention whatever of troubling itself about *mens rea*. If it had, the thing could have been settled long ago. All that Parliament would have to do would be to use express words that left no room for implication. One is driven to the

conclusion that the reason why Parliament has never done that is that it prefers to leave the point to the judges and does not want to legislate about it.'   (Devlin 1958: 208)

The related concept of vicarious liability is even more obviously a judicial creation. Parliament scarcely ever states that one person is to be liable for crimes committed by others; but by a remarkable feat of interpretation the courts have held that many regulatory offences can be committed through others acting in the course of employment by the defendant or failing to perform the statutory duties which the defendant has delegated to them.

Of course, not all judges over the years have taken the same view about these matters. Some rely much more strongly on the presumption in favour of *mens rea* than others. Even the same judge may appear to take different attitudes on different occasions. This explains why the law in this area is so inconsistent and why it is difficult to state any satisfactory general principles. At the present time there is a remarkable difference of judicial opinion between the 'objectivisits' (though some of them would object to being so described) who would severely restrict the operation of the doctrine of *mens rea* and the 'subjectivists' who favour its more general application.

'Real crimes' and 'quasi crimes'

It is then the lawyers, and particularly the judges, who are responsible for the present state of affairs in which offences can be divided into two categories, offences requiring fault, whether *mens rea* or negligence, and offences of strict liability. How, if at all, can this distinction be justified? The judges have commonly sought to distinguish offences of strict liability as not being 'real crimes'. In the leading case of *Sherras* v. *De Rutzen* [1895] 1 QB 918 at p. 922 J. Wright distinguished 'a class of acts . . . which are not criminal in any real sense, but are acts which in the public interest are prohibited under a penalty'. In the case of such offences the court will more readily find that the presumption in favour of *mens rea* is excluded. In the first case concerning strict liability to reach the House of Lords, *Warner* v. *Metropolitan Police Commissioner* [1969] 2 AC 256, Lord Reid expressed his reluctance to hold that the offence of possessing prohibited drugs was one of strict liability because it was an offence to which a stigma attached. The House has now on several occasions accepted as valid the principle of strict liability and, almost invariably, one of the grounds stated is that the offence is not 'a real crime'. In so saying, the judges are not talking law. In law, all offences are 'real crimes'. When Parliament creates a new offence it does not say that it is, or is not, a 'real crime'. If Parliament declares certain conduct to be an offence triable in the criminal courts and punishable with a fine, or imprisonment, or in some other way, it is, in law, a crime like any other. The courts are really saying, not that it is not a crime, but that the plain man would not regard it as such. Judges see themselves as plain men who know what other plain men feel and think. If this distinction is, as it is often stated to be, the foundation of the categorization of offences and it is baseless, then it may be argued either that all offences should require *mens rea*; or that all should impose strict liability. Lady Wootton, of course, takes the latter view. She states two objections to the 'real crime' argument. 'In the first place the statement that a real crime is one about which the good citizen would feel guilty is surely circular. For how is the good citizen to be defined in this context unless as one who feels guilty about committing the crimes that Lord Devlin classifies as "real"?' (Wootton 1981: 39). If this criticism is well founded, then the lawyer's world is indeed crumbling about his ears. Throughout the law, civil as well as criminal, we constantly have to look for standards of conduct. The standard has to be that of the good citizen in the particular circumstances. None other is available. It is only by this device that we can distinguish negligent from prudent conduct; but the good citizen's standards are invoked in branches of the law other than negligence. For example, a statement is defamatory if it 'would tend to lower the plaintiff in the estimation of right-thinking members of society generally' (*Sim* v. *Stretch* [1936] 2 All ER 1237 at p. 1240, per Lord Atkin).

The intuitive method of determining the standards of the good citizen is, no doubt, unscientific and may well appear unsatisfactory to the social scientist; but, given that such a standard exists, at least in the minds of the judges, there is nothing 'circular' about applying it to particular types of conduct. The good citizen is not merely a person who would feel guilty about committing 'a real crime'; he is the reasonable man, L. J. Bowen's celebrated 'man on the Clapham omnibus', who always behaves with prudence, who does not lose his self-control in the face of provocation (except of an extreme kind), who firmly resists threats (except of an extreme kind) aimed at compelling him to commit crime, and so on. But Lady Wootton continues:

'And in the second place the badness even of those actions which would be most generally regarded as *mala in se* is inherent, not in the physical acts themselves but in the circumstances in which they are performed. Indeed it is hard to think of any examples of actions which could, in a strictly physical sense, be said to be bad in themselves.'

(Wootton 1981: 42)

This, with respect, is obviously right; and no lawyer who understood his subject would deny it. The law does not judge acts without regard to the circumstances in which they are performed. Within the definition of every crime there is unexpressed but implicit provision for circumstances of justification or excuse. Conduct is not 'reckless' unless it is unreasonable in the circumstances. The circumstances may also excuse the conduct on the ground of a particular defence, such as duress or self-defence. If the concept of *malum in se* or 'real crime' is to have any utility it must be applied, not to the mere movement of the body, but to the action in all the relevant circumstances. The insertion by the surgeon of the knife into his patient on the operating table is an act of a wholly different quality from the insertion of the same knife into the same part of another's body in the heat of a quarrel.

'Wickedness' must be a mental element

Merely to take account of the relevant circumstances does not, however, get over the difficulty raised by Lady Wootton. To her question, 'can we . . . in the modern world identify a class of inherently wicked actions?' (Wootton 1981: 38), the answer must be in the negative; and this is no less true of the ancient world. Notwithstanding her opinion that 'the badness . . . is inherent not in themselves, but in the circumstances in which they are performed' (Wootton 1981: 42) it is submitted that the *action*, even in the broadest sense, is not 'inherently wicked' if no account is taken of the state of mind with which it is done. No stigma attaches, or should attach, to the person who kills another, or a hundred others, or who causes any other unhappy result, 'by sheer accident'. *Ex hypothesi* he is blameless and deserves only sympathy. But the action may perhaps be considered wicked if done negligently, certainly if done recklessly, and still more so if done intentionally. This does create a difficulty for the application of the 'real crime' test.

Take Warner's case. His story was that he collected two parcels which he believed to contain scent and which had been left at a café for him in connection with a part-time business he carried on. One of the parcels contained 20,000 amphetamine tablets. The Divisional Court [1967] 3 All ER 93, held that the offence of possessing controlled drugs was one of strict liability and upheld his conviction. Even if his story was true, even if his belief was based on reasonable grounds, he was still guilty. But if his story was true he had done nothing wrong. No stigma should then have attached to Warner from his conviction on these facts. Why should Lord Reid think it would attach? The answer must be that the conviction would not proclaim, 'This man is blameless'; instead it would class him with those who intentionally possess large quantities of controlled drugs, and who, no doubt, are stigmatized by the 'right-thinking members of society generally'. The trouble about strict liability offences is that conviction of them does not distinguish between different degrees of fault and no fault at all.

It appears then that, in order to test whether an offence is one which attracts such stigma that it ought to be treated as 'a real crime', we should consider the case where the proscribed act is done intentionally. If this attracts stigma, then, by holding the offence to be one of strict liability and convicting a blameless person we subject him to the same stigma; for the same legal label is attached to him as to the intentional offender. Does this provide a workable test? If Parliament prohibits the causing of results which are in some measure harmful, the intentional causing of the harm deserves some measure of condemnation. Some stigma attaches, or should attach, to the motorist who deliberately leaves his car in a parking space for longer than is permitted by law – it is an anti-social act and one which causes inconvenience to others. So is keeping out a library book beyond the permitted time. But few people, however 'right-thinking', would consider these acts so iniquitous, even when done intentionally, that the actor should be locked up or even shunned and avoided.

If this is true, no clear line can be drawn between offences carrying stigma and offences not doing so. Any distinction drawn must be one of degree; since most of the distinctions which the law has to draw are matters of degree, that is not a fatal objection. Moreover, it is clear that this is by no means the only factor involved in the court's decision. For example, the court will more readily impose strict liability in the case of an offence which applies only to persons engaged in a particular occupation – a 'regulatory offence'. If you choose to take part in that particular activity, then you infringe the law at your peril.

'Where penal provisions are of general application to the conduct of ordinary citizens in the course of their everyday life, the presumption is that the standard of care required of them in informing themselves of facts which would make their conduct unlawful is that of the familiar common law duty of care. But where the subject-matter of a statute is the regulation of a particular activity involving potential danger to public health, safety or morals, in which citizens have a choice whether they participate or not, the court may feel driven to infer an intention of Parliament to impose, by penal sanctions, a higher duty of care on those who choose to participate and to place on them an obligation to take whatever measures may be necessary to prevent the prohibited act, without regard to those considerations of cost or business practicability which play a part in the determination of what would be required of them in order to fulfil the ordinary common law duty of care.'

(Lord Diplock in *Sweet* v. *Parsley* [1970] AC 132 at p. 163)

So we find most instances of strict liability in offences regulating the sale of food and drugs, the conduct of licensed premises, and the like. But the 'particular activity' may be one in which citizens generally engage, like driving a car. Still, this is something which we choose to do and as it involves potential danger it is not inconsistent with this statement of principle that some offences regulating the activities of motorists should be strict.

Judging the intentions of others

The law relating to responsibility, Lady Wootton rightly says, 'presumes an ability to make judgments about other men's intentions and the degree of their iniquity, the validity of which cannot ever be objectively demonstrated' (Wootton 1981: 64). It is certainly true that the doctrine of *mens rea* does presume this ability. If the presumption is baseless the doctrine is a sham and should be abolished as soon as possible. It should not be accepted that it is baseless, however, because its validity cannot be 'objectively demonstrated', in the way that the rules of science may be demonstrated in a laboratory. We can often be as certain that a man had a particular state of mind as we can be certain of anything. Does any rational being doubt that armed men who enter a bank and demand money at gunpoint intend to steal, that they dishonestly intend to appropriate property belonging to the bank and permanently to deprive the bank of it? that a man who lies in wait for a girl in a dark lane, knocks her down, and has sexual intercourse with her, intends to have sexual intercourse with her without her consent? that a man who applies a loaded shotgun to another's knee and pulls the trigger intends to cause grievous bodily harm? In such cases we can be just as certain that the defendant had the intention as that he did the act. That, indeed, is what the law requires. The judge tells the jury that they must be convinced not only that the defendant did the act, but that he did it with *mens rea*. Evidence is always admissible to challenge the inference and, if it casts doubt on even the most overwhelming inference of *mens rea*, the defendant is entitled to be acquitted.

Moreover, Lady Wootton herself assumes that these matters would be taken into account at the sentencing stage. 'The prevention of accidental death presents different problems from those involved in the prevention of wilful murders' (1981: 48). But it is no easier to answer the question at the one stage than the other. While we retain our present procedures it will be the magistrates who will have to answer the question at whatever point it arises. In the Crown Court it becomes a question of whether the matters which really determine the fate of the defendant are to be decided by the judge or by the jury. It would not be appropriate here to attempt to assess the relative virtues of the judge and jury in matters of fact-finding; but there would certainly be grave disquiet in many quarters if the jury were relegated to the role of answering only the question, 'Did he do it?'

No doubt there is a greater difficulty in answering the second point: can we properly assess the degree of iniquity? We can, however, assess reasonably objectively the gravity of the harm caused; and, if the defendant chose to cause that harm, or to take a risk of causing it, this seems to afford a reasonable measure by which to assess 'iniquity'. This assumes that the defendant could and did choose.

Could the defendant choose?

Lady Wootton's conclusion that the concept of responsibility should be allowed to wither away was based on her penetrating study of the operation of the law relating to diminished responsibility (1960: 76 LQR 224). There are, however, dangers in drawing general conclusions about the criminal law from such material. Diminished responsibility is a concept unknown to the common law and imported from the law of Scotland for the purpose of mitigating the unacceptably severe results of a mandatory penalty for murder – at the time of its importation, death, and now, life imprisonment. Offences for which the penalty is fixed by law are quite exceptional in our system; in practice, murder is the only such offence in peacetime. In the case of other offences the matter which would constitute diminished responsibility in murder are taken into consideration only at the sentencing stage. There is much to be said for abolishing the mandatory sentence for murder and, if it were abolished, there would be a strong case for abolishing the defence. It should be added, however, that the Criminal Law Revision Committee, who were almost evenly divided on whether the mandatory penalty should be abolished, were disposed to retain the defence in any event (1980: 19, 33).

Diminished responsibility creates a special problem in determining whether the defendant is liable to conviction, because it requires the jury to take into account the difficulty or impossibility which a mentally abnormal person may have in controlling his conduct. In cases other than murder the law simply assumes, in the absence of evidence of 'automatism', that the defendant is able to choose, and it is left to the court to take account in sentencing of any special difficulties he may have. If responsibility for a forbidden result is imputed because the defendant chose to cause it, or to take the risk of causing it, it would be wrong to impute liability unless we were sure he was able to choose. In the case of the vast majority of crimes, it is submitted that we can be as sure of this as we can be sure that the defendant did the act. In the absence of evidence of duress no one will seriously doubt that the bank robber, the rapist, and the knee-capper discussed above were able to choose to do, or not to do, the act in question. It is notoriously difficult to prove the general deterrent effect of particular sentences or patterns of sentencing but there can be no doubt whatever that the general system of law enforcement acts as a very significant deterrent.

Andenaes (1965: 70–1) points out that when, in 1944, the Germans arrested the entire Danish police force, criminality increased immensely, though there was a great difference in the various types of offences; and that a short-lived police strike in Liverpool in 1919 resulted in the plundering of 400 stores in the course of a few days. Great numbers of people are choosing not to commit crimes every day because of the deterrent effect of the criminal law. Others choose to take the risk of being caught. The reported increase in crime in many cities during the recent coal strike when large numbers of police were diverted from their normal duties shows that some potential burglars choose to stay at home when the risks of being caught are high but are willing to go to work when they are low. But surely it needs no demonstration. Lady Wootton pours a little gentle scorn on 'the optimism which expects common sense to make good the deficiencies of science' and thinks that 'no objective criterion which can distinguish between "he did not" and "he could not" is conceivable' (1981: 77–8). This is said in the context of mentally abnormal offenders; but, in the case of those who are not mentally abnormal, the common sense and the experience of the jury or magistrates are surely a sufficient guide. A defendant's claim that he acted 'involuntarily' is approached with under-standable scepticism by the law. Unless the defendant introduces credible evidence of 'automatism' the jury will not be invited to, and the magis-trates need not, consider the question. Once the issue is properly raised, however, it is established that it is for the prosecution to prove beyond reasonable doubt that the defendant's act was voluntary.

If the prosecution fails to achieve this and the defendant goes free, it may be said that the law is failing in its purpose because it is turning loose on the public a person who, because he involuntarily does harmful things, is a danger. There is force in this criticism but much of the sting is taken out of it by the legal distinction between insane and non-insane automatism and the relatively small scope allowed to the latter. If the condition arises from an 'internal factor', for example, epilepsy, arteriosclerosis, a brain tumour, or even diabetes, it is classed as 'insanity' and will result in the special verdict of 'not guilty on the ground of insanity' and the indefinite detention of the defendant. If the condition arises from an 'external factor', for example a blow causing concussion or an anaesthetic, the defendant will be entitled to a simple verdict of not guilty. Obviously 'internal factors' are likely to be continuing conditions with consequent continuing danger to others whereas 'external factors' are generally transitory.

TWO CASES

The theory of universal strict liability might be usefully examined in the light of two cases. The first is *Ball* (1966) 50 Cr App R 266. The defendant was the civilian driver of a military scout car, so constructed that he could see only to the front and not to the side. He stopped at a T-junction with a major road. His colleague standing in the turret of the vehicle advised him that the road was clear. Ball drove forward into the path of a motor cyclist who was killed. He was charged with causing death by dangerous driving (an offence abolished by the Criminal Law Act, 1977) and the judge directed the jury as follows:

> 'once you are satisfied looking at it objectively that it was what you think it right to describe as dangerous driving, well, then, it does not matter whether the driver was being deliberately reckless, whether he was being careless, whether he was being what you would call momentarily inattentive, whether he was a most incompetent person doing his best, or whether he was a good driver doing his best in very difficult circumstances. The question is: Was it in your view, whatever the reason for it may have been, a piece of dangerous driving?'

Ball was convicted. The judge granted him an absolute discharge. He appealed against his conviction. The appeal was dismissed; the direction to the jury was correct.

It will be noted that the direction corresponds closely with Lady Wootton's refusal to draw a distinction between the results 'of sinister malicious plotting, of negligence or of sheer accident'. Like her, the court takes account of these factors in sentencing. Since he gave the defendant an absolute discharge, the judge was presumably of the opinion, from his own view of the evidence (because the jury's verdict of 'Guilty' told him nothing), that he was concerned with 'a good driver doing his best in very difficult circumstances'. It is worth noting that the driver, although given an absolute discharge, which for most purposes does not count as a conviction, still thought it right to appeal. No doubt there is considerable stigma attached to a conviction for causing death by dangerous driving because it lumps the defendant together indistinguishably with those who kill by deliberate recklessness, whom right-thinking members of the community very properly condemn.

This decision did not survive as an authority for long. In *Gosney* [1971] 2 QB 674 a lady drove her car at a gentle pace in the wrong direction along the fast lane of a dual carriageway until she encountered a police car coming in the opposite direction. The trial judge, following *Ball*, rejected evidence that the conditions at the junction might have led a competent and careful driver to suppose, as Mrs Gosney had done, that she was entering a single carriageway road. This was irrelevant because, if her driving was dangerous (as was obvious) it was irrelevant to liability (though not to sentence) that she was a good driver doing her best. The Court of Appeal found her conviction offensive to their sense of justice. They overruled *Ball* and held that fault – in effect, negligence – was an essential element in the offence. After *Gosney*, a person acting as Ball did would almost certainly not be prosecuted. Lady Wootton's theory faces us with the question whether the law ought to allow, or require, him to be prosecuted – or subjected to whatever form of legal process might be put in the place of prosecution.

The second case, *Tolson* (1889) 23 QBD 168, is one of great importance in the development of the criminal law. Martha Ann Tolson was deserted by her husband on 13 December, 1881. She and her father made enquiries about him and learned from his elder brother and from general report that he had been lost on a vessel bound for America which went down with all hands. Five years went by and then, on 10 January, 1887, Mrs Tolson went through a ceremony of marriage with another man. The circumstances were well known to the second husband and the ceremony was quite open. Then in December, 1887 Mr Tolson returned from America. Mrs Tolson was charged with bigamy and convicted by the jury who, in answer to a question put by the judge, said that they thought that she, in good faith and on reasonable grounds, believed her husband to be dead at the time of the second marriage. The judge sentenced her to one day's imprisonment so that she was immediately released. He reserved for the Court for Crown Cases Reserved the question whether, on these facts, Mrs Tolson was rightly convicted of bigamy. By a majority of nine to five the court held that she was not.

It has always seemed to me that the reasonable being from another planet, knowing nothing of our legal history, would be astonished at the story of Mrs Tolson – first, that she should be prosecuted at all, let alone convicted of a felony punishable with a maximum of seven years' imprisonment; second, that after protracted debate five learned judges should actually have been in favour of upholding her conviction. Her conduct seems to have been eminently reasonable. She made appropriate enquiries about her deserting husband and then, reasonably believing himself to be a widow of five years' standing, she, as she thought, remarried. She *intended*, being a widow, to marry; but in fact, being married she had gone through a ceremony of marriage during the lifetime of her husband. The 'harm' at which the offence of bigamy is aimed had occurred. She was not liable, the majority decided, only because she believed in good faith and on reasonable grounds that she was a widow.

If we are to apply universal strict liability until 'after what is now known as a conviction', unfortunate people like Ball and Mrs Tolson would presumably have to be subjected to what is now known as prosecution and conviction so that the person whom we now know as the sentencer could consider what were 'the appropriate measures to be taken to prevent a recurrence of the forbidden act'. It is difficult to see what that person could do in respect of Ball or Mrs Tolson except to make sympathetic noises.

SOME PRACTICAL DIFFICULTIES

This brings me to what I regard as the major difficulty in Lady Wootton's theory. It is essentially a practical one. The only question for the court of trial is to be 'Did he do it?' Whether he did it intentionally, recklessly, negligently, or by sheer accident is irrelevant. In any event the person who did it is to be passed on to the 'sentencer' who will consider what should be done to ensure that he does not do it again. Now if the court of trial has to disregard the question of fault, so too surely do the police and the prosecuting authority (or whatever takes its place). If we allow the police or prosecutor to decide to proceed or not on the basis of whether or not the defendant was at fault, we do indirectly what we will not permit to be done directly. We allow the crucial decision which is now made formally and openly on proper evidence in court to be made informally, privately, and on whatever evidence the prosecutor, in his wisdom, or lack of it, considers relevant. The logic of the system requires the prosecution of *all* cases because even if the forbidden result has resulted from 'sheer accident', the sentencer is under a duty to consider whether there is anything to be done to ensure that the 'offender' does not have such accidents again. Everyone who causes an injury to another person, everyone who damages another's property, could, and should, be brought to court. Every buyer or seller of goods who makes an innocent misrepresentation, every bona-fide purchaser of goods in fact stolen, the surgeon whose patient dies on the operating table, the Good Samaritan who innocently gives help to a person escaping after committing an arrestable offence – all these have brought about the harm which it is the object of the law to prevent; so they should be subject to process of law so as to ensure that they do not cause the harm again. The business of the courts would be enormously multiplied. And to what purpose? What is to be done with all those who (like Ball and Mrs Tolson) have behaved reasonably and have had the misfortune to cause the forbidden result by sheer accident – except to tell them to continue to behave reasonably?

It is reasonably safe to assume that what would in fact happen is that, however illogically, the fault test would be applied at the police or prosecution stage. This would be prompted, not only by the natural sense of justice of those operating the system, but also by their realization of the futility of invoking legal process against one who has behaved entirely reasonably.

A further practical difficulty is that the system would put enormous discretion into the hands of the sentencer. He would apparently have the same power in law over one who caused death accidentally as over a murderer. It is difficult to believe that such a large discretion would be tolerable. It would dilute, if not destroy, the criminal law as a moral force and that at a time when the decline of religious belief has, as Lady Wootton herself says, created a dangerous vacuum. The shift from punishment to prevention may be intended to remove the moral basis of the law; but if, as some believe, one of the major reasons why people do not commit crimes is the sense of guilt which attaches to them, should not the aim be to enhance the sense of guilt rather than otherwise? To remove the element of fault is to empty the law of moral content. If murder were, in law, no different from accidental death, should we be so inhibited from committing murder as most of us are?

Strict liability and negligence

The advocates of strict liability sometimes confuse it with liability for negligence. Even Lady Wootton lapses when, in the midst of her argument in favour of strict liability, she writes: 'But now, perhaps, the time has come for the concept of legal guilt to be dissolved into a wider concept of responsibility or at least accountability, in which there is room for negligence as well as purposeful wrongdoing' (1981: 50–1). And at the conclusion of her chapter she remarks that she has been chiefly concerned with cases of negligence (1981: 51). Liability for negligence is plainly not the same thing as strict liability. It excludes the person who has caused the proscribed result 'by sheer accident'. There may be some point in subjecting the negligent person to compulsory legal process to encourage him, and others, to behave with greater care in the future.

The objections rehearsed above to strict liability do not apply to liability for negligence. Indeed it is submitted that this is the proper criterion of responsibility in regulatory offences which have as one of their objects the protection of the public from carelessness. There is, furthermore, weighty authority for using the same criterion in the case of 'real crimes' – offences likely to be visited with imprisonment. In the two famous, or notorious, cases of *Caldwell* [1982] AC 341 and *Lawrence* [1982] AC 510 the House of Lords extended the concept of recklessness so as to extend well beyond *mens rea*, as described above, and to embrace such negligent conduct. The defendant is 'reckless' not only when he is aware of the risk of causing the harm in question but also when he is not aware of a risk which would have been obvious to a reasonable and prudent man who gave thought to the matter. The writer is strongly of the opinion that this extends liability for serious crime too far – and it has in fact caused confusion and disquiet in lower courts – but it is clearly a tenable view.

I make no apology for the fact that this essay in honour of Barbara Wootton is somewhat critical of her views, for it is a great tribute to her that lawyers should still be worrying about her criticisms of their theories more than twenty years after they were published.

REFERENCES

Andenaes J. (1965) *The General Part of the Criminal Law of Norway.* London: Sweet & Maxwell.

Criminal Law Revision Committee (1980) *Fourteenth Report* (Cmnd 7844). London: HMSO.

Devlin P. (1958) Statutory Offences. *Journal of the Society of Public Teachers of Law.*

Packer, Herbert (1969) *The Limits of the Criminal Sanction.* Oxford: Oxford University Press.

Wootton, Barbara (1960). Diminished Responsibility: A Layman's View. *Law Review Quarterly,* April: 224–39.

—— (1981) *Crime and the Criminal Law* (2nd edn). London: Stevens.

10

CRIME AND PENAL POLICY
Howard Jones

The range of Barbara Wootton's work has been impressive. It includes important contributions to methodology, the economics of wages determination and the trade cycle, the critical examination of the role of the 'helping professions', such as psychiatry and social work, and a contribution sustained over many years to the development of humane and rational judicial and penal policies. All of this work has displayed a firm grasp of theoretical considerations, but with a commitment to common sense and usefulness which must have dismayed the more dogmatic theoreticians. She has provided the most convincing evidence possible for the Lewinian dictum that there is nothing so practical as a good theory (Marrow 1969), but with the emphasis on the word 'good'.

Nowhere is this typically British empiricism better exemplified than in the book whose title has been borrowed (with great trepidation) for the title of this paper (Wootton 1978). Modestly she addresses the book to 'people like myself . . . a non-professional public with an interest in penology', but it is no penological cook book. It is (as ever) free of the jargon and tortuous syntax which lesser scholars apparently need in order to bolster up their academic self-image. But this simplicity only imperfectly conceals her mastery of the theoretical considerations and research upon which a sound penal policy must be founded.

She has never been afraid of controversy, and therefore, for example, does not scruple to take issue with the 'moralists', whose noisy denunciation of rehabilitative approaches so often drowns other voices (Wootton 1981: 94). For many years it had been argued that the most rational and compassionate way to deal with offenders was to attempt to 'correct' them, but this has now been challenged on the grounds that correction is both ineffective and unjust. Instead we are urged to return to an older aim emphasizing legalism, and punishment according to 'desert'. This 'justice model' (Bottomley 1980) clearly has important practical implications, and any discussion of penal policy must deal with it first.

As Lady Wootton points out (1978: 37), its claims are moral: that the judicial and penal machinery should aim at fairness and not at the reduction of crime – which it is argued, they cannot achieve. So there should be no penal action until the guilt of the accused person has been established by due process of law. This done, a sentence should be imposed which is related to the amount of blame attributable to him. This sentence should also be a judicial act, and should then be implemented strictly in accordance with the order of the court, leaving very little scope for administrators or social workers to allow for changed or personal circumstances (Hood 1974). This rigorous control by the courts over sentencing, like the similar adherence to due process in the determination of guilt, is advocated as a protection for offenders from arbitrary or unfair treatment, but it also effectively prevents any individualized attempts at rehabilitating them.

But is this 'justice model' as just as all that? First of all does conviction for a crime imply blame, such as to justify punishment? Or does it not depend instead on a traditional distinction between retributive and distributive justice – the familiar but untenable separation of the punishment of criminals from the distribution of welfare. If there is one thing which challenges the moral pretensions of the justice model, it is this purely negative aspect. How can it reasonably be claimed that adding one 'bad', the infliction of pain, to another, the committing of crime, somehow produces a 'good'? Even in elementary algebra: $-x + -x = -2x$.

Meanwhile the more comprehensive and positive concept of social justice is available to us. The statistical correlations of various forms of social deprivation with arrests are well established. Arguments about the 'dark figure', and differential rates of arrest only serve to strengthen these affiliations. It is probable that criminological researchers will continue to discover other associations of this kind. It is not necessary to deploy determinist arguments in order to claim that the existence of these factors reduces, to an unknowable extent, the degree of an offender's responsibility. Marx, so often seen as an arch-determinist, put it very well: 'Men make history, but not in circumstances of their own choosing.' Because the amount of blame left for imputation to the offender is unknowable, the attempt, in the name of justice, to graduate severity of punishment to desert becomes very unreal.

Nor is it an attack on his autonomy, as protagonists of the justice model would claim, to take account in this way of factors which contribute to his criminality but are outside the control of his own will. It is in fact a defence of that autonomy. Indeed a related but wider, and therefore even more conservative, formulation is dissolved by making this link between freedom and social justice. This is the dichotomy, propounded by Rawls (whom the retributionists have often conscripted in their support), in which freedom is given priority over distributive justice (Rawls 1971: 43). Freedom is impossible in the presence of social injustice, including freedom in relation to the committing of crime.

However, if society accepts no responsibility in respect of the criminal's diswelfare, he is relieved of the moral obligations of citizenship, including obedience to the law (Murphy 1979: 102ff). One is reminded of Rawls's hypothetical social contract (Rawls 1971: 11ff): because this is entered into by 'free and rational persons concerned to further their own interests', it commits them to assuming all the obligations which the contract brings with it.

It is inconceivable that any 'free and rational person' would enter into such a contract knowing that it would be as much to his disadvantage as it is for many criminals. Rawls adds the revealing presumption that in entering into the agreement none of the parties is aware of his social-class position, his status, or his personal physical or psychological abilities. Such assumptions are reminiscent of the most unreal models of 'economic man', and transform the decision to enter into a contract into one in which the much-vaunted freedom and rationality are totally irrelevant. Instead of a rational choice we have a blind gamble. If hypothetical social contracts are to carry any conviction at all, it must be on some assumption of a choice based on knowledge. Otherwise such a contract can have little legitimacy for those who afterwards discover that its terms were so framed as to enable others to exploit them.

To sum up, the debt alleged to be due to society on the part of the criminal, a debt which is used to justify punishment, is seen not to exist if retributive justice is replaced by the more tenable concept of social justice (Murphy 1979: 109). This would justify the replacement of punishment by a policy of helping the offender to keep out of further trouble – what is usually called rehabilitation. Realistically speaking, there is no possibility of eliminating punishment entirely. Psychoanalysts (Alexander and Staub 1956: 214–23) suggest that there will continue to be a public demand for the punishment of criminals because they are convenient social scapegoats. But there is no reason to capitulate entirely to these primitive motivations. It is the task of leaders to lead. Experience in Britain with the death penalty has shown that this is practicable in the penal field. If, on the other hand, there is no commitment at all to social justice on the part of society, then those who suffer as a result cannot be held to have any corresponding social obligations. Assuming that they knew what they were doing, they would not have put their names to Rawls's hypothetical social contract.

What is to be said about that part of the justice model which is concerned with preserving due process and the dominance of the courts, ostensibly to protect the rights of the individual? There is no doubt about the importance of due process at the stage of determining guilt or innocence, though one might have some doubt about the use of such a term as justice, implying as it does moral guilt or innocence, rather than the factual question of whether or not the accused person committed the act complained of.

Against this, Lady Wootton argues persuasively that the present adversarial system can lead to 'opposite distortions', and may not always, therefore, be the best way of getting at the truth. An alternative could be an inquisitorial system like that found in many European countries (Wootton 1981: 32). Nevertheless all possible safeguards should be available to ensure that an innocent person is not convicted, including the right to hear what is being alleged against him, and to be adequately represented. It must be remembered that even a purely rehabilitative approach to offenders will make heavy demands on convicted offenders, while in the mixed system which is the more likely outcome, conviction could bring with it heavy punishment.

Sentencing is a different matter entirely. If rehabilitation is to enter into these decisions at all, sentencers will have to be much more knowledgeable about the relevant considerations than they are at present. It is now almost a quarter of a century since the Streatfeild Committee on the Business of the Criminal Courts expressed this view (Home Office 1960), and although the training of magistrates has improved since then, there has been much less progress in the training of judges officiating in the higher courts. Nor has this training led to any greater rehabilitative efficiency in sentencing (Brody 1976) perhaps because the training has been aimed more at improving performance in administering retributive justice, than in implementing a policy of rehabilitation.

We ought perhaps to be giving serious consideration to practice in some European countries, where the office of magistrate is not a reward for local prominence or public service, or the office of judge for achievements at the Bar, but a profession in its own right. Aspiring judges would undertake from the outset an education which was related to the functions (including sentencing) which they would be expected to perform. And recruited as magistrates, their further progress in the hierarchy would depend on their performance as judges and nothing else. By itself, this would not solve all the problems. Because educational opportunities are so unequal, recruitment to the new professional judiciary would be class-biased, unless steps were taken to prevent this.

Another Streatfeild recommendation, that greater use should be made by the courts of social inquiry reports compiled by probation officers, in order that relevant consideration about an offender might be brought to their attention, was more widely implemented, but these reports themselves have been very much under attack (Bean 1976: 90ff). It is argued, for example, that the attempts of probation officers, in these reports, to assess the personalities and social circumstances of accused persons are unjustifiable. They include damaging statements about the accused, which are based either on hearsay or prejudice, or on ideologies disguised as psychological theory; an American lawyer went so far as to call them 'character assassinations' (Blumberg 1967: 158). They also usurp the role of the courts by including recommendations for sentence.

If these strictures were justified it would be a serious matter, though some might find comfort in another criticism sometimes levelled against them: that the courts are not greatly influenced by them. If this is the case, they could hardly have played as malevolent a role as is alleged.

Lady Wootton, though doubting if the reports did have much effect, commended them to 'help fill the enormous gap that separates those at the elevation of the judicial and magisterial bench, from those standing in the dock whose lives and liberties they can control' (Wootton 1978: 45). It is true that most judges come from the middle and upper classes, and most accused persons from the working class. The differences between them in education, economic security, lifestyle, and values, make for a gap in understanding which is very difficult for either to bridge. In using social enquiry reports to remedy this ignorance, a clear distinction should be drawn between facts and the inferences drawn from them. This is not a guarantee of objectivity, for the probation officer has to make a selection from the many facts which the contingencies of life generate, and he will do this on the basis of what is relevant to the correctional task. Nevertheless it would remove one source of confusion, and the situation would be further clarified, if the report were prefaced by a clear statement of the theoretical or other assumptions which guided both the selection of information and the interpretations based upon it.

Sentencers would then be in a position to evaluate the content of a report for themselves, though some people will doubt whether that is in itself necessarily a gain. Research (Bottomley 1973: 130–70) and the idiosyncratic statements made by some of our most senior judges, give reason to doubt the fairness and objectivity of their judgement. As to its wisdom, they remain lay persons in the field of rehabilitation, with little relevant knowledge. Their naïvety here is not even relieved by practical experience, for as Lady Wootton points out (1978: 42), they rarely come into further contact with those they have sentenced, and so cannot study the effects of their decisions and thus 'learn by doing'.

Evidence has been presented to suggest that the reports are no answer: that they do not improve the effectiveness of sentencing. This could be because they do not contain the right kind of information, or because sentencers do not take enough notice of them. Or it could be because they form part of a total sentencing process which blunts or nullifies any useful effect they might have. What is surely indisputable is that the more information any decision-maker has, the better his decisions are likely to be, and sentencers are no exception to this.

The challenge to the rehabilitative effectiveness of social inquiry reports is only part of an onslaught on the effectiveness of rehabilitation in general. Since Lipton and Martinson's celebrated negative evaluation of correction a decade ago (Lipton, Martinson, and Wilks 1975), the conventional wisdom has been that 'nothing works'. This pessimistic view has not remained unchallenged (e.g. Palmer 1978; Jones 1981a), and it is not indispensable for the validity of the 'social justice' ideal that correction should work. The moral superiority of that ideal is in its recognition of a broader basis for fairness, and its replacement of punishment by sympathy and understanding. However, its moral case is even stronger if the offender is actually helped to a better social adjustment. Experience, moreover, shows that a burgeoning crime problem does increase punitive attitudes in the public at large, making it more and more difficult to secure the acceptance of a policy based on social justice rather than on fear and revenge.

With the progress of science and technology man has gained a high and increasing degree of control over his physical circumstances; it is almost a cliché to say that he still has achieved by comparison very little control over his social environment, and therefore continues to suffer the grievous effects of such social problems as war and the fear of war, poverty, mass unemployment – and crime. Why should we not attack these misfortunes with the rational tools which have paid such dividends elsewhere? In relation to crime, this would mean research and experimentation aimed against the crimogenic forces at work in society, but it would also require similar efforts directed towards the rehabilitation of offenders. Always assuming, of course, that the measures adopted are consistent with the aims of freedom and social justice.

In particular it is necessary to counter the view that the rehabilitation of offenders is a form of 'brainwashing' or of ethnic imperialism. This particular charge depends on an argument with which the present writer has much sympathy: that laws are the weapon of a dominant class, and are used to maintain their economic position at the expense of the rest of the community. Crime is therefore defined in a partisan way, so as to include acts committed by other classes which threaten the interests of the governing class, while excluding acts of the privileged where these do not represent such a threat (Vold 1958: 203–19). Rehabilitation could then be a programme for 'cooling out' the underprivileged, persuading them to accept the laws which support their exploitation. Rehabilitation is the 'soft sell', reducing the divisive tensions which the 'hard sell' of punishment is bound to intensify in a class society.

Against such a background, there could be no moral basis for punishment of the kind claimed by the doctrine of retribution, because there would be no moral obligation to obey the law. Punishment would be a form of intimidation to enforce obedience, and would continue to be so as long as such conflicts in society continued. Experience in the communist countries gives no reason for believing that revolution eliminates them. In the context of social conflict, punishment robs people of their autonomy no less than does retributive punishment, in an ideology of consensus.

Is there no acceptable alternative? Must rehabilitation necessarily be a 'con-act' in support of privilege? Could one conceive of an approach which sought to help offenders to reduce the material, cultural, and emotional deprivations which gave rise to their criminality? In the best traditions of social casework, the emphasis would be on helping them to emancipate themselves, rather than on doing it for them, for they have also to be strong enough to hang on to their gains afterwards. This would be done by casework aiming, in the classical tradition, at giving them a greater insight into the nature of their social and personal predicaments, and then leaving them, as sovereign individuals, to choose their own course of action for themselves.

Although this would be a libertarian approach it would be operating within an unequal and illiberal social framework. One of the facts which the offender would come to see more clearly, and have to take into account in charting his own course, would be the power of the law to punish him if he maintained his resistance. He might then decide to yield to *force majeure*, but if he did not, he would at least no longer be inclined to accept the retributive ideology that the punishment was 'deserved'.

The analysis of the nature of society undertaken above would be acceptable to many Marxists, but they would deny the possibility of rehabilitation on such a basis. The ruling classes would not permit the emergence of such a challenge to their power and interests. As students of history, Marxists should pay more attention to the history of the last 200 years in this country; they would find that it did not bear them out. Although the Webbs' dictum about the 'inevitability of gradualness' is not often invoked nowadays, it seems to have been vindicated by events.

There are in any case many forms of crime in which class interests are involved only in the very broadest sense, as when, for example, it is argued that the protection of anybody's property legitimates the accumulations of the rich. Such considerations would be more relevant if the task in hand were the reform of society rather than the rehabilitation of criminals. However desirable the wider objective may be, criminals should not be used as cat's-paws in its attainment. Much criminal violence is, in this sense, of only marginal significance in class terms. So are many property crimes: they are committed as often against the poor as the rich – and sometimes by criminals who are richer than their victims. It is a romantic myth that property crime is a way of achieving a more equitable distribution of property (Birkbeck 1982).

But the main case raised against correction, apart from that from the viewpoint of retribution, is that it does not work: a charge which is based on the results achieved by rehabilitation in the past. They by no means prove the point. As Palmer (1978) points out, rehabilitation in the cases studied has often been inappropriately applied, i.e. to offenders with whom it was unlikely to be successful. This was either due to the court's slender knowledge about the requirements for rehabilitation, or to their mixing it up with retributive or sometimes deterrent aims. Inevitably its effect has been largely neutralized.

It would be no exaggeration to say that in the present state of judicial innocence, rehabilitative, retributive, deterrent, and preventive sentences are imposed more or less at random, in relation to the objective of rehabilitation. If all of the four aims of sentencing were of equal importance in the minds of the sentencers, this should produce an expectation of 25 per cent rehabilitative success – a level of achievement which is easily surpassed. In fact, our expectations ought to be even lower than 25 per cent, as courts usually seem to rate rehabilitation below the other sentencing objectives.

However, there is a more serious fallacy in the argument that if rehabilitation has failed in the past, it must therefore also fail in the future. Surely all that can be deduced from past failures is that our knowledge and skill need to be improved by further research and experimentation. If, instead, we take it for granted that correction cannot work, and give up trying, this assumption becomes a self-fulfilling prophecy.

Even if there is a joker in the human pack, in the shape of an element of free will, making the application of the scientific method less predictable in its effects, this is no reason for assuming that the behaviour of criminals cannot be influenced. Just as there are factors outside the individual's volition which contribute to the change in his behaviour in the direction of criminality, so we may assume that there are factors which could contribute to a change in the opposite direction. After all we run our daily lives on the assumption that we can influence the behaviour of other people, and nobody has ever produced any evidence to suggest that criminals are different in this respect from everybody else.

Hostility to rehabilitation is strongest in discussions of the role of the prison. There is now almost general agreement that reforming the prisoner should not be seen as part of its function. Because prison cannot rehabilitate, and indeed does harm to the social adjustment of inmates, it is important that its use should be kept to a minimum. It is particularly important that the courts should not impose a prison sentence on the grounds that it has correctional value for the person concerned. Such a justification is sometimes used, resulting in people being committed to prison who should not and would not otherwise be there.

There can be no doubt that prison is a very difficult place in which to attempt to rehabilitate. The corrupting inmate culture, the institutionalizing effect of insular, rigid, and depersonalized regimes, and the damage done by separation and labelling to the family relationships and other outside networks which should be the prisoner's main purchase on normal life after discharge: all these work against any correctional aims which a prison might have.

This is not a new discovery. Over thirty years ago, Sir Lionel Fox, then head of the British prison and Borstal systems, declared that prisons do more harm than good (Fox 1952). But it is the new doctrinaire attack on rehabilitation *per se* which has converted this scepticism, which had previously provided grounds for penal reform, into an assumption that nothing can be done (Cross 1971). Some even go further, opposing certain prison improvements on their own account, on the grounds that this may make courts more willing to send people to prison instead of imposing the more desirable non-custodial sentences. On such grounds, for example, it is argued that a moratorium should be imposed on new prison building – even though this would mean keeping some prisons which do not provide civilized conditions of confinement, and would also leave some prisoners still 'doubling-up' in cells originally intended for single occupation (King and Morgan 1980: 114–21).

These arguments are regrettable for at least two reasons. First of all they weaken the prison reform movement, taking the heat off those both within and without the prison service who still believe that imprisonment should be a harsh experience. These 'backwoodsmen' usually try to justify themselves by saying that prisons should be retributive and deterrent, but these arguments resemble nothing quite so much as the 'techniques of neutralization', with the aid of which, according to Sykes and Matza (1957), juvenile delinquents attempt to rationalize their law-breaking. If Zilboorg (1956) and others (Alexander and Staub 1956: 220), are right in saying that the urge to punish the criminal derives its strength from the same roots in instinctual aggression as does crime itself, one might well want to clothe such motives in more acceptable garb.

As justifications, retribution and deterrence certainly carry little conviction. Reasons have already been advanced for rejecting the former. As for deterrence, current research gives little reason for believing in its general effectiveness (Beyleveld 1979, 1980). And in those cases in which it might have been effective, the corrupting influence of present-day prisons will offset it as much as it does rehabilitation. For example, a criminal who is sent to prison will not only be reinforced in his criminal identifications by his contact with the mature criminals around him, but will also be in a position to learn new criminal skills from them, which will give him confidence (however misplaced) in his ability to avoid arrest in the future.

An unregenerate prison system is clearly a grave probable outcome of the retreat from rehabilitation. Cross denies this. Prison reform, he says, must continue, but should content itself with removing the bad effects of imprisonment instead of attempting rehabilitation (Cross 1971). It is difficult to visualize such a neutral condition, neither corrupting nor aiming to 'improve'. Measures like better inmate–staff relationships, personal and group counselling, education, and a realistic work programme would only succeed in dislodging apathy and 'crimogenic' loyalties if they replaced them by something else more desirable. And even if it were possible, the status quo represented by an unrehabilitated criminal is hardly an attractive target to aim at. The May Report on the United Kingdom prison services (Home Office 1979) attempted to square this circle, and showed how unreal the task was by coming up with that extraordinary hybrid 'positive custody'.

The second reason for deploring this rehabilitative nihilism is that no matter how actively we pursue a policy of 'decarceration', there will still be offenders in prison. In some instances they will be there to 'protect the public' – incapacitation. In others it will be at the insistence of a public whose vengefulness or sense of justice (if these two can really be separated) will lead them to insist that certain serious crimes be punished in this way. It may be impossible to resist such a demand, but at least we should not compound the offence by allowing the gap between convicted criminals in prison and those outside to widen even further. This would hardly be in accord with the ideals of the retributivist model of justice espoused by so many of the anti-correctionalists. Nor would it meet the more defensible requirements of social justice or the claims of humanity.

In spite of the severe handicaps with which rehabilitation in a prison setting is confronted, there is some evidence that it can be successful. A case in point is the study of social work in prison carried out by Margaret Shaw (1974). Much more could probably be achieved if the corrupting influence of the inmate culture could be reduced, and the artificial and regimented nature of life in prison be alleviated. More open prisons would be one way forward, although they have their own shortcomings, mainly owing to the fact that their staffs have been recruited and trained (and indeed socialized by their peers) for a system which is still orientated towards bolts and bars (Jones and Cornes 1977).

Much smaller institutions, or self-contained small units within existing institutions, also do much to weaken the structural obstacles to rehabilitation. When numbers are small, helpful relationships are more likely to develop across the staff–inmate divide and unnatural regimentation becomes unnecessary. The success of the Special Unit in Barlinnie Prison in Edinburgh is instructive in that regard (Boyle 1977), though it ought not to be necessary to operate on such a small scale.

Structural changes like these are more important than specific rehabilitative measures. Nevertheless it is possible to discuss the latter, if in very general terms. What is required is a rich environmental experience to provide a background for individual and group counselling. That environment would include programmes of work, education, recreation, and interpersonal relationships, against which the individual could measure himself and set himself objectives for the future, in other words, gain insight into the nature of his personal and social predicament. It would all be a waste of time, of course, if the sort of life waiting for the prisoner outside, after discharge, were neglected, but earlier discharge might legitimate social-work support at that stage also.

Although it would be undesirable to give up rehabilitative programmes in prisons, it is not suggested that incarceration should continue on its present scale. There are many reasons why this is undesirable. For one thing prisons are very expensive, partly because of the cost of maintaining security and control. They require high staffing levels, and costly buildings and equipment. Incidentally it does not have to be assumed that adopting a correctional policy will increase the cost. Security will be more easily maintained, for example, if numbers are small, and if better relationships with inmates enable staff to know more about what is going on.

Imprisonment is also expensive because of what are sometimes euphemistically called 'hotel costs'. And there is also the further loss to the community because the prisoner is often either engaged in unproductive work during his sentence, or in producing objects of low value by unproductive methods for only a few hours a day. This is on the assumption that an alternative to prison would enable him to work at some non-criminal activity, a condition which the level of unemployment and the criminal's own motivation will often not permit to be met.

The existence of certain other kinds of cost have also to be noted, however. These are the personal costs paid by the prisoner and his family. Sometimes they are of a financial kind – the wages he might have earned if he had not been imprisoned, and the financial loss resulting from his employment difficulties after discharge. These would be reflected in the current and possibly the future standard of life of his dependants and himself. The reality of this may be a wife and children living on Supplementary Benefits while the breadwinner is in prison – and after his release if he is unable to get a job. To these have to be added the very heavy human costs: the separation, the stigma, and the deprivation of autonomy, of heterosexual expression, and of personal comfort. And all to facilitate a process in which the scales are weighted against any gain to the prisoner through rehabilitative success.

In any social justice ledger these personal costs have to be debited against imprisonment, and together with the financial costs referred to earlier, they constitute a formidable case against its use even if its structure and methods were reformed and made more effective. The case for a rehabilitative programme must rest on the needs of that minority for whom prison is seen as unavoidable.

Two devices in particular have been used to try to limit imprisonment: suspended sentences and parole. The relevance of the suspended sentence seems obvious. The criminal does not go to prison immediately, which is a gain. The threat of imprisonment if he does not observe the law during the period that the sentence is suspended should deter him from future crimes at least during the period of suspension, and ensure that he does not finish up in prison later on.

It has been suggested that this is not in fact what happens (Bottoms 1980). The law provides that if the person so sentenced commits another offence during the period of suspension, the suspended sentence is activated and added to a further sentence of immediate imprisonment for the new offence. The court has the discretion not to enforce the whole of the suspended sentence, but if it were reduced too often, offenders would cease to take it seriously. On the other hand, if too many received increased sentences, the effect, over a period, would be to increase rather than reduce the number of people in custody. This is precisely what is said to have happened.

This effect, according to Bottoms (1979: 439), has been worsened by the way in which the suspended sentence has been applied by the courts. Instead of using it as intended, solely as an alternative to imprisonment, it has sometimes been used instead of probation. Like probation, it does not involve immediate incarceration, and could conceivably be more deterrent than probation because of the threat of imprisonment contained in it. This usage is not of course in accordance with the law: only if a court has first decided that a custodial sentence is appropriate should it go on to decide whether it is to be served immediately or suspended. If this illegal practice is continuing, the Lord Chief Justice should issue instructions to have it brought to an end.

There still remains the question of whether or not the number of failures among those legitimately given suspended sentences is so large that it cancels out any effect that suspension might have had upon prison populations. This is a matter of statistics, but it would not be very surprising if it turned out to be true. As the device is applied, it relies for its effect almost entirely on deterrence. Serious doubts have been voiced about the general effectiveness of deterrence. The law does provide for supervision in association with a suspended sentence, and this could be useful, both in increasing its deterrent effectiveness through closer surveillance, and in providing casework to support the offender in keeping out of trouble. But it is not often used, largely because of the reluctance of probation officers to be so closely linked to imprisonment.

Suspended sentences operate so as to keep offenders out of prison from the outset. Parole does not, of course, do that, but it can substantially shorten the length of a sentence, reducing both the financial costs to the community and the personal costs to the prisoner and his family. Nevertheless it has been assailed on a number of grounds, not least by prisoners themselves. Before release on parole can even be considered by the national Parole Board, a prisoner has to have completed at least one-third of his sentence, and also to have secured the approval of a Local Review Committee at the prison in which he is confined. As the governor of the prison is an influential member of the local committee, it is argued that good behaviour while in prison, and co-operation with the staff, loom largest in its deliberations. In other words it is really a disciplinary device for the prison, rather than a genuine attempt to predict a prisoner's post-discharge behaviour. Dark suggestions are made that the easiest way to secure parole is to 'grass' on your fellow prisoners (Jones and Jones 1979).

It is not necessary to go along with the more paranoid of these suspicions to see that prison behaviour is not the best predictor of behaviour after release. The regimentation and social isolation of the prison constitute a way of life which is very different from that outside. Thoroughgoing adjustment to it will make eventual adjustment to normal society very much more difficult, as is shown by the speedy return to prison after release of the more institutionalized old lags.

Others protect themselves from such a fate by their involvement in the inmate society of the prison, which at least bears some resemblance to the life of criminals outside the walls. As control, in closed prisons at any rate, is achieved by a delicate balance between staff and inmate authority – the so-called 'custodial compromise' (Jones 1965) – it is possible for a man whose criminal record and attitudes earn him high status in the inmate community to present no problems of discipline, and therefore be considered a 'good prisoner' by the prison authorities.

For such reasons as these it would probably be better if parole were automatic rather than resting on behaviour while in prison (Williams 1975) except in those few kinds of case which could be precluded by a specific court order. The Local Review Committee would have no place in such a scheme, and dealing with parole defaulters would become the main function of the Parole Board. Careful supervision would be necessary, not only to help with rehabilitation, but also to ensure that failure did become immediately apparent, and lead, if necessary, to a speedy return to prison. The Parole Board would, of course, deal by its present methods with those for whom automatic parole was forbidden. With all its faults, even this would be better than no possibility of parole at all.

The other major criticism of parole harks back to the 'justice model', with its assumption that sentencing is the job of judges, and not of administrators or lay members of a Parole Board (Hood 1974). The justification for such legalism is that the traditions and training of judges, and the limits imposed on their discretion by the law, ensure that they operate as the guardians of our liberties, and should therefore be in the driving seat when decisions like those about imprisonment, which affect those liberties, are being made. It is easy to see how such ideas apply to sentencing itself, but more difficult to apply them to parole, which is concerned with increasing not limiting freedom.

More plausible is the argument that judges, with their commitment to a retributive tariff, are the best people to ensure that justice is done as between one prisoner and another when decisions are being made as to who should be released. As they would already have imposed a 'just' sentence, there ought to be no room for parole, but if it has to exist in order to give a downward impetus to sentences while maintaining equity, then it should be in their hands.

Being committed to retribution, they would presumably base their rulings about early release (or reincarceration, in an 'automatic parole' system), on considerations of 'desert' rather than the likelihood of rehabilitation. This is only to be expected; the proposal is an integral part of a 'justice model' which is anti-correctionalist in its essence. It is no answer, however true it might be, to say that non-judicial experts should be able to make better rehabilitative decisions if such decisions are not what is being aimed at. Non-correctional parole, however, is a very curious concept.

But there is one respect in which parole could learn from due process as this is understood in the courts of law: the right to know what you are being charged with, and to meet your accusers face to face. At present, those rejected for parole are not told why, and personal appearance at the meetings of the Parole Board, and access to its dossier on the case, are not permitted (Williams 1975). These limitations accord as little with the requirements of social justice as they do with justice of the more retributive kind. They also reduce the amount of information available to the Board, making it more difficult for them to reach sensible decisions, whether of a rehabilitative or a retributive kind. The Star Chamber nature of such procedures would become obvious if a system of automatic parole was in operation, but even under the present system it seems optimistic to expect parole to serve as an incentive to good institutional behaviour, if you refuse to tell prisoners exactly in what respects they are at present falling short. Better understanding of the criminals coming before them might also be obtained if a former prisoner was added to the membership of the Parole Board. This is less revolutionary than it might seem, and is provided for in the Parole Law of Jamaica.

At the administrative level, Hall Williams (Williams 1975) has pointed to the delay between the stage in a sentence when parole becomes theoretically applicable, and the time when a case is brought before the Parole Board. As a result, periods of actual parole are often very short. There is a feeling, also, that the Board is too cautious, giving parole in too few cases, although this seems to have improved, as the Board has gained greater experience and confidence. It might also be accused of being too retributive in its decisions. The refusal of parole to certain notorious criminals seems to be influenced more by the nature of the crimes they originally committed than by evidence of their correctional progress since.

There seems little doubt that parole can play an important part in reducing the length of prison sentences and thus improving the rehabilitative effectiveness of the penal system, and that it can do this without threatening our liberties, especially if release on parole can become automatic for most cases, default being assessed according to the prisoner's performance in the normal world outside, rather than in the artificial society of the prison. But if there is to be any dramatic reduction in the size of the custodial population in Britain, it can only be achieved by the imposition of fewer prison sentences: and that in its turn will depend on the availability and correctional effectiveness of the alternatives.

Fines are used widely as one of those alternatives, and they do have the advantages of convenience and of being easily graduated according to the requirements of a retributive tariff. They are also very cheap, almost certainly producing more revenue than they cost to administer, even taking into account the expense involved in imprisoning defaulters. Fines do not pretend to rehabilitate. So far as they purport to have any effect on the course of crime, it is as deterrents. For crimes in which motivation is uncomplicated and there is a high level of certainty of detection and punishment, they probably do deter. It is this which must account for any success they achieve as compared with other forms of sentence.

These achievements notwithstanding, there must be doubts about greater reliance on fines for any except the more trivial crimes. Is it desirable to base obedience to the law, in the more serious types of case, on fear rather than on understanding? If non-conformists are to be compelled to 'toe the line', as a 'conflict' theory of criminality must imply, it should be after a correctional process in which the nature of the choices involved have become clear to them.

Fines also offend against the canons of both social justice and retribution, for a fine of a given size is much easier for a rich man to pay than his poorer fellow. One way sometimes proposed for dealing with this is through 'day-fines' (Thornstedt 1975). Under this innovation, developed originally in Sweden, a fine is of so many days' pay, rather than a fixed sum of money. This could reduce the inequities involved, but only up to a point. Quite apart from the difficulty of assessing a day-fine, say, for a rich man whose income is made up in a complicated and not always open way, income differences may sometimes be so large as to indicate fines for the same offence which are so different as to seem in the public view to be very unfair. Such public attitudes are retributive in character, and often at odds with social justice, but they cannot be ignored in any realistic penal policy. They certainly are not in Sweden (Thornstedt 1975).

If a fine remains wilfully unpaid, the usual resort of the courts is to imprisonment. The role of the fine as a non-custodial alternative is then lost, and it is probably worth considering the possibilities available for avoiding such an outcome. They include a court order for the attachment of part of an offender's earnings. There is also the possibility of ordering him to 'work off' his fine by service to the community. The latter would be very controversial. Trade unions would have to be consulted about it, and it might be in breach of international conventions about forced labour. However, the principle has already been accepted in the case of Community Service Orders, to be discussed below.

More attention should, however, be given to non-custodial alternatives which offer the promise of rehabilitation, and in the forefront of these must be probation. The offender stays at home, keeps his job, preserves his social relationships intact, but is required to report regularly to his probation officer, who not only ensures that he keeps to the terms of his probation order but also uses casework skills to help him to rehabilitate himself.

In terms of reconviction rates, probation appeared for a long time to be a highly successful penal measure; but this was partly due to the fact that offenders put on probation were usually of a less serious and confirmed type than those sentenced, for example, to imprisonment. This has become clear from research comparing like with like, in which, in spite of the many drawbacks of prison as a milieu for correction, it was shown to achieve results comparable with those of probation (Wilkins 1958). This, together with what are considered to be the illiberal and unfair features of correction as such, has led to proposals for radical changes in the traditional pattern of probation.

In the 'paradigm' presented by Bottoms and McWilliams (1979), any rehabilitative pretensions are to be abandoned in favour of using probation (as it appears), as a way of achieving some mild retributive punishment – the aim of the justice, rather than the correctional model. So both the length of the period of probation and the frequency with which the probationer has to report to his probation officer are to be based on a judgement about the seriousness of his crime rather than, as in the past, on some assumption about the time needed for rehabilitative casework to be effective.

Although compulsory casework under the terms of the probation order would be ruled out, probation officers would make themselves available to provide help for those who asked for it, though such 'help' would be defined by the probationers themselves rather than by the caseworker. The latter may well feel this to be unreal: that there often are 'needs' which a probationer himself has not yet come to recognize, but which have to be met if he is to stand a chance of being rehabilitated. A great pioneer in the understanding of crime, August Aichhorn has pointed out (Aichhorn 1951) that because the offender lacks any feelings of personal 'dis-ease' he will not initially even consider the possibility that he 'needs' to give up crime.

The inconvenience involved in simply 'signing on' at the probation office is so light that it is difficult to see what retributive value it could have. The same comment could be made about its use as a deterrent. Nor is there any incapacitative effect, because there is no real surveillance of the offender's behaviour.

Other schemes place more emphasis on surveillance. In a programme put forward a few years ago by the Muldoon government in New Zealand, this was to become the sole role of probation officers, who would enlist the assistance of volunteers from the general public to help them carry out this task. This raised horrifying possibilities, but quite apart from civil-rights issues, the scales were weighted against its being success-ful. It set up a conflict from the beginning between the supervisors of offenders (the new name for probation officers) and their wards, placing a premium on attempts to escape their eye.

General distaste for the New Zealand proposals led to their aban-donment, and in spite of a favourable reception for the Bottoms and McWilliams scheme from the chief officers of probation departments throughout Britain, it seems so far to have made little difference to the way in which probation is actually practised. Rank-and-file probation officers still see themselves as caseworkers, performing a correctional task. In the course of the casework relationship surveillance also takes place. A close and frank relationship with a probationer is the best guarantee that both you and he know what he is up to – the best basis, in other words, for a defensible form of surveillance. If retribution and deterrence have any place in this discussion, it could be argued also that the stresses implicit in rehabilitating yourself impose more burdens on the offender than 'signing on' could ever do.

None of this should be taken as implying that no changes are required. The poor correctional performance of probation makes it clear that they are. The service was established in the nineteenth century, when the belief in the individual's personal responsibility for his behaviour was unquestioned. The aim of the probation officer was to convince the criminal under his care of the error of his ways. The arrival of casework following the war of 1939–45 acknowledged the limits, largely of an attitudinal kind, on the offender's free will, but still sought to help him through individual casework aimed at changing his attitudes.

What was still insufficiently recognized was the role of the offender's social context in creating and perpetuating his criminal pattern. A juvenile offender living in a high-delinquency area, whose friends are all members of delinquent gangs, or an adult criminal whose social life, status, income, and possibly even family are derived from his involvement in crime, will be difficult to rehabilitate if the probation officer confines himself to the traditional method of the individual interview. A shift in orientation is required, which retains the individual focus while using methods which have an impact on key elements in the probationer's social situation (Jones 1981b).

Although probation will remain the most important form of non-custodial disposition, there is a great need to develop new and imaginative forms of correctional disposition, in order that the need to have recourse to imprisonment may be minimized. One such is to try to achieve the training advantages of a prison sentence without either incurring the financial and personal costs usually involved, or risking criminal contamination or institutionalization. This might be done, for example, by means of the day prison, or, in Britain, the day training centre. Regrettably day training centres have not found favour with the courts, and so few have been established. They offer opportunities for offsetting some of the social handicaps, in, say, education, vocational training, and even diet and health, which contribute to the criminality of some people, as well facilitating insight-giving group discussion. But they will need to be promoted by the Home Office more vigorously than they have been so far if they are to be successful.

The only other major innovation of the last decade or so has been the Community Service Order, under which the offender is required to do unpaid work for the community, prescribed and supervised by a probation officer, and to do this in his leisure time. This has proved much more attractive to the sentencers, so much so that it has been used as a rather more onerous alternative to probation, rather than as the alternative to imprisonment which it was intended to provide (Willis 1977). As with the suspended sentence, judicial education seems to be called for here.

Various problems associated with Community Service Orders have been noted (Pease and McWilliams 1980). One is the difficulty of finding suitable work at a time of high unemployment like the present. Even in the absence of mass unemployment, there would be a need to negotiate schemes with the trade unions concerned, but the large number of jobless makes this even more imperative. There is also the difficulty of deciding what level of performance is to be accepted as meeting the requirements of the Order. How hard must the individual work to avoid being reported to the court as in default?

The emphasis could be placed on the deterrent element in a Community Service Order: on the fact that the individual has to give up some of his spare time to do this work, and that it might be chosen for its laboriousness or unpleasantness. This would be as much a mistake as the similar former attitude towards 'hard labour' in prison. Nothing is gained if a person comes to see work, and especially work for the community, as a punishment. The Community Service Order should be seen as enabling the law-breaker to do something for other people for once.

This has profound possibilities for changing the criminal's self-image. He can come to see himself as having made some restitution for his crimes. It offers him a way of 'paying' for his crime which unifies him with respectable society as much as punishment is likely to alienate him from it. A man who spends his weekends decorating an old lady's cottage might be expected to value her words of appreciation afterwards in spite of the fact that the work was done under a court order. He could come to see himself as no longer a predator, but as a person who has paid his debt to society, and now has a positive and socially rewarded contribution to make. The rewards of conformity would have become apparent to him, and therefore seem more attractive. It would be difficult not to see such a process, if it occurred, as anything other than insight: progress in his understanding of himself and his social predicament.

In view of the small part of the total of crimes committed which end in conviction, the effect of penal policy on the social problem of crime can only be marginal. This in no way derogates from its importance. How a society treats its criminals may be an even clearer indication of its moral qualities than the incidence of crime. And on the grounds of social justice, both to victims and criminals, something should be done to rehabilitate the latter. But when all is said and done, the roots of crime have to be sought in broader social and economic influences, perhaps arising, as Marxists and others would argue, out of the very nature of that society. If nothing else made that clear, changing trends in crime would do so. This may not be relevant to penal policy in its narrower sense, but it certainly is to the control of crime.

REFERENCES

Aichhorn, A. (1951) *Wayward Youth*. London: Imago.

Alexander, F. and Staub, H. (1956) *The Criminal, the Judge and the Public*. Glencoe: Free Press.

Bean, P. T. (1976) *Rehabilitation and Deviance*. London: Routledge & Kegan Paul.

Beyleveld, D. (1979) Deterrence Research as a Basis for Deterrence Policies. *Howard Journal of Penology* 18(3): 125–49.

—— (1980) *A Bibliography on General Deterrence Research*. London: Saxon Books.

Birkbeck, C. (1982) Property Crime and the Poor: Some Evidence from Cali, Columbia. In Colin Sumner (ed.) *Crime, Justice and Development*. London: Heinemann.

Blumberg, A. S. (1967) *Criminal Justice*. Chicago: Quadrangle Books.

Bottomley, A. K. (1973) *Decision in the Penal Process*. London: Martin Robertson.

—— (1980) The Justice Model. In A. E. Bottoms and R. H. Preston (eds) *The Coming Penal Crisis*. Edinburgh: Academic Press.

Bottoms, A. E. (1979) The Advisory Council and the Suspended Sentence. *Criminal Law Review* 437–46.

—— (1980) *The Suspended Sentence after Ten Years: A Review and Reassessment*. Leeds: University of Leeds Department of Social Work and Applied Social Studies.

Bottoms, A. E. and McWilliams, W. (1979) A Non-Treatment Paradigm for Probation Practice. *British Journal of Social Work* 9(2): 159–202.

Boyle, J. (1977) *A Sense of Freedom*. London: Pan Books.

Brody, S. (1976) *The Effectiveness of Sentencing*. Home Office Research Study No. 32. London: HMSO.

Cross, A. R. N. (1971) *Punishment, Prison and the Public*. London: Stevens.

Fox, L. (1952) *The English Prison and Borstal Systems*. London: Routledge & Kegan Paul.

Home Office (Streatfeild Committee) (1960) *Report of the Interdepartmental Committee on the Business of the Criminal Courts* (Cmnd 1289). London: HMSO.

—— (May Committee) (1979) *Report of the Committee of Inquiry into the United Kingdom Prison Services* (Cmnd 7673). London: HMSO.

Hood, R. G. (1974) *Tolerance and the Tariff*. London: National Association for the Care and Rehabilitation of Offenders.

Jones, H. (1965) *Crime in a Changing Society*. Harmondsworth Penguin Books.

—— (1981a) A Case for Correction. *British Journal of Social Work* 11(1): 1–17.

—— (1981b) Old and New Ways in Probation. In Howard Jones (ed.) *Society Against Crime*. London: Penguin Books.

Jones, H. and Cornes, P. F. (1977) *Open Prisons*. London: Routledge & Kegan Paul.

Jones, S. and Jones, H. (1979) A Study of Dispersal Prisons. An unpublished report for the Home Office by the Department of Social Administration, University College Cardiff.

King, R. D. and Morgan, R. (1980) *The Future of the Prison System*. Edinburgh: Gower.

Lipton, D., Martinson, D., and Wilks, J. (1975) *The Effect of Correctional Training – a Survey of Treatment Evaluation Studies*. Springfield: Praeger.

Marrow, A. J. (1969) *The Practical Theorist: The Life and Work of Kurt Lewin*. New York: Basic Books.

Murphy, J. G. (1979) *Retribution, Justice and Therapy*. Dordrecht: Reidel Publishing Co.

Palmer, T. (1978) *Correctional Intervention and Research*. Lexinton: D. C. Heath.

Pease, K. and McWilliams, W. (eds) (1980) *Community Service by Order*. Edinburgh: Academic Press.

Rawls, John (1971) *A Theory of Justice*. Oxford: Clarendon Press.

Shaw, M. J. (1974) *Social Work in Prison*. Home Office Research Study No. 22. London: HMSO.

Sykes, G. M. and Matza D. (1957) Techniques of Neutralization: A Theory of Delinquency. *American Sociological Review* 22: 664–70.

Thornstedt, H. (1975) The Day-Fine System in Sweden. *Criminal Law Review* 307–12.

Vold, G. B. (1958) *Theoretical Criminology*. New York: Oxford University Press.

Wilkins, L. T. (1958) A Small Comparative Study of the Effects of Probation. *British Journal of Delinquency* 3: 201ff.

Williams, J. E. H. (1975) Natural Justice and Parole. *Criminal Law Review* 82–91, 215–23.

Willis, A. (1977) Community Service as an Alternative to Imprisonment: A Cautionary View. *Probation Journal* 24(4): 120–26.

Wootton, Barbara (1978) *Crime and Penal Policy*. London: Allen & Unwin.

—— (1981) *Crime and the Criminal Law*. London: Stevens.

Zilboorg, G. (1956) *The Psychology of the Criminal Act and Punishment*. London: Hogarth Press.

11

CONTEMPORARY TRENDS IN CRIME AND ITS TREATMENT

Terence Morris

The idea that there is such a thing as the 'treatment' of crime is beginning to have an old-fashioned ring about it. In the world of the 1980s the term most commonly used is 'law and order'. Quite how the change came about is not entirely clear though the distinction tells us a good deal about the changes that have occurred in the climate of politics and penal policy since the end of the Second World War forty years ago. Although in Britain the coming of peace brought no immediate relaxation of the material privations that had become a commonplace part of wartime life, the predominant atmosphere of the era was that of social optimism. In 1919 the war-weary survivors of the military imbecility commonly known as trench warfare returned not to a land 'fit for heroes but to unemployment, industrial strife, and the emiseration of the great depression with its wage cuts and humiliatingly adminstered Public Assistance. The two decades after the defeat of the Kaiser culminated in the rise of fascism and the outbreak of yet another world war. In 1945 there was a resolution that this time, things would be different.

At first it might seem that such social optimism could never have been grounded in experience; only in hope. But perhaps it was because the hopes of those who had lived through the first half of the century were based upon a passionate longing for some alternative that there was this conviction that there could and ought to be a better, altogether more morally decent society. The twin emphases were on social justice and planned social policies. The experience of the war had shown, and conclusively (when comparisons were made with the war of 1914–18), that rational planning in the allocation of scarce resources produced a more effective result than the operations of the free market. Naturally, such issues as employment, health, housing, and education were regarded as priorities, but in penal affairs the predominant mood of the times could still be discerned. Over-arching almost all the social and economic changes of the first ten years after 1945 was a commitment to the utility of the social sciences as a basis for the formulation of social policies. It was not always explicit and it was not without its critics. Almost from the time of the formation of the Labour government of Clement Attlee (with its landslide majority) there were those who advocated the end of rationing and controls and demanded the return of a 'free' market in scarce resources. The political opposition, overshadowed by the great brooding figure of Churchill, had to wait six years before he once more became Prime Minister but what was remarkable was that so little, indeed hardly anything that had been legislated by the Attlee government, was cast aside. The things that had been done in health, housing, education, and social welfare generally were left for the most part entirely as they were notwithstanding the bitterness of the opposition to them as they had been debated in Parliament.

It was widely believed by the optimists of reform that if the conditions of social life materially improved, then there could not fail to be a corresponding improvement in the general level of social morality. This was not a new idea. It had been firmly believed in the nineteenth century when such problems as drunkenness, prostitution, and child abuse were thought to be the automatic products of poverty and the generally deprived state of the lower orders. In short, decent social conditions would result in people behaving better.

What happened in post-war Britain was that the material conditions of social life improved in almost every way. But crime, the great index of morality, far from showing signs of disappearing along with malnu-trition, rickets, infant mortality, and the slums, demonstrated not only a remarkable persistence but a discouraging propensity to increase. Those who had opposed the social redistribution implicit in the Welfare State, deriding it as providing something for nothing from the cradle to the grave, were not slow to point out that far from reducing crime, all the evidence indicated that it did the very reverse. Each year until 1951, penal reformers who had felt that the Attlee government had been altogether too cautious in its great Criminal Justice Act of 1948 anxiously watched as the figure of recorded crime rose, and with it, the size of the prison population.[1] It was a dispiriting experience, not least because critics were able to rub salt into the wounds of disappointment. From 1945 to 1950 life in Britain remained markedly austere. Rationing of food and many other commodities continued. In 1951 the figure of recorded crime for England and Wales reached an all-time high of some 500,000 indictable offences. For a brief period of some four years the level of recorded crime began to fall until in 1955–56 it resumed its upward movement. Crime, as known to the police, has increased sixfold in the last thirty years and shows no signs of declining in the immediate future.

Yet if we look at other social trends since 1950 it is clear that there is no simple correlation between levels of crime and the social condition of society. The period of immediate post-war austerity characterized by increasing crime was followed by a period of affluence which lasted until at least 1970. These were the years during which Harold Macmillan proclaimed that we had 'never had it so good'. He was almost certainly right. Living standards in real terms were at their highest. The economy was booming (some said it could do even better but for the fact of 'over-full employment'), more youngsters than ever before were entering higher education, more houses were being built, more people were acquiring motor cars for the first time. And yet, as in the preceding years of austerity, crime continued – after the brief respite mentioned earlier – to rise. Once more critics blamed the Welfare State for having sapped the moral fibre of the nation. They were not slow to blame penal reform. Admittedly, the penal system had come a long way since the end of the war. The Criminal Justice Act of 1948 had taken away the power of the courts to order corporal punishment though the abolition of flogging for offences against prison discipline was to wait for more than a decade, albeit falling into desuetude in consequence of the Home Secretary (and especially Rab Butler when he held that office) declining to confirm the awards of visiting magistrates. Prisons, it was said, had become like holiday camps and the powers of the courts had been too much diminished. It was true that in some respects prisons had become marginally less uncomfortable places. At the convict prison at Parkhurst for example, where as late as 1954 inmates wishing to read on winter evenings were compelled to stand by a glass panel near their cell doors through which shone the meagre light of a gas jet outside, electric light had been installed for the comfort of the malefactors. Prison food was, and some would say remains as, one of the subtler pains of imprisonment although the present writer can recall a delegate member of the Council of the Magistrates' Association at a meeting in the early 1970s stoutly maintaining that in the prison where he was a member of the Board of Visitors the inmates 'ate like fighting cocks'. The 'holiday camp' jibe has persisted but there is no evidence that their guests were ever confined three to a room for up to 23 hours in the 24 with little but boredom and the stench of their own ordure to pass the time.

The persistence of crime in the affluent post-war years giave rise to a variety of explanatory theories as distinct from the kinds of assertion already mentioned. For my own part in a broadcast on the BBC Third Programme in 1955 entitled 'The Carrot out of Reach' I argued along functionalist lines derived from the work of Robert Merton's 'Social

Structure and Anomie' (1949). The materially disprivileged, subjected to the same relentless public pressures to consume material goods as the affluent and persuaded that social status was inextricably linked to their conspicuous consumption, dealt with the problem by sneaking round the back, so to speak, to get at the prizes. Given that most crime was property crime the theory had some plausibility. It was reinforced by the fact that those apprehended for property offences came overwhelmingly from the lowest orders of society and could be seen to have benefited least from all the various advantages that attended upon social change in post-war Britain. As a theory, it was probably altogether too simple. It was insufficiently distinguished from the theory current in the thinking of the American social-work pioneers at the end of the last century who saw juvenile crime as much as a technique of subsistence in conditions of extreme poverty as a manifestation of moral depravity. Albert K. Cohen, on the other hand, as a result of his researches in the Indiana State Training School, looked at the problem of status in another way (1956). His theory was based upon the notion that denied access to status systems that were dominated by middle-class values, working-class boys simply created status systems of their own in which delinquent acts acquired the character of what Thorstein Veblen would have termed a 'conspicuous exploit' (1899). It made and still makes sense of some of the seemingly pointless things that some juveniles are liable to do, such as trespassing on the railway in situations of great risk. In this period too, the relationship between crime and delinquency and unemployment was explored, albeit not very widely. But in retrospect the most profitable work was probably that of Leslie Wilkins (1964) whom history will surely recognize as the founding genius of criminological research in the modern Home Office. Wilkins's concept of 'delinquent generations' focused attention for the first time upon the demographic aspects of the crime problem. Although it had been clear from the statistics of prosecuted offenders that crime and delinquency were essentially activities of the young, and especially those under 25, what had not been truly appreciated was the extent to which the proportion of the most crime-prone age-groups in the total population would have a bearing upon the total incidence of crime. The period between 1920 and 1940 was one of falling birthrates, the era of the one-child or the no-child family. After 1940 an increase in the birth rate continued to a climax in the so-called post-war 'bulge' – due in part no doubt to the increased fecundity of couples no longer separated by the demands of war. Thus even if the propensity for offending remained the same in the most crime-prone age-groups there would be an increase in the total volume of crime. What Wilkins demonstrated was that not only was this the case, but that there had been an increase in the propensity to commit offences.

The period between 1950 and 1970 was characterized not only by an increase in the proportion of the young in the population but by conditions of material affluence that established new norms about consumption patterns. While in the 1930s the possession of a new bicycle would have been regarded as a sign of material advantage, the young of the 1960s had motor bikes and cars. Record players, clothes, and cosmetics became everyday purchases. The emergence of this new market was described by Mark Abrams in his *Teenage Consumer* (1959).[2] But by 1970 the party, to use a popular phrase, was almost over. Within three years the economies of the western industrial societies moved into recession; the use of the 'oil weapon' by the Middle Eastern potentates who came to form OPEC as a political counter in their contest with Israel dealt them a hammer blow. Roaring inflation fuelled by rises in the price of the oil on which the west had become excessively dependent combined with technological change in which the societies of the Pacific Basin forged ahead while Britain along with western Europe plunged into mass unemployment. Nor did the United States escape. By the end of the decade the mood in the western democracies had been characterized by a pronounced shift to the right of the political spectrum and in Britain, as in the United States, a new faith in the values and practices of what was essentially nineteenth-century econ-omic liberalism echoing through the voices of von Hayek and Milton Friedman[3] precluded any return to Keynsian devices for the control of mass unemployment and reflation. Far from finding work through public-works projects and their 'multiplier' effects, the workless were to experi-ence both restriction upon their access to public welfare and a redefinition of their putative social desert. According to some of the evangelists of the new right the unemployed are to be thought of as being *voluntarily* unemployed since what they are doing, in effect, is to price themselves out of work by demanding too high a price for their labour.

The phenomenon of unemployment in contemporary Britain is com-plex. While in the areas of declining heavy industry, the old labour-intensive ports, and the textile industries, the effects of recession are manifested in what at first seems like a landscape of infinite dereliction, areas of the Golden Triangle of the south-east of England are booming. The new private housing estates grow month by month. The company car-driving vendors of insurance and computer software multiply. But whereas the traveller from, say, Hull to Liverpool will view from the train window scenes of apparently unremitting desolation – empty factories with smashed windows and chimneys from which the smoke no longer billows – a journey from London to Poole through an altogether greener and more pleasant land would give an impression of affluence and activity concealing the deprivations of the minority. Not far behind the railway tracks as the train left Waterloo would be found the mean streets of

Lambeth and Vauxhall but perhaps more important would be the discovery that for the poor and the unemployed the fact of living in proximity to affluence does not do much to improve one's lot. The Land of UB40 has no geographical boundaries.

Besides important regional variations in unemployment there are distinctions to be drawn between the position of the young who are seeking work for the first time and that of the middle-aged who on becoming redundant discover that they face the prospect of unemployment for the remainder of their lives. What is perhaps most masked is the position of the ethnic minorities. In Britain there is a strange convention against speaking about such things. Those who do so openly are often racists who for the most part might be regarded as pretty vulgar in any event. Those who speak out for racial equality, however, not infrequently find themselves castigated as 'do-gooders' by the organs of right-wing populism. For the most part we tend to behave as if the existence of black people, like that of gynaecological ailments, ought to be a matter for restrained conversation among restricted audiences. Yet it is the unfortunate case that the evidence suggests that the consequences of recession have borne upon ethnic minorities with even more deleterious results than on the most vulnerable groups in the indigenous population. In areas where unemployment among white school-leavers is high, that among their black contemporaries is higher – certainly if they are male.[4]

The relationship between crime and unemployment is far from clear. The Prime Minister, at the time of the riots in Brixton and Toxteth in 1981, was quick to deny that there was any connection. Certainly there seems little to connect crime and unemployment in the depression years of the 1930s, but there were fewer young people, the unemployed were older, and school-leavers were often employed as cheap labour (Mannheim 1940). Contemporary data seem to suggest that the connection is not with crime as such but with imprisonment (Brenner 1976; Gladstone 1979; Box and Hale 1982). Increases in unemployment, both in this country and the United States, seem to be related to increases in the numbers of persons incarcerated rather than to the incidence of crime *per se*. Whether this is because the unemployed commit the offences that are more deserving of imprisonment or because the judiciary is reluctant to deprive any offender of a job that has been hard to acquire by sending him to prison is not at all clear. When, at the time of the riots, the Prime Minister maintained that 'nothing could excuse' these manifestations of public disorder she seemed to suggest that nothing could explain them either, save presumably the presence of some intrinsic social malevolence on the part of the participants. From subsequent analysis of the Brixton scene it is clear that this was no latter-day bread riot by the starving poor but an altogether more complex social phenomenon involving a range of factors from the specificity of police harassment of young blacks to a more general sense of alienation.

Inner-city riots are essentially extreme manifestations of social *malaise* but in a sense more troubling are the instances of vandalism and gratuitous violence towards vulnerable targets, both human and animal, to which Patricia Morgan referred in her *Delinquent Fantasies* (1978). Although such things as theft and burglary and the taking of motor cars are often troubling and invariably infuriating, they are at least readily capable of some rational understanding. But to gang-rape a young woman and then for each of her assailants to urinate over her, or to hang a cat from a lamp post, soak it in petrol, and then set it alight, is to behave in a way which defies understanding on the same plane. Such things appear so repellent as to make sense in the context of psychopathology rather than merely the extremes of moral turpitude. Property crime at least makes sense, even if it is a form of wealth redistribution on the wrong side of the law. Yet even within the context of property crime there are new dimensions that were unknown a generation ago. Drug-related crimes, including burglary from domestic premises as well as pharmacies, and robbery from the person (popularly referred to as 'mugging') are an established part of the crime scene. Like many of the phenomena associated with crime they are often presented in terms of social stereotypes. The myth of the 'dope fiend' identified by Alfred Lindesmith (1947) almost forty years ago has re-appeared as the teenage addict driven to crime to pay for the habit. 'Mugging' has become associated with the activities of black youth on the streets of the inner city, an image with which the events in Brixton were closely associated.

The so-called 'moral majority' has sought to express its concern for such things in a variety of ways. Yet however transparent the sincerity of many of the social reformers, and however forceful the arguments that pornography degrades the status of women and the portrayal of sadistic violence debases the currency of human dignity, elevating to the level of the commonplace things which ought to be regarded at best as behavioural aberrations and at worst as inimical to the interests of a civilized and caring society, the fact is that they have at times coaxed from the social wainscoting a reactionary and illiberal puritanism. It is an irony of the situation that those among this 'silent' or 'moral' majority who have taken comfortably to themselves the catechism of right-wing populism have often failed to perceive that much of the traffic in these materials is the very archetype of capitalist enterprise – the reflexive supply of goods and services freely demanded in the market-place.

In looking at Britain in 1985 one cannot fail to experience a depressing disquiet about what has happened in the last forty years. If the social optimism of 1945–50 was not immediately fulfilled, the self-confident affluence of the 1960s did much to disguise the fact. But in the harsh economic climate of the 1980s that fact, and much else, has been laid painfully bare. Not only did improvements in social welfare fail to result in moral improvements of the kind that would reduce crime; newly found affluence seemed to make it worse. Faced now not merely with the depredations of economic recession but with the fact that the social divisions that the post-war planners sought to reduce are now more marked and promise to become even more so, it is possible to perceive a society in which the prospects have seldom been more pessimistic. At a time when the structure of the Welfare State is about to undergo major surgery the controversial Bishop Jenkins has observed: 'To return to the ethics of 19th Century entrepreneurial individualism is either nostalgic nonsense or else a firm declaration that individual selfishness and organised greed are the only effective motivations for human behaviour' (1985).

It is an uncomfortable thought that the rational motivations of those who live by crime are so close to those who operate on the other side of the thin and often unclear line between the lawful and the illegal. It is, after all, only legislation about consumers' rights that has turned the sharp car dealer into a criminal when he sells the proverbial 'good runner' that boasts a gearbox filled with sawdust and old oil. Before that the principle of *caveat emptor* embodied the freedom of the market-place. There is an argument which, if not wholly persuasive, is at least deserving of an answer, that the behaviour of those who are seen to succeed in society and whose values are projected as worthy of emulation may well become a perversely distorted gauge for those without access to the advantages of social privilege. It is a quasi-Mertonian argument in which bank robbery appears as a form of adventure capitalism and the fencing of stolen MOT certificates as a variety of cottage industry. What, too, of vandalism and a general disregard for the environment? There was a time in the 1960s when academics in the University of London could observe both the petty destruction wrought by self-styled student revolutionaries and the demolition of a significant part of early nineteenth-century Bloomsbury in order that modern buildings could be raised alongside the existing neo-Stalinist Senate House.[5] And what of the behaviour of the consumers of fast 'food' from the ubiquitous take-away shops who carelessly throw down the unwanted plastic containers? How do they compare with those who would allow the seas to become a nuclear rubbish bin? O *tempora! O mores!*

The austere atmosphere of post-war Britain was characterized by a commitment to social order, or at least conventionality, that is largely lacking in the Britain ruled over by Margaret Thatcher and even she, for all the promotion of her image as *mater et magistra*, cannot be blamed for all that has befallen. But she has undoubtedly focused on the issue of public order in a way in which no political figure since the war has done. Indeed, one would need to return to the General Strike of 1926 and the enrolment of large numbers of Special Constables to see anything to equal the more recent response to the miners' strike. As early as 1979 it became clear that alone among those in the public service the police were largely to be exempted from cuts in real income. Not only are the police at full strength, but they are paid better than at any time in their history.[6] The miners' strike of 1984–85 came perilously close to a form of civil war at times and the prolonged use of the National Reporting Centre enabled large numbers of police to be deployed on a national basis for the purpose of containing not only serious disorder but in some instances legitimate trade union activity. The turning back of Kent miners at the Dartford Tunnel in case they were intending mischief in Yorkshire has already entered the oral history of trade unionism. The existence of a police force in Britain, at full strength and handsomely paid, with substantial access to modern technology, ought to have done something to reduce crime. Not only has crime continued to rise but the proportion of serious crime cleared up has fallen between 1979 and 1984 from around 43 per cent to about 37 per cent. The effective control of crime may well lie elsewhere than in the area of police surveillance.[7] But this same well-furbished police force is now attuned to respond to public disorder. Riot shields, protective headgear, staves, visors, flame-proof overalls, and adapted vehicles that are protected from missiles against their windows and Molotov cocktails beneath their chassis together with firearms are part and parcel of available equipment. Where the bulk of operational experience was once drawn from the north of Ireland, the lessons of pitched battles between police and striking miners are more recently at hand.

There is a subtle but important distinction between the control of crime and the maintenance of public order but the new right seems not always to make it. In a society that is socially divided, not merely in terms of employment and unemployment – and consequently relative wealth and poverty – but in terms of ideological commitment, it becomes important to ask 'who is for and who is against us?' Margaret Thatcher's telling reference to the 'enemy within' during the miners' strike revealed how close can be a definition of dissent to a definition of treasonable rebellion. If there is crime in the inner city it might be thought the manifestation of social alienation and a rejection of conventional approaches to the institutions of private and public property; but if there is disorder it might be conceived as an albeit inchoate rejection of the legitimacy of the power of the state. This would be no novel thing. Mayhew's accounts of the courts and alleys of Victorian Holborn and Westminster, and the portrayal of the Old Jago in Arthur Morison's novel of that name, or the East End of the childhood of Arthur Harding tell similar stories.[8] Meanwhile private security organizations flourish, not merely to protect cash in transit but to keep order in the shopping precincts and strangers out of apartment blocks. A walk round a leafy suburb on a summer evening reveals not just a range of horticultural skills but an infinite variety of burglar alarms.

But how reliable are the images of crime that we derive either from statistical sources or the more selective accounts in the communications media? The latter, by their very nature, are biased towards the exceptional if not the sensational. 'NO CATS KILLED ON MOTORWAY' was never a scoop headline. Official criminal statistics, on the other hand, suffer from other, no less limiting biases. Just as it has become a truism that they reflect only the tip of the iceberg it is now generally recognized that they are more reliable as an index of the activities of law enforcement agents than of crime. Many factors bear upon the decision to report crime and still more upon the decision to prosecute. Since the clear-up rate is so low – and for some property crimes it may fall to 20 per cent or even less – very few reliable inferences about the social characteristics of offenders can be drawn from them. Still less can there be much confidence that what the courts may decide to do with these apprehended miscreants will have much bearing upon the behaviour of those who escape detection and relax in the knowledge that until they are caught for the first time they have a good chance of staying anonymous. The British Crime Survey (Hough and Mayhew 1983) whose first report appeared in 1983 went a long way towards providing an indication of the relationship between recorded and unrecorded crime, and was able to provide some useful comparisons with the data derived from the General Household Surveys in 1972 and 1973 and again in 1979 and 1980 on the more specific topic of household burglary. The magnitude of the 'iceberg' phenomenon emerges clearly. But no less importantly the British Crime Survey indicated that the risks of victimization of ordinary householders were much lower than commonly supposed. Thus the statistically average person might expect: a robbery once every five centuries; an assault once every century; the family car to be stolen or taken by joyriders once every sixty years; a burglary in the home once every forty years (Maxfield 1984).

In terms of the likelihood of victimization it is clear from other studies that there tends to be an excess of fear over risk.[9] Crime is an urban problem and certainly the kinds of crime that may excite the greatest levels of fear, such as robbery and assault, are more likely to occur in urban areas. But while fear is marked among both women and the elderly it is not the case that they are prime targets. Indeed, the young male who spends his time drinking in pubs and clubs is dominant among both victims and offenders. What is undoubtedly important in all this is the extent to which the press tends to exaggerate reality. The security industry is not without blame either and complaints have been made to the Advertising Standards

Authority about the presentation of the statistics of domestic burglary in the context of advertisements for alarm systems.

When we examine the various images of crime that are presented, whether through the media of the press and TV, or through official statistics that are the more refined results of crime surveys, it remains that the picture is essentially that of the malfeasance of the lower orders of society. In part this is due to the fact that their use of public space results in their higher visibility to law enforcement agencies but it is also a consequence of the fact that the illegal activities of the privileged sections of the population tend to be dealt with in other ways. The present government in its determination to root out false social security claims has increased the number of Department of Health and Social Security staff to deal with the problem and the notorious 'hit squads' have made their presence felt as far apart as Oxford and Brighton. In the Department of Inland Revenue there have been staff cuts making it more difficult to trace tax dodgers. As a political statement about social and moral priorities the message could not be plainer: those among the poor who try to screw the state for a few extra pounds must be hunted down and rigorously prosecuted while those fortunate enough to need to make tax returns are to be left more often on 'Cub's Honour' to tell the truth. Just as there is a dangerous obfuscation of the distinction between the control of crime and the maintenance of public order, so too is there a discernible trend towards the identification of social dependency with minimal desert and, ultimately, turpitude.[10] To this might be added the proposals contained in the government White Paper of May, 1985, to reshape the law governing public order. If they become law they will represent the most regressive peacetime restrictions on political freedom this century and possibly since the infamous Six Acts of Lord Liverpool's government after the Napoleonic wars. Both marches and 'static' demonstrations will be subject to prohibition. To pretend that the intention is other than to limit political dissent such as is manifested by the Campaign for Nuclear Disarmament, or the women of Greenham Common, or industrial picketing – whether peaceful or otherwise – is absurd and the Thatcherite press has given the White Paper an enthusiastic welcome. Whether middle-ranking police officers, let alone chief constables, relish the prospect of a new role as political commissars is doubtful. Judging by the Police Federation Conference of 1985 the rank and file have had enough of being the infantry in the government's war against the trade unions. The document, it may be noted, came not long after the Prime Minister's references to the 'enemy within'.

The picture presented by those parts of the criminal justice system that deal with the definition of crime and its prosecution are, it can scarcely be denied, undergoing fundamental change whether in such practical details as the new Police and Criminal Evidence Act or in those more general terms which enable priorities – or some would say targets – to be identified. Within the penal system proper, change has been slower. The Prison Service with an *esprit de corps* generated by Paterson in the 1930s firmly believed and went on believing in the idea of rehabilitation for almost all the period under discussion. Only in the late 1970s did the reality of overcrowding, the effects of economic recession on the viability of prison workshops, and the disaffection of the basic grades of staff finally persuade many prison governors that if they could run a prison from which no one escaped and in which there were no disturbances they were meeting the greater part of the job specification. Of course, the rehabilitative ideal is not entirely extinguished but its practice has become more difficult and its objectives could be hardly less well regarded. It has been one of the consequences of the unashamed political polarization of penal policy by the Thatcher administration that containment and the provision of experiences that might be seen as a variant of aversion therapy have become the subject of popular demand by the rank and file of the Conservative Party. Thus the jewel in the crown of the new 'tough' detention centre regime would appear to be the monotonous scrubbing of floors; military-style drilling has taken a lower place since it was discovered to be one of the few features of the regime from which the inmates derived any positive satisfaction. In spite of legislation to establish a presumption of bail the number of remand prisoners and the conditions of their detention have never been worse.[11] When in October, 1983, Leon Brittan, newly appointed to the post of Home Secretary, announced at the Conservative Party Conference a new policy for parole which, albeit by reducing the minimum period of eligibility, offered an immediate general gaol delivery of short-termers, set out an altogether more rigorous prospect of longevity of incarceration for those convicted of certain crimes that in his view were especially heinous. The speech to the party, and the subsequent statement in the House of Commons, deserve careful study by those interested in the decline of the bi-partisan approach to penal questions.

There are those who argue that the sure way of reducing the prison population is to reduce the availability of prison places to the courts; however, without some statutory restriction on overcrowding to make it illegal to exceed certified accommodation this would seem unlikely. The building of new prisons, on the other hand, will almost certainly encourage the expansion of the prison population. The government's proposals, set out in *Criminal Justice* in May, 1984 (Central Office of Information 1984), include plans for a building programme that, while providing further space for long-term prisoners, will fall short of providing for those serving short terms who make up the bulk of those incarcerated. That the crisis of the prison system would focus on the local prison used for both short-termers and remands was a point forcefully argued by Richard Sparks (1971) more than a decade ago. For all the impact that his carefully prophetic analysis has had upon policy-making during the period he might have saved his energies.

The shortcomings of the prison system are so numerous that it is difficult to discover many grounds for optimism. The reports of the Inspectors General have in recent years read like those of their nineteenth-century counterparts in identifying both inadequacy and unacceptability of provision. Ironically, those whose shorter sentences would imply a lesser degree of moral turpitude must spend their time in conditions substantially worse than those whose crimes are sufficiently bad to send them to prison for a very long time. The worst of the squalor is in the old decaying 'locals'. The reconviction rates among young offenders sentenced to detention centres and the youth custody that has taken the place of Borstal present a dispiritingly pessimistic prospect. But the temper of the times is such that under the tutelage of a right-wing press that is contemptuous of what it calls 'do-gooding' there are many who would see little about contemporary prison conditions over which to lose sleep. Since offenders are 'bad' – and generally presumed to include violence in their repertoire of depravity – is not the faecal stench of a multi-occupied cell some adequate and richly deserved consequence of their free choosing?

Nor is the area of non-custodial penalties by any means free from problems. Throughout the post-war period the fine became established as the basic penalty, even for indictable offences. But the growth of unemployment in the last six years from 1 million to over 3 million (some would say nearer to 4 million) and the increasing pauperization of the lower orders from among whom the majority of convicted persons are still drawn has meant that the paying of fines has become more difficult. Many courts, in consequence, have been compelled to think carefully about the size of fines, having regard as they must to an offender's ability to pay. For those in inner cities where a steady job is the exception rather than the rule fines paid from welfare benefits must invariably be on an instalment basis: by coming close to the form of other 'easy payments' the punitive cutting edge of the sanction may be much diminished.

The notable innovation of the Community Service Order, which owes much to the work of Barbara Wootton's work on the late Advisory Council on the Penal System, may go some way to resolving the question posed by a reduced capacity to pay an appropriate fine. Although some people imagined that the scheme would involve such things as groups of convicted vandals cleaning *graffiti* from bus shelters it has not proved to be what Benjamin Rush of the Pennsylvania Prison Society described in the 1780s as a form of enforced labour 'publicly and disgracefully imposed'. The wide variety of schemes whereby young offenders have been given the opportunity of performing useful and worthy tasks has encouraged some of them to continue in a voluntary capacity. The device is open to two criticisms. Firstly, because participants have to be suitable, there is an element of selectivity in favour of those with the better prognoses. On this score it does not always represent an alternative to imprisonment except in the narrowly technical sense that those who are eligible for imprisonment may be considered. Secondly, it does not provide any direct opportunity for the offender to make reparation to a particular victim. Still, Community Service provides a bridge between offenders who would otherwise be isolated by the rejection of society – a phenomenon which the admonitory remarks of some judges and magistrates may well reinforce – and those in the community who in the course of 'doing good' still believe that it is both possible and desirable that offenders should be encouraged to think themselves capable of better things.

Whether the term 'treatment' has much meaning in the context of supervisory non-custodial measures such as Community Service or probation is doubtful. The days when trainee probation officers were raised on a diet of psychoanalytically orientated casework[12] to the exclusion of virtually anything else are long gone although a later, more rebellious generation regarded it with as much savour as a diet of brimstone and treacle. When the heretical Geoffrey Parkinson nailed his famous thesis *I Give Them Money* to the symbolic door of Rainer House[13] he was perhaps redirecting the probation service to its London Police Court Mission roots: those that sought to turn people away from crime by restoring their moral dignity in the course of giving them practical help. But the assumption of responsibility for the practical needs of the offender can easily blur into a form of control, and nowhere is this more marked than with regard to juvenile offenders.

The Children and Young Persons Act of 1969, following as it did from a fundamental reorganization not only of local-government social services but of the boundaries of local authorities, would have encountered difficulties in its practical operation even if it had not been controversial. At the heart of the criticism was the fact that the assumption of powers by local authority social-service departments was perceived by the magistrates of the juvenile courts to have been entirely at the expense of their own hitherto acknowledged supremacy. Juvenile court magistrates, especially those in London who were appointed directly by the Lord Chancellor specifically for the task, have long been led by highly articulate women of strong and confident views. It was not long before the Magistrates' Association had espoused many of their criticisms. No longer able to commit to approved schools whose demise was finally precipitated by the scandals at Court Lees, they were faced with making care orders over whose precise conditions they had no control. And although subsequently they have been empowered to make residential orders it would be foolish to suggest that local authority social workers, however brightly shine their CQSW's, enjoy the kind of magisterial confidence that was once vested in the probation service. How well founded are the criticisms of present practice is hard to assess. What we do know is that the demands on local social services have probably never been greater and the pressures towards retrenchment originating in the policies of central government never more unrelenting. There are inner-city areas where one can only wonder that those concerned to reduce the sum of human misery have not buried their hopes in old copies of the *Sun* and *Mail*, and departed.

To say that we 'treat' offenders in the sense of prophylaxis must surely be a deception. The bald fact of the matter is that we are no nearer to answering the question of whether what we do with offenders can be subsumed under one or a variety of objectives. And if we opt for the variegated model what order of priority must be accorded to punishment, deterrence (both general and individual), therapy, restitution, and the public denunciation of crime? Even that, in our increasingly pluralistic society, is becoming increasingly difficult. There has been no unqualified and universal condemnation of the violence in the miners' strike acceptable to the nation as a whole; on the left the pickets were seen as defending their communities against a para-military police action while on the right excesses of police behaviour were either ignored or applauded as both a necessary and richly deserved lesson for what was seen as political insurrection.

Barbara Wootton, who became a magistrate before she was old enough to vote, entitled her charming autobiography *In a World I Never Made* (1967). If she never made the world in which she lived, she has certainly made her mark on it in those places where men and women sit in judgement on each other. That those in judicial office and those who operate other parts of the criminal justice system do not in fact do more harm to their fellows than they do is in part a result of the adoption of what might be termed the minimalist approach in dealing with law-breakers. In past ages even petty offenders suffered dreadfully from the penal enthu-siasms of the powerful[14] but within Barbara Wootton's working life the judiciary and the magistracy have altogether drawn back from that position. Sentencers are not only constrained but continually enjoined to consider what they are about. To say that she has played a major part in the process would be little better than a bald understatement. But apart from her public contributions to the reform of penal practice her *Testament for Social Science* was for many of us an inspiration in our undergraduate years; the fact that she has uttered no cry of disillusion or despair in these bleak and terrible times is an inspiration to us in our middle age when not only the propagation of liberal notions about how society might be decently ordered but the very profession of learning itself are reviled and under attack from the apostles of the new philistinism. If crime, in so far as it is the manifestation of the darker, uncaring side of human nature, is some gauge of our moral condition, then how we deal with our offending fellows is no less a measure of both justice and intelligence. Winston Churchill, when Home Secretary in 1909, suggested that it was a mark of civilization. And the chance of getting it right has not yet been extinguished.

NOTES

1 The Prison Commissioners, a most liberal collection of public servants, watched the rising tide with anxiety and dismay. Many of them had served as governors and Borstal housemasters under the inspiring leadership of Alexander Paterson. See the post-war *Reports* of the Prison Commissioners for England and Wales from 1950 to 1960.

2 See also Mays, J. B. (1965) *The Young Pretenders*. London: Michael Joseph.

3 While Friedman will be remembered for his contribution to the transformation of monetarist theory into fiscal practice by governments of a right wing persuasion faced with tackling inflation, von Hayek's contribution has been on an altogether broader plane. His *Road to Serfdom* (1944) London: Routledge and University of Chicago Press) was widely employed by critics of the Labour Government of 1945–51 in its attempts to found a welfare state on the principles of socialism and Keynsian economics. His later writings focused upon the problems of individualism in the context of the economic order and the inter-relationship between philosophy, politics, and economics. See: *Individualism and the Economic Order* (1948) London: Routledge; *The Constitution of Liberty* (1960) London: Routledge; and *Law, Legislation and Liberty* (3 vols): Vol. 1: *Rules and Order* (1973); Vol. 2: *The Mirage of Social Justice* (1976); Vol. 3: *The Political Order of a Free Society* (1979) London: Routledge and University of Chicago Press.

4 Various estimates were made at the time of the Scarman Inquiry into the Brixton disorders. The position had not improved by the time of the riots of 1985.

5 Both property developers and farmers have taken advantage of loopholes in the law to destroy deliberately the flora and fauna of sites about to be designated as being of special scientific interest (SSSIs). Bulldozers and plant sprayers have invariably enjoyed a police escort and those seeking to prevent the destruction by sit-down protest have found that the obloquy of 'offender status' has been applied not to the commercial vandals but to them.

6 The Police Federation, representing the rank and file, thinks otherwise. Any hopes the government might have entertained that the
   British police could be relied upon as a faithful praetorian guard were
   dashed at the Federation Conference in May, 1985, when Leon Brittan,
   the then Home Secretary, whose views on public order were thought
   to reflect those of the Prime Minister, was subjected to boos, jeers, and
   derisive laughter.

7 Notwithstanding the constant reminder by government spokesmen of
   the undoubted truth that it has put more policemen into uniform and
   more policemen on the streets.

8 Henry Mayhew (1862) *London Labour and the London Poor*. Henry
   Mayhew and John Binny (1862) *The Criminal Prisons of London and
   Scenes from Prison Life*. Arthur Morrison (1896) *A Child of the Jago*. One
   of the most excellent social histories of crime in the inner city – the area
   covered by Morrison's 'Jago' which was actually the infamous Nichol
   – is Raphael Samuel's (1981) *East End Underworld: Chapters in the Life of
   Arthur Harding*. London: Routledge.

9 The present writer who lived in London for forty years experienced
   something very like the chance described in the BCS: a burglary in
   1936 in Croydon committed by a young unemployed man and another
   in Kensington in 1961 committed by a juvenile of 14 on the run from
   Stamford House Remand Home.

10 One wonders what Churchill, whose slogan at the 1950 election was
   'Set the People Free', might have thought of recent moves to prevent
   the young unemployed from living in bed and breakfast accommodation in one place for more than a limited time and to the linking of
   payment of benefits to participation on Youth Training Scheme
   programmes.

11 Towards the end of 1983 the scandal of holding men in police cells
   rather than prison – in London this could mean in *underground* cells
   occupied by three prisoners without access to fresh air, daylight,
   showers, or baths for up to a week – was such that the Home Secretary
   promised that it would come to an end with the year. And so it did, for
   just three weeks until in January, 1984, the practice began again.

12 Are we really to think of burglary as symbolic incest or jewellery as
   representing the female genitalia?

13 Rainer House in Chelsea was for many years a national training centre
   for the probation service. Time, the need for economy, and the
   pedagogic imperialism of generic training in social work have rendered
   it a redundant church. It closed in 1983.

14 Among cases known personally to the present writer (in consequence
   of his father's interest in penal reform in the 1930s) two first offenders
   come to mind. One served six months with hard labour for receiving a

stolen pocket watch, the other, a teenager, was sentenced to Borstal for breaking open a domestic gas meter.

REFERENCES

Abrams, M. (1959) *Teenage Consumer*. London: London Press Exchange Ltd.

Box, S. and Hale, C. (1982) Economic Crisis and the Rising Prisoner Population in England and Wales. *Crime and Social Justice* 17.

Brenner, M. H. (1976) *Estimating the Social Costs of National Economic Policy*. Washington: US Government Printing Office.

Central Office of Information (1984) *Criminal Justice*. London: HMSO.

Cohen, A. K. (1956) *Delinquent Boys: The Culture of the Gang*. London: Routledge.

Gladstone, F. (1979) Crime and the Crystal Ball. (Home Office Research Unit) *Research Bulletin* 7.

Gottfredson, M. R. (1984) *Victims of Crime: The Dimensions of Risk*. Home Office Research Study No. 81. London: HMSO.

Hough, M. and Mayhew, P. (1983) *The British Crime Survey: First Report*. Home Office Research Study No. 76. London: HMSO.

Jenkins, D. (1985) The God of Freedom and the Freedom of God. Hibbert Lecture 1985. *Listener*, 18 April.

Lindesmith, A. (1947) *Opiate Addiction*. Granville, Ohio: Principia Press.

Mannheim, H. (1940) *Social Aspects of Crime in England between the Wars*. London: Allen & Unwin.

Maxfield, M. G. (1984) *Fear of Crime in England and Wales*. Home Office Research Study No. 78. London: HMSO.

Merton, R. K. (1949) Social Structure and Anomie. In *Social Theory Social Structure*. Glencoe, Ill.: Free Press.

Morgan, P. (1978) *Delinquent Fantasies*. London: Maurice Temple Smith.

Morris, T. (1955) The Carrot out of Reach. *Listener*.

Sparks, R. (1971) *Local Prisons: The Crisis in the English Penal System*. London: Heinemann.

Veblen, T. (1899) (rev. edn 1953) *The Theory of the Leisure Class*. New York: New American Library.

Wilkins, L. (1964) *Social Deviance: Social Policy, Action and Research*. London: Tavistock.

Wootton, B. (1967) *In a World I Never Made*. London: Allen & Unwin.

—— (1950) *Testament for Social Science*. London: Allen & Unwin.

12

BACK TO BASICS: REFLECTIONS ON BARBARA WOOTTON'S 'TWELVE CRIMINOLOGICAL HYPOTHESES'

David Downes

Barbara Wootton's *Social Science and Social Pathology* was the first book on academic criminology I read. Hot, indeed blistering, from the presses of 1959, it was both an exhilarating and a dismaying experience. It exhilarated because it conveyed a sense of urgency, a biting scorn for waffle, and a clear sense of direction. It dismayed because it laid bare the general poverty of criminology, showing it to be a set of rusting clichés and sloppy generalizations. For the novice expecting to enter a field gleaming with theoretical sophistication and methodological rigour, it presented instead a picture of half-baked and rather third-rate propositions cumbersomely 'tested' against data culled from a weird array of 'samples' of diverse deviant populations. The twelve hypotheses examined by Barbara Wootton in the light of twenty-one studies judged by her to be of suitable quality and range were quickly and efficiently despatched. It was an impressive ground-clearing job, carried out with wit and a down-to-earth, no-nonsense empiricism which were in direct line of descent from Dr Johnson's kicking a stone: 'Thus I refute Berkeley.'

Even back in 1959, there were, however, a few qualifications that had to be entered against the overall success of this formidable critique. It may seem churlish to elaborate them here, particularly with the clear advantage of twenty-five years' hindsight, but the occasion demands it. First of all, the ground to be cleared was defined in a very precise but rather odd way: the twelve hypotheses were selected in the light of 'popular' theories, so that one simply had to take the author's word for it that the following factors were to be taken as keys to the then most 'fashionable theories' (Wootton 1959: 83–4): 1) the size of the delinquent's family; 2) the presence of other criminals in the family; 3) club membership; 4) church attendance; 5) employment record; 6) social status; 7) poverty; 8) mother's employment outside the home; 9) school truancy; 10) broken homes; 11) health; and 12) educational attainment.

Though there was little doubt that factors 1, 2, 5, 6, 7, 8 (especially 8), 10, and 12 had much currency, 3, 4, 9, and 11 were far less prominent than such timeless favourites as 'lack of parental discipline', which was strangely omitted from the list. The point, however, is that no evidence for 'popularity' or 'fashionableness' was given.

A second problem was the choice of studies on the basis of whose data the hypotheses were to be tested. These were 'selected in accordance with the requirements that each should deal with at least 200 subjects; should contain data on not less than half, or nearly half, the hypotheses under review; and should be sufficiently substantial to include accounts both of the findings and the methods used' (Wootton 1959: 81). The stringency of the first two criteria unfortunately ruled out such sources as Shaw and McKay's famous ecological study and Lander's Baltimore investigation, which are discussed elsewhere in the book, but not in relation to the twelve hypotheses. All in all, however, one felt that the yardsticks employed amounted to a self-denying ordinance regarding some of the more searching studies available even in the late 1950s, and included too much that was quantitatively relevant but qualitatively highly problematic.

Barbara Wootton's summary of the upshot of this exhaustive analysis of the twenty-one studies' findings in relation to the twelve hypotheses was that 'the results of this review are strikingly negative, in the sense that they hardly enable us to prove or disprove any of the currently fashionable theories.' However,

> 'the whole exercise has not, I think, been altogether unprofitable. For on the one hand, it includes a wholesome scepticism; and on the other hand it shows up many of the major technical weaknesses in the work so far undertaken in this field; and, since such work is still hardly out of the pioneering stage, concentrated attention on technical improvement can be a most constructive operation.'   (Wootton 1959: 83)

Thus, the direction in which she clearly pointed was that what was needed was more, but better, research of the same kind. Such a directive was, with a few major exceptions, to be massively ignored over the next two decades. And, ironically, it was the very success of her own ground-clearing critique which helped pave the way for theorizing and research which in general took very different forms from her own recommendations. Her own directive was for a more refined and rigorous criminological positivism, and that paradigm was decisively rejected by the majority of academic criminologists who came of age in the 1960s and 1970s. A turbulent period ensued in which a diverse array of theories and methods, loosely assembled for a time under the aegis of the 'sociology of deviance', was propagated by protagonists who agreed on one thing only: the exhaustion, if not the evils, of criminological positivism. It may be, however, that Barbara Wootton will have the last laugh, for over the past few years something of a revival has occurred of work which picks up the threads of the tradition she espoused, albeit on scathingly critical terms, in her own contribution. There is a move back to theoretical parsimony, to rigorous empiricism, and to clear-cut hypothesis-testing. It is time to review the interim, and explore how far the wheel has come full circle.

It would be a mistake, however, to imply somehow that criminological positivism, of a sophisticated Woottonesque variety, was nowhere to be found in the period from 1960 to 1980. It did flourish in certain milieux, notably the Cambridge Institute of Criminology, and found perhaps its most developed expression in the longitudinal study of delinquency undertaken by Donald West and his colleagues from the mid-1960s to the mid-1970s (West and Farrington 1973, 1977). This project embodied all the canons of positivism at its best: it was longitudinal to avoid the confounding problems of selective recall and the dangers of mistaking consequence for cause; it sampled well over 200 subjects; it tested well over half the hypotheses considered by Wootton, as well as a host of relatively novel propositions, some culled from labelling theory (see below, p. 206); and its theories and methods were exhaustively documented. The culminating volume, *The Delinquent Way of Life*, established beyond reasonable doubt the greater propensity of delinquents, compared with their non-delinquent peers, to smoke, drink, gamble, and engage in sexual activity. But the antecedents of delinquency remained stubbornly resistant to the discernment of any neat lineage, so that, to adapt Barbara Wootton's phraseology, beyond establishing that delinquents tend to come from impoverished lower working-class backgrounds, and pursue a relatively self-indulgent if not enjoyable way of life, 'we cannot go'.

Now the interesting feature of this conclusion to a really quite prodigious amount of hard criminological research is that it brought us back to the point, the 'delinquent way of life', at which Albert Cohen began his theory of delinquent gangs some thirty years ago in a book (Cohen 1955) uncharacteristically omitted by Barbara Wootton from her overall coverage of the field. It is perhaps now pertinent to assemble a dozen criminological hypotheses of a variety rather different from those which Barbara Wootton reviewed, most of which emerged only after her book was written, and to subject them to appraisal along lines she herself adopted. We may then find both that we are hardly more secure in any generalization we may care to make about delinquency than we were in 1959; and that the most exciting theories intellectually have of late been giving ground fast to those more amenable to prosaic canons of proof and disproof. In the process, however, our knowledge of the problems inherent in the task has increased immensely; and a great deal, albeit of a partial and situated character, has been learnt.

The twelve hypotheses which have preoccupied criminologists in the post-1959 era have been principally of a sociological variety, though not exclusively so. Those I wish to consider are: 1) anomie theory; 2) early subcultural theory; 3) ecological theory; 4) culture of poverty theory; 5) working-class culture theory; 6) differential association; 7) functionalism; 8) labelling theories; 9) radical criminology; 10) late subcultural theory; 11) social control theory; and 12) situational control theory. Clearly these are not all hypotheses in the sense of the term as it was used by Barbara Wootton. They are theories, even meta-theories, that encompass many subsidiary hypotheses around a core set of domain assumptions (Gouldner 1970). They each have their naïve and sophisticated versions, and often have resisted, with varying degrees of success, that consignment to oblivion which is held by Popper to accompany empirical falsification. Rather, they rise and fall in terms of fashionableness for reasons that are, curiously, little explored, but may have much to do with an academic culture that venerates creativity far more highly than 'normal' science (Kuhn 1961). However, normal science now appears to be winning out, and the search for new permutations and approaches has become correspondingly less heated. This may represent an opportunity for many of the theories to be evaluated rather more appropriately than has been the case in the past; or it may reflect a growing sense of entropy, of criminology as an extractive industry of declining salience, whose intellectual seams are now uneconomic. That would, however, be to mistake exodus for exhaustion: for one of the primary sources of both theoretical and empirical innovation in the field, graduate researchers, has been massively cut back; and, among the ageing band of practitioners who remain in the field, a marked shift of emphasis has occurred in their work from the focus on deviance and its causes that obtained in the 1960s and 1970s, to a stress on the realities and trends in control of the 1980s.

However, it is worth attempting to distil the theoretical core from these approaches to produce a latter-day criminologist's dozen. It is not my intention to repeat the second half of Barbara Wootton's achievement, the testing of the hypotheses against evidence culled from twenty-one or any other number of studies. The best source for such an exercise is Rutter and Giller's recent book *Juvenile Delinquency: Trends and Perspectives* (1983). All that can be attempted here is a citation of what seem to be the most pertinent forms of evidence or argument against which to evaluate the theories.

1. *Anomie*   That increasingly high material aspirations, commonly held, generate rates of crime directly related to the extent of economic inequality

Barbara Wootton was briskly dismissive of anomie theory, finding it 'suspiciously tautological . . . a high-sounding name for the attempts of the poor to get rich quick in the only ways that may be open to them' (Wootton 1959: 69). She also noted the naïvety of Merton's (1938) acceptance of the official view that crime is more a property of the poor than of the rich. However, that aspect of the theory can be discarded if we pay more attention to Durkheim's original notion that anomie (or a state of normative confusion) is more common among employers than employees: 'Those who have only empty space above them are more likely to be lost in it' (1897: 247); i.e. the lower one's class, the more subdued one's aspirations. Merton, however, was pitching his theory in terms of the 'American Dream', and its continuing appeal (most recently as an undertow to Lea and Young's *What Is to Be Done about Law and Order?* (1984)), is due to its addressing a central paradox of crime trends: their rise and rise in the context of affluence. While Barbara Wootton would probably see all this as a sociological rendering of the commandment 'Thou shalt not covet thy neighbour's goods', or that greed, once stimulated, knows no bounds, there are, of course, quite proper sociological questions to be asked about the variability of greed, the nature of its stimulants, the contexts of its arousal, etc. Since the capitalist show can only be kept on the road by the constant fostering of the propensity to consume, and since its pattern of income and wealth distribution remain resolutely inegalitarian, it is not altogether surprising that the USA, for the half-century since Merton's theory was published, has complied with his thesis. Indeed, it may be that his thesis applies only to America, as he intended at the time. But a theory with only one case to offer is not much of a theory, and it seems necessary to extend coverage to other capitalist societies. Two recent attempts to do so have produced mixed evidence. Braithwaite (1979) found some limited support for such an approach in a survey of comparative inequalities in income and crime rates; and another comparative survey found the approach worked well only in relation to the USA (Stack 1984). The difficulties in testing the theory are notorious, since 'aspirations', 'income', 'crime', and a host of mediating variables such as 'class', 'status', and 'success', present immense problems of measurement which are compounded by any cross-cultural survey. For example, Stack's highly sophisticated cross-national survey is based on Interpol rates for crimes against property which show Sweden to have eight times the crime problem of Italy and over ten times that of Hong Kong.

There is a sense in which anomie theory is Marxism shorn of the dialectic, but that could be an advantage, since its scope is broadened in principle to cover all industrial societies, including those which (with deference to Trotsky) lack the formal attributes of capitalism. It will in all likelihood continue to animate a great deal of sociological work in this field, but that work should attend more carefully to the need to monitor certain subsidiary clauses, such as the impact of advertising on the level, character, and implications of material aspirations. Such sub-themes remain virgin territory outside the field of market research.

2. *Subcultural theory (early)*   That juvenile delinquency of an expressive variety is the manufacture of excitement by illicit means

Most crime is property crime, and most property crime is petty theft. The working model of the average criminal is therefore usually that of failed Economic Man. Yet a considerable amount of crime does not conform to that stereotype, especially at the juvenile age-range. Vandalism, violence, 'joy-riding', in short 'hooliganism', have an expressive rather than an instrumental set of connotations, much as its detractors label it 'meaning-less', 'motiveless', 'animalistic', and the like. Even acts of theft can take this form, as in shop-lifting sprees where risk-taking and defiance of convention seem more to the point than sheer acquisitiveness. That theorists had ignored this crucial aspect of the 'delinquency way of life' was Albert Cohen's starting-point for his theory of delinquent subcultures (1955). He argued that the delinquent gang provided status for those denied it in conventional contexts, especially schools. Indeed, the rules of the delinquent game were those of respectable society turned upside down. Later theorists found his stress on both gangs (though see Horowitz 1983) and school too pronounced. Delinquency usually took more mundane forms than wrecking the classroom. And delinquents usually cared not at all about schooling, much as they might resent its imposition on their time. Matza (1964) proposed a version of subcultural theory which favoured an image of delinquency as born of drift and the pursuit of toughness, excitement, and pleasure. Much ethnography has dwelt on delinquents' accounts of illegal acts as varied responses to boredom (Downes 1966; Marsh 1978; Parker Corrigan 1979). But what differentiates the boredom of adolescent boys from that of girls, businessmen, and old-age pensioners? (Barbara Wootton constantly reminded her readers that simply to raise this kind of question was enough to demolish most theories.) The stress on conspicuous self-assertion as a defining characteristic of the male gives part of the answer. Traditionally, though now diminishingly so, women were assigned the self-effacing role. Yet the young, especially lower-class and ethnic-minority young males, are disproportionately denied ways of demonstrating prowess. Perhaps

Goffman's (1972) notion of 'character' is what is fundamentally at stake: 'character' is won through action, and the scope for action of any legitimate sort that might be honorific is in short supply in such contexts. Hence, 'making things happen' comes to embrace law-breaking. The critical point made by Rutter and Giller, that most delinquency is theft of a minor kind, and that this is also common to middle-class youth, rather misses the point. The theory can stretch to accommodate those middle-class youth who are – for whatever reason – adrift; and such material as we have on e.g. mods and rockers (Little and Barker 1964) and soccer hooligans (Marsh 1978) confirm their working-class backgrounds.

3. *Ecological theory*   That criminal areas generate more crime than would exist if their offenders were integrated into less crime-prone communities

'Even the most unprejudiced sociological eyebrows will hardly be raised at the discovery that delinquency tends to be concentrated in particular areas, and that in general those are the slummy areas' (Wootton 1959: 65). Barbara Wootton pays closer attention to ecological theory than this might suggest, but she none the less found it severely wanting. A few years later, Peter Cook and Dudley Moore returned from the USA with the line: 'There's a great deal of poverty in America, but fortunately it's concentrated in the slum areas.' Such consensus clearly had to be wrong, and in 1976 Peter Townsend demonstrated that the area basis for so much social policy towards poverty was massively misconceived. 'However economically or socially deprived areas are defined, unless nearly half the areas in the country are included, there will be more poor people or poor children living outside them than in them. There is a second conclusion. Within all or nearly all defined priority areas there will be more persons who are not deprived than there are deprived' (Townsend 1976: 18). Though no similar exercise has been carried out in relation to crime, one would expect broadly similar conclusions. As with poverty, inner-city areas – as the British Crime Survey has shown – are considerably more at risk than other areas. But the dispersion is too great to warrant the conclusion that more than a small proportion of crime is reducible to specifically ecological factors. Such studies as those by Gill (1977) and Morris (1957) have shown the significance of housing policies in congregating a 'critical mass' of 'at risk' groups which generates unusually high delinquency rates (and stigmas). We still await, however, the kind of study recommended by Barbara Wootton: 'It is indeed only to long-term studies extending over more than one generation . . . that we must look for answers to the really vital questions as to the concentration of anti-social attitudes at the bottom of the social scale' (1959: 73). In this respect, West's finding that delinquency rates fell among emigrants from London is of especial interest (1982: 111–12).

4. *Culture of poverty*   That poverty, regardless of context, promotes a culture highly productive of crime and delinquency

That poverty causes crime was one of the hypotheses examined by Barbara Wootton in 1959. She concluded that the studies then available showed that 'most delinquents come from the lower social classes, but the evidence as to the extent to which they can be described as exceptionally poor is conflicting' (1959: 134). Donald West's study found a strong relationship between 'deprivation' (of which low income, large family size, and poor parenting were among key indicators): 'In truth, the surprising concentration of delinquent individuals, especially recidivists, among a small minority of families in our sample, and the strong tendency for criminal fathers to have criminal sons, were among the most important observations to come out of our study. . . . The worse the background, the worse the likely outcome' (1982: 116). He is, however, the first to acknowledge that 'deprivation applies only to a section of delinquents, and how deprivation operates to produce delinquents is far from clear' (1982: 118).

Oscar Lewis (1959, 1961) provided one such explanation in terms of a 'culture of poverty' that was transmitted intergenerationally and apparently formed a response to extremes of poverty wherever it existed. Thus, in Mexico City, New York, Glasgow, and Calcutta, the collective response is essentially the same: fatalism, *machismo*, and an inability to defer gratification. Lewis was, however, emphatic that the *root* cause of the 'culture of poverty' was structural, though the 'culture of poverty' impeded the scope for advantage to be taken of improved opportunities. Liebow (1967) described in vivid detail how such a culture is lived and reproduced in one small corner of Washington, DC. Unfortunately, policy-makers reversed the causal sequence of such work to end up, in effect, 'blaming the victims' for culturally sealing their own fate, as, for example, in Sir Keith Joseph's 'cycles of disadvantage' speech of 1973. Their inability to grasp how poverty could persist in an 'affluent' society was in part due to their reluctance to accept the view that relative rather than absolute indices of poverty are the more appropriate measure of its extent as standards of living in general rise (Townsend 1979). The poor may become more marginalized, isolated, and apathetic in a context where even the institutions once available to the poor, in a vigorous 'culture of poverty', are mopped up by the commerce of economic change: it is infinitely more difficult in England now to find cheap lodgings, cheap cafés, cheap entertainment, than it was even twenty years ago. Perhaps for that reason the most deprived subjects of Donald West's study did not articulate a culture of poverty of the complexity of those described by Lewis, Liebow, and Horowitz for the USA. Their career options, however, lay in a dismal choice between petty, persistent criminality and apathetic conformity on the margins of casual labour and institutional life.

5. *Working-class culture*   That working-class culture is a 'generating milieu' of delinquency

Although this approach had its heyday in the 1950s and early 1960s, in the work of John Mays in England and Walter Miller in America, it has continued to exert considerable if diminishing sway, and has certain affinities with the otherwise very different work of, for example, Paul Willis. In some ways, it is difficult to differentiate this approach from ecological theory on the one hand, and 'culture of poverty' theories on the other, especially since so much of the focus is on the *lower* working class, whose way of life is often counterposed to that of the ultra-respectable working class (see, for example, Elias and Scotson 1966). Working-class culture is seen by both Mays and Miller as a solidary, distinctive culture evolved over two centuries of shared experience of manual labour. The common experience of at best a precarious prosperity and, at worst, a grinding exploitation, has given rise to a sharp awareness of the differences between 'Them' (the bosses) and 'Us' (the workers). The high premium placed on physical strength and stamina invests 'toughness' with unusual value. Toughness, smartness, fate, excitement, trouble, and autonomy were seen by Miller as six 'focal concerns' of working-class culture. Such a culture, acted out by male adolescents on the inner-city streets, inexorably involved them in a state of normalized conflict with the police and the authorities. Evidence for the enduring character of the culture is seen by Miller in the relatively unchanging nature of gang delinquency in America, despite the apparent potency of such phenomena as youth culture, 'black power', and drug abuse, which were all heralded, at the time of their maximum media coverage in the past two decades, as signalling the end of gang traditions. Empirically, official crime data consistently show markedly higher rates of delinquency in the lower working class than in other social groups, though the association is usually much weaker when self-report data are used. Of late, however, self-report data are viewed with some scepticism, not least because the school populations from whom such self-reports are usually culled exclude a substantial minority of drop-outs and truants whose delinquency is commonly more pronounced. Some criminologists (e.g. Box) see the disparity between official and self-report data as a symptom of class bias on the part of the police, though as the community activates most police responses, that effect has serious limitations. Here it is necessary to address the paradox which, to Kornhauser, seems to dispose of the theory: 'The belief that powerless people will endorse in their sub-cultures actions by which they are grievously injured is unreasonable. . . . No *groups* of people will construct a culture or a sub-culture that makes their own lives impossible. . . . That is why the search for sub-cultures that differ markedly in their orientation to crime is doomed to failure' (1978: 218). It seems necessary to point out that none of the theories under review in cultural terms subscribes to this position. What is argued is that values having distinctive roles in some social groups but not others exert, at several removes, an influence which carries a high risk of involvement in delinquency. The kind of research currently being done on lifestyles in relation to victimization (Gottfredson 1984) stresses the much greater risks of victimization within certain working-class, inner-city neighbour-hoods, among young males who drink in pubs. But people don't go to pubs with the aim of getting thumped in the face; nor – for that matter – do drivers who accelerate nerve and speed necessarily wish to have fatal crashes; nor do businessmen who wish to cut 5 pence off the price of a hamburger aim to hasten the deforestation of Latin America: but the high valuation placed on some forms of conduct and not others increases those risks. The problems with the theory are otherwise: that it accounts rather badly for trends (the crime rate increasing while the working class is shrinking); that it accounts only partially for the character of much delinquency, especially theft; and that it accounts not at all for delinquency in social groups other than the lower working class.

6. *Differential association* That persons become delinquent because of an excess of definitions favourable to violation of law over definitions unfavourable to violations of law

Differential association (d.a.) theory, which most criminologists had come to regard as cumbersome, untestable, and obsolete, has of late staged something of a revival, not least due to its continued championship by Donald Cressey (Sutherland and Cressey 1979). Barbara Wootton rephrased d.a. theory as proposing that 'the question of whether you go straight or crooked depends mainly upon the company that you happen to be thrown with' (1959: 84), though she regretted that not one of her twenty-one studies made any serious attempt to examine it. Shortly after she wrote, Glaser (1960) and Short (1960) ingeniously tested the theory by such means as equating the 'frequency, intensity, priority and duration' of 'definitions favourable to violations of the law' with friendship patterns. A sample of young offenders were asked questions related to delinquent and non-delinquent friends in terms of their number, who their *best* friend was, which friends they had made first, and how long such friendships lasted.

The findings were generally in line with d.a. theory, the intensity of friendships being most strongly associated with delinquency. Later studies found mixed results, once controls were introduced for parental supervision (Bahrs 1979). Rutter and Giller concluded that 'differential associations with criminal patterns do influence the development of delinquent activities, but they interact with family variables, and [these] have an independent direct influence of their own' (1983: 250). Differential association theory thus remains an active if reduced magnet for research, in part because its precepts underlie much that is elaborated in cultural and subcultural theories. Its own very high level of abstraction, however, precludes explanation in terms of just how and why, other than in terms of chance, such associations arise and are subject to change. Perhaps fortunately, the 'new right' in Britain has never got hold of d.a. theory, since the so-called 'permissive society' would no doubt have been cast as a potent source of 'an excess of definitions favourable to law violation', and of a weakening of definitions unfavourable to law violation. Against such a view, one might simply note that crime has risen, if anything, faster under a 'law and order' government than before.

7. *Functionalist approaches* That normal rates and types of crime are essential for social order

There is no mention in Barbara Wootton's book of Durkheim's famous theorem: 'Crime is normal. . . . It is a factor in public health, an integral part of all healthy societies' (1895). One suspects she would have quickly teased out its teleological, tautological, and strictly untestable character. Durkheim's whole point was that crime had the effect of eliciting a heightening of common sentiments against it, thus clarifying and reinforcing the community's most central norms and values. If crime rates, comparatively, rose too high, or fell too low, something was wrong: either crime was swamping a community's capacity to respond appropriately to it, or the controlling sentiments were too powerful. But Durkheim's functionalist leanings led him to imply that normally crime arose *in order* to bring about a regeneration of social norms, much as a muscle grows flabby if it is not used; and that implies some sort of collective unconscious at work: causality can be assigned to beneficial consequence. It is also strictly speaking untestable, since, whatever happens, some functional significance can be read into it. In his day, Durkheim's views were seen by some as immoral, for seeming to justify crime; in our day, they are more likely to be seen as pointless, since no criminological research can be mounted on that basis.

None the less, functionalist notions continue to pervade much sociological work on deviance (Scott 1972; Marsh 1976) and that suggests its logical problems may not matter too much by comparison with its richness as a source for conjecture. After all, Darwin's theory of natural selection is seemingly tautological, since if a species has survived, it has clearly evolved in ways appropriate to its environment, the main indication of its failure to adapt being its non-survival. One source of evidence by which to test natural selection is the fossil record, where species change should be discernible in graduated phases rather than sudden metamorphoses. Though enormous gaps exist, at least the theory is in principle testable. The fossil record for crime and delinquency is similarly patchy, but such as it is, it lends some credence to functionalist axioms. For example, Pearson's (1983) unearthing of 'moral panics' about hooliganism over the past few centuries is replete with contemporary-sounding alarms about 'children no longer respecting their elders' and the like. This would all be grist to the functionalist mill: 'moral panics' simply represent that heightening of collective sentiments against deviance without which the social order could not be preserved. But why should deviance arise in the first place? Presumably because of a prior weakening of collective sentiments against deviance, arising from a variety of causes (or the sheer diversity of consciousness). The approach remains awesomely circular, and resists the clear assignment of causal priorities. From the best of the recent work which draws on functionalist notions (Scott 1972; Marsh *et al.* 1978), what seems most worthy of scrutiny is the sheer variation in the reactions of different societies to deviance of apparently comparable kinds, some repressive, others restitutive. How far hidden or informal controls of a repressive character may obtain where formal controls are weak, and vice versa, seems to demand far more attention than it has so far received.

8. *Labelling theory*   That processes of social control generate more deviance than would otherwise exist

Functionalist concerns were either absent from or actively opposed by labelling theorists. The tone and character of much work in this tradition is best exemplified in its single most influential work, *Outsiders* by Howard Becker (1963). A part-time jazz musician, Becker became preoccupied with such problems as how it came about that users of a relatively benign substance, marijuana, should become vilified as dope fiends in a society that promoted such potent killers as alcohol and tobacco, rewarding their manufacturers with large sums of money and high honours. His dismay at the inability of existing theories to account for, or even take account of, such selective regulation was matched only by his incredulity at theories which consigned marijuana users to anomie, status frustration, or other unlikely states. He argued that considerable social bias was mobilized by 'moral entrepreneurs' who attempted to legislate morality on such issues, for idiosyncratic reasons but with dire results: for those labelled as deviant tended to become confirmed in that status. It seemed to Wilkins also that control 'amplified' deviation: and Ditton (1979) has more recently argued that criminology should itself be relabelled 'controlology' to reorientate inquiry in this direction. The labelling theorists were the first to take seriously the spirit of Joe Orton's remark that there is something deeply suspicious about a society that loves its police force.

It is to Barbara Wootton's eternal credit that much of her book is laced with insights of this sort, and that she went on to chair a government inquiry into cannabis use and its regulation, recommending that social prejudice be counteracted by substantial decriminalization. But for a reactionary Home Secretary, James Callaghan, burying that report, it might have led to tens of thousands of people being protected from undue interference with their liberty by the police and prison authorities, improving race relations in the process. Even so, a blow was struck for social policy to be better informed by the rational sifting of research evidence.

From modest beginnings, labelling theory became rapidly elaborated to redress the legacy of neglect of traditional criminology in terms of the study of the actual workings of institutions and agencies of control as causally implicated in deviance. Its naïve version – that labelling a person deviant entails a simple 'self-fulfilling prophecy' – was found wanting when put to the test (Gove 1975). In favour of the proposition, Stan Cohen found backing for the view that the 'mods and rockers' riots were greatly amplified by media, police, and court reactions. Jock Young went far (Notting Hill) to demonstrate that drug use was amplified by police harassment, since drugs became the symbol of group cohesion under threat. Cohen has moved on to view contemporary trends in social control as blurring, deepening, and broadening the grip of the state over 'deviant' lives (1979; 1985). Though some case-studies have found contrary trends, as in Damer's (1974) study of a Scottish housing estate *not* falling prey to amplified deviance despite intense stigmatization, the use of interactionist methods to study deviance and control has momentously enlarged the scope of the field, and redeemed it from the kind of naïve empiricism excoriated by Barbara Wootton. How well the 'punitive city' image of control trends stands up to closer examination is perhaps the most urgent issue in this field at present (Bottoms 1983).

9. *Radical criminology*   That capitalism is uniquely 'criminogenic'

Radical criminologists set out with panache to do to the subject what Albert Cohen argued young delinquents did to respectable morality: turn it upside down. Thus, in Britain, the real crime problem lies with the Woking class rather than the working class; corporate crime victimizes on a scale that dwarfs the efforts of those committing an inferior class of crime; tax evasion (anything from £4 billion p.a. to £15 billion) puts social security fraud (£200 million) into the shade; police crime is at least as bad as policed crime trends (Taylor, Walton, and Young 1973; Box 1983). Violence is no exception, since the rate of avoidable deaths caused by neglect of health and safety regulations at work and by consumer products greatly exceeds the official murder rate. Moreover, 'accidents' are no accident: capitalism generates such crimes on so vast a scale as the result of its overriding stress on profits at (almost) any cost. Yet somehow criminology came to view the theft of sweeties from Woolworths as more deserving of serious analysis than the killing and maiming of people by pollution, automania, and industrial injury, a view largely shared by the criminal justice system.

There is more than enough truth in this line of attack to justify the 'New Criminology's' attempt to call the subject's practitioners to task. Their preference for a Marxist analysis of political economy as the only possible basis for a relaunched criminology has, however, deflected a great deal of energy and talent away from the research task into theoretical infighting. For example, the insistence on capitalism as somehow uniquely tainted finesses the problem of the misuse of power and knowledge in other forms of society, notably self-styled socialist systems. Also, is it that useful to treat capitalism, or any other form of political economy, as a single entity, an invariant variable, when some capitalist societies are far more profligate than others with their citizens' lives and health? A related problem for 'idealist' left-wing criminologists is the awkward reality of 'street crime' for working-class communities. A more 'realist' left-wing criminology has recently emerged (Taylor 1981; Lea and Young 1984) in which such problems are addressed, and policy solutions are explored in shorter-term thinking than revolutionary praxis allows. Such problems are indeed urgent, and also addressed by those to the right of the radicals. Lea and Young have presented an unrivalled analysis of just why, in the context of the technologically based 'emancipation of Capital from Labour', with its implications for endemic mass unemployment, the problem of police accountability matters even more urgently than before. In London, for example, 98.6 per cent of complaints against the police are not upheld – a level of saintliness unknown among the twelve apostles; and when the average number of serious crimes cleared up by police officers is four annually, at a cost of roughly £5,000 per crime, something slightly uneconomic is going on. One can hardly fail to agree with the general point of radical criminology that crime and its control are a regressive tax on the community; that the powerful are, relatively speaking, over-protected and under-controlled, and the powerless under-protected and over-controlled. Such a situation makes for respectable hypocrisy (the rich uphold the law) and working-class authoritarianism (only tougher punishments can stem 'street crime'), the recipe for 'Thatcherism'. Testing such propositions covers a broad range of research tasks, as yet more effectively carried out in the USA by such non-radical criminologists as Marshall Clinard, working in the Sutherland (1924) tradition, than by radical criminologists here. It is difficult to see, however, how such an agenda could be a basis for research without a Freedom of Information Act.

10. *Subcultural theory (late)*   That delinquency is best explained as sym-
                                   bolic resistance to class hegemony

By the early 1970s, the promise of early subcultural theory had been blunted by, *inter alia*, two major limitations: first, it was cast in essentially deprivational terms, and had difficulty in accounting for emergent forms of middle-class deviance, such as drug use and student revolt; second, it never really made sense of the bewildering succession of youthful styles that were variously associated with delinquency or, at least, 'anti-social' behaviour. Phil Cohen persuasively resolved part of the problem by linking such styles to changes in political economy at both local and national levels. Teds, mods, rockers, skinheads had improvised subcultural styles 'to express and resolve, albeit "magically", the contradictions which remain hidden or unresolved in the parent culture' (1972). Thus, for example, the mod style could be interpreted as 'an attempt to realise, *but in an imaginary relation*, the conditions of existence of the socially mobile white-collar worker'. This mode of analysing what Melly called 'revolts into style' (1972) became elaborated and extended in the work of Hall, Willis, and others at the Birmingham University Centre for Contemporary Cultural Studies (1975–78). Middle-class as well as working-class forms of youthful deviance could be decoded as modes of differentiation from, and resistance to, contradictory aspects of the worlds of school and work in which they were emmeshed. Though decoding style in this way can too easily degenerate into facile over-interpretation, these were valuable projects, though exceptionally difficult to evaluate empirically. Stan Cohen has argued forcefully that the elements of struggle and resistance have indeed been over-drawn (1980). Hebdige (1979), for example, could equate 'putting the boot in' with 'resolving contradictions'; drug abuse can be seen as rioting by needle, or chemical Thatcherism. Some empirical work, however, lends credence to the view that delinquency need not be devoid of political meaning. For example, in analysing the backgrounds of offenders in the 1981 Toxteth riots, Paul Cooper concludes that it was an 'extraordinary event', not (as the police claimed) simply an outbreak of hooliganism: 'At certain points, members of marginalised communities may be provided with the motivation and the opportunity to assert their rights to equal concern and respect by means of violence' (1985). John McVicar has argued similarly in relation to prison violence (1982). Such readings may lean heavily on inference: but we are far from the point at which they can be dismissed out of hand.

11. *Social control theory*   That crime is the product of weak or ineffective social bonds

For a considerable time, from roughly the late 1930s to the mid-1970s, sociologists of crime and deviance managed to hold at bay the view that crime arose chiefly where social controls were weak or absent. Such a view did not appeal because it placed virtually the whole weight of causality on internal, psychological factors, reducing the social and environmental to a merely secondary role. Psychologists and psychoanalysts were naturally wedded to this view, which meant that it could be safely dismissed as 'individualistic', and therefore hardly worthy of discussion, by sociologists. The slow heretical fuse of opposition to this view was really lit by Travis Hirschi (1969), though precedents existed in abundance in the work of Matza, Shaw, and McKay's concept of 'social disorganization', the Gluecks, Durkheim's anomie, Freud, Hobbes and Aristotle. Hirschi put all these strands together again on the basis of a large self-report study which found little correlation between class, ethnicity, 'cultural deviance', and crime, but significant links between delinquency and measures of what he termed 'attachment, commitment, involvement and belief': indices of the bonding of the individual to the family, school, and society. Box (1971) wrote persuasively in the same vein, and Wilson (1978, 1980) lent substance to the approach by her finding that 'chaperonage', the close parental monitoring of children, linked strongly with absence of delinquency among a group of poor large families living in overcrowded conditions in an inner-city area. Hagan and colleagues (1979) provided a *coup de grâce* by establishing strong links between gender, parental discipline, attitudes favourable to risk-taking, and actual involvement in delinquency. The sex difference in delinquency, which had been addressed only rather tortuously by subcultural theory, was convincingly grounded in the far greater exposure of girls to familial processes of *informal* social control. Barbara Wootton had pointed in 1959 to the 'relative rarity of women offenders . . . for the most part tacitly ignored by students of criminology. . . Yet if men behaved like women, the courts would be idle and the prisons empty' (Wootton 1959: 31–2). The major shortcoming of social control theory is that it persistently avoids issues of motivation and meaning which have preoccupied theorists of the more expressive forms of delinquency, in particular, over the past thirty years; but in the work of Box and Hagan, some affinities exist with themes and theories of subcultural approaches.

12. *Situational control theory*   That rates of crime correspond to the presence of opportunities and the absence of constraints

Despite the common emphasis on controls as the key variables governing crime rates, social and situational control theories differ in one crucial respect: in the former, the environment is secondary to *internal* control variables derived from child socialization processes; in the latter, environmental variables are virtually *all* that need to be taken into account. Offenders are seen as exercising rational choices in relation to perceived risks, costs, and benefits. The question of *dispositional* bias is regarded as too arcane for inquiry to be profitably employed any longer in that direction; *situational* variables, however, are (rightly) said to have been unduly neglected in criminological research (Clarke 1980). For example, the installation of North Sea gas appears to have been crucial in dramatic falls in the suicide rate in English cities in the 1970s (Mayhew *et al.* 1976). Had a sociologically informed policy produced that result, we would all be announcing the arrival of the millennium. Quite adventitiously, the enforcement of the wearing of crash helmets by motor cyclists reduced the rate of motor bike theft to negligible proportions. It is part of the appeal of situational control theory that it generates relatively clear-cut policy leads in the realm of crime prevention. It is much more salient to suggest precise technical solutions to messy social problems than messianic solutions to technical problems. Locking doors at night, creating 'defensible space' (Newman 1972) vandal-proofing phone boxes: these kinds of measures are seen as preferable, cheaper, and more readily monitored than people-changing on the one hand, or society-changing on the other. Neither of the latter have been very intelligently handled in the past. 'Nothing works' (Martinson) could well be the verdict on revolutions as well as rehabilitation, though – as Donald West notes in Chapter 13 – such unrelieved pessimism may well be premature.

The fact that there is considerable mileage in situational control theory should not blind one to its very real limitations. Stopping or staunching crime is one thing: understanding and explaining it another. And even stopping and staunching awaits proper evaluation. Displacement of crime, either from one area to another (as seems to have been the result of local neighbourhood watch schemes), or from one kind of target to another (as may have occurred with vehicle theft), could well be the chief effect of situational control. On the other hand, suicide seems non-displaceable: you either live or die, though 'quality of life' would emerge as the issue on that score. And the more opportunistic the crime, the greater the scope for situational controls to work: much hinges here on the reality of purely opportunistic crime. For the fact remains that even though our society is positively bristling with security, surveillance, and controls, the crime rate continues to climb.

CONCLUSION

Subcultural theory was the most significant development of the 1950s; labelling theory of the 1960s; radical criminology of the 1970s; and control theories of the 1980s. It would be pleasant to record this sequence as a series of progressive problem-shifts, each superseding the other as the result of proven accretions of knowledge. But that is not the case. Theoretical systems may rise and fall, or bloom and fade, but they seem to do so more for reasons of poorly analysed fashionableness than on grounds of rigorous falsification. In truth, we are only negligibly less ignorant about crime than we were twenty-five years ago: but we are now far more knowledgeable about our ignorance, especially in terms of control processes. Of the theories reviewed, I suspect Barbara Wootton would approve at all enthusiastically only of control theories, for their relatively precise formulation and empirical grounding, though *obiter dicta* scattered throughout her work suggest a strong affinity with aspects of labelling theory and radical criminology. Her trenchant criticism helped usher in a far more adventurous phase of criminological inquiry; and even if that phase seems largely spent, the insights it afforded should not be lost in the return to relative orthodoxy.

REFERENCES

Bahrs, J. (1979) Family Determinants and Effects of Deviance. In W. R. Burr *et al.* (eds) *Contemporary Theories about the Family*. Vol. 1. New York: Free Press.

Becker, H. (1963) *Outsiders*. New York: Free Press.

Bottoms, A. E. (1983) Neglected Features of Contemporary Penal Systems. In D. Garland and P. Young (eds) *The Power to Punish*. London: Heinemann.

Box, S. (1971) *Deviance, Reality and Society*. New York: Holt, Rinehart & Winston.

—— (1983) *Power, Crime and Mystification*. London.

Braithwaite, J. (1979) *Inequality, Crime and Social Policy*. London: Routledge.

Clarke, R. V. G. (1980) Situational Crime Prevention. *British Journal of Criminology*.

Clinard, M. B. and Yeager, P. C. (1980) *Corporate Crime*. New York.

Cohen, A. K. (1955) *Delinquent Boys: The Culture of the Gang*. New York: Collier Macmillan.

Cohen, P. (1972) Working Class Youth Cultures in East London. *Working*

Papers in Cultural Studies. Birmingham: University of Birmingham, Centre for Contemporary Cultural Studies.

Cohen, S. (1979) The Punitive City. *Contemporary Crises.*

—— (1980) *Folk Devils and Moral Panics.* 2nd edn. Oxford.

—— (1985) *Visions of Social Control.* Cambridge: Polity Press.

Cooper, P. (1985) Competing Explanations of the Merseyside Riots of 1981. *British Journal of Criminology,* January.

Corrigan, P. (1979) *Schooling the Smash Street Kids.* London: Macmillan.

Damer, S. (1974) Wine Alley: The Sociology of a Dreadful Enclosure. *Sociological Review.*

Ditton, J. (1979) *Controlology.* London: Macmillan.

Downes, D. M. (1966) *The Delinquent Solution.* London: Routledge.

Durkheim, E. (1895) *The Rules of Sociological Method* (translated 1964). New York: Free Press.

—— (1897) *Suicide* (translated 1952). London: Routledge.

Elias, N. and Scotson, E. (1966) *The Established and the Outsiders.* London: Frank Cass.

Erikson, K. (1966) *Wayward Puritans.* New York: Wiley.

Gill, O. (1977) *Luke Street: Housing Policy, Conflict and the Creation of the Delinquency Area.* London: Macmillan.

Glaser, D. (1960) Differential Association and Criminological Prediction. *Social Problems,* Summer.

Glueck, S. and E. (1950) *Unravelling Juvenile Delinquency.* Cambridge, Mass.: Harvard University Press.

Goffman, E. (1972) Where the Action Is. In *Interaction Ritual.* London: Allen Lane.

Gottfredson, M. R. (1984) *Victims of Crime: The Dimensions of Risk.* Home Office Research and Planning Unit Report No. 81. London: HMSO.

Gouldner, A. (1970) *The Coming Crisis in Western Sociology.* New York: Avon.

Gove, W. (ed.) (1975) *The Labelling of Deviance.* London: Halsted Press.

Hagan J., Simpson J. H., and Gillis, A. R. (1979) The Sexual Stratification of Social Control. *British Journal of Sociology,* March.

Hall, S. and Jefferson, T. (eds) (1976) *Resistance through Rituals.* London: Hutchinson.

Hebdige, D. (1979) *Subculture: The Meaning of Style.* London: Methuen.

Hirschi, T. (1969) *The Causes of Delinquency.* Berkeley: University of California Press.

Horowitz, R. (1983) *Honor and the American Dream.* Chicago.

Kornhauser, R. (1978) *Social Sources of Delinquency.* Chicago: University of Chicago Press.

Kuhn, T. S. (1961) *The Structure of Scientific Revolutions.* Chicago: University of Chicago Press.

Lea, J. and Young, J. (1984) *What Is to Be Done about Law and Order?* Harmondsworth: Penguin.

Lewis, O. (1959) *Five Families*. New York: Basic Books.

—— (1961) *The Children of Sanchez*. New York: Random House.

Liebow, E. (1967) *Tally's Corner*. London.

Little A, and Barker, P. (1964) The Margate Offenders: A Survey. *New Society* 30 July.

McVicar, J. (1982) 'Violence in Prisons' in P. Marsh and A. Campbell (eds) *Aggression and Violence*. Oxford: Blackwell.

Marsh, P. , Rosser, E., and Harré, R. (1978) *The Rules of Disorder*. London: Routledge.

Martinson, R. (1974) What Works? Questions and Answers About Penal Reform. *Public Interest* 35.

Matza, D. (1964) *Delinquency and Drift*. Chichester: Wiley.

Mayhew, P., Clarke, R. V. G., Sturman, A., and Hough, J. M. (1976) *Crime as Opportunity*. Home Office Research Study No. 34. London: HMSO.

Mays, J. B. (1954) *Growing Up in the City*. Liverpool: Liverpool University Press.

Melly, G. (1972) *Revolt Into Style* Harmondsworth: Penguin.

Merton, R. K. (1938) Social Structure and Anomie. *American Sociological Review*.

Miller, W. B. (1958) Lower Class Culture as a Generating Milieu of Gang Delinquency. *Journal of Social Issues*.

—— (1976) Youth Gangs in the Urban Crisis Era, in J. F. Short, Jr (ed.) *Delinquency, Crime and Society*. Chicago.

Morris, T. P. (1957) *The Criminal Area*. London: Routledge.

Newman, O. (1972) *Defensible Space*. London: Architectural Press.

Parker, H. (1974) *The View from the Boys*. Newton Abbott: David & Charles.

Pearson, G. (1983) *Hooligan: A History of Respectable Fears*. London.

Reiss, A. (1975) Inappropriate Theories and Inadequate Methods as Policy Plagues: Self-Reported Delinquency and the Law, in A. Demerath *et al.* (eds) *Social Policy and Sociology*. New York.

Rutter, M. and Giller, H. (1983) *Juvenile Delinquency*. Harmondsworth: Penguin.

Scott, R. (1972) A Proposed Framework for Analysing Deviance as a Property of Social Order. In R. Scott and J. Douglas (eds) *Theoretical Perspectives on Deviance*. New York: Basic Books.

Shaw, C. and McKay, H. (1942) *Juvenile Delinquency and Urban Areas*. Chicago: University of Chicago Press.

Short, J. F., Jr (1960) Differential Association as a Hypothesis: Problems of Empirical Testing. *Social Problems*, Summer.

Stack, S. (1984) Income Inequality and Property Crime: A Cross-national Analysis of Relative Deprivation Theory. *Criminology*, May.

Sutherland, E. H. (1924) *Principles of Criminology*. Chicago. Extensively revised as Sutherland, E. and Cressey, D. (1979) *Criminology*. New York: Lippincott.

—— (1949) *White Collar Crime*. New York: Holt, Rinehart & Winston.

Taylor, I. (1981) *Law and Order: Arguments for Socialism*. London: Macmillan.

Taylor, I., Walton, P., and Young, J. (1973) *The New Criminology*. London: Routledge.

Townsend, P. (1976) *The Difficulties of Policies Based on the Concept of Area Deprivation*. London: Queen Mary College.

—— (1979) *Poverty in the United Kingdom*. Harmondsworth: Penguin.

West, D. J. and Farrington, D. P. (1973) *Who Becomes Delinquent?* London.

—— (1977) *The Delinquent Way of Life*. London: Heinemann.

—— 1982 *Delinquency: Its Roots, Careers and Prospects*. London: Macmillan.

Wilkins, L. (1964) *Social Deviance*. London.

Willis, P. (1977) *Learning to Labour*. Farnborough: Saxon House.

—— (1978) *Profane Culture*. London: Routledge.

Wilson, H. (1980) Parental Supervision: A Neglected Aspect of Delinquency. *British Journal of Criminology*.

Wilson, H. and Herbert G. (1978) *Parents and Children in the Inner City*. London.: Routledge.

Wootton, Barbara (1959) *Social Science and Social Pathology*. London: Allen & Unwin.

Young, J. (1971) The Role of the Police as Amplifiers of Deviance. In S. Cohen (ed.) *Images of Deviance*. Harmondsworth: Penguin.

13

YOUNG OFFENDERS
D. J. West

The extent to which criminal behaviour in general, and youthful delinquency in particular, are responses to social pressures, or are reflections of
individual weaknesses or peculiarities, remains a controversial issue.
Criminological fashions change, and there has been a marked swing away
from interest in the personal characteristics and family backgrounds of
delinquents towards concern with the social situations that provide the
stimulus and the opportunity for the commission of offences. To be
realistic and complete, however, explanations of delinquent behaviour
need to take into account the interaction between the individual and his
family on the one hand and external, environmental factors on the other.

At a time when fashion ran to a different extreme, and glaringly obvious
social influences were neglected in favour of investigations of family
pathology and searches for unconscious intra-psychic conflicts or obscure
physiological disturbances, Barbara Wootton stood out against such
foolishness. For instance, she was swift to point out the anomalous
consequences of the use of 'psychopathy' as a ground for evading responsibility for criminal acts, namely that the moderately wicked were to be
punished for their misdeeds, while the extremely wicked could claim to be
sick. In her influential book *Social Science and Social Pathology* (Wootton
1959), she exposed the weaknesses in the empirical evidence that was then
available in support of prevailing beliefs about delinquency, that it was
determined by such factors as large-sized families, criminal parents or
siblings, low social class, poverty, broken homes, working mothers, or
poor health. She found that the better controlled studies failed to substan-
tiate the importance of the last two factors, and although the others were
all supported to some extent by most of the published surveys, the

strength of the associations varied wildly according to the operational definitions chosen by investigators and the origins of the samples under scrutiny.

Those comments were made a long time ago. It may be timely to reconsider the evidence that, after all, factors reflecting individual temperament and family climate can make a substantial contribution to the likelihood of becoming a delinquent, especially a recidivist delinquent. The issue is more than academic. If individuals are not merely passive reactors to external pressures there is hope that preventive or therapeutic measures directed at them might change their patterns of behaviour and reduce the incidence of recidivism. The increasingly popular view that nothing of this kind works, and that the only hope lies in a proliferation of locks and keys, or in the faint prospect of some Utopian changes in society, may be unduly pessimistic.

Results indicating the high degree of vulnerability to delinquency of particular types or groups of persons are sometimes so obvious that they are overlooked. Males are certainly more vulnerable than females. In 1983, in England and Wales, over five times as many males as females under the age of 21 were cautioned or found guilty of indictable offences, that is over 250,000 males against less than 50,000 females.

The concentration of criminal convictions among a relatively small minority of males has been noted again and again. In the male cohort survey known as the Cambridge Study in Delinquent Development over a half of all the convictions recorded against young offenders were attributable to a recidivist minority comprising less than a quarter of the delinquents (West 1982: 16). In a cohort studied in Philadelphia 18 per cent of offenders were responsible for 52 per cent of all recorded offences (Wolfgang, Figlio, and Sellin 1972). To a very considerable extent the work of the courts in regard to young offenders reflects the activities of a hard core of persistent recidivists.

Persistent delinquents tend to transgress against the law in more ways than one, what is sometimes called 'cafeteria delinquency'. Offences such as violence against the person, criminal damage, or drug infractions are mostly to be found interspersed among the more common acquisitive offences in the criminal records of young recidivists. In the Cambridge study most of the thirty-two young males who were convicted of an offence of violence were recidivists, each with at least four convictions. Only four of them were free from convictions for offences other than violence. In a recently published survey of a Swedish birth cohort a minority of 6.6 per cent of arrested males were found to be intravenous drug users, but this minority accounted for 36.9 per cent of all the arrests of males in the survey (Fry 1985). Klein (1984) reviewed thirty-three published reports that gave data on the issue of versatility and found that twenty-one of them were strongly supportive of the hypothesis that delinquency is predominantly unpatterned offending. Particularly important was the result of the large Philadelphia study (Wolfgang, Figlio, and Sellin 1972) showing that the type of offence for which a delinquent gets arrested bears no relation to the type of offence for which he was arrested before. Klein observed that in a few self-report studies factor analysis had unearthed a slight tendency to specialization in some unusual offences, such as deviant sexuality, but lack of specificity remained the dominant feature. There was a clear indication that the persistent young offender's law-breaking is heterogeneous.

The Cambridge study went a step further and showed that the typical delinquent is anti-social in many aspects of attitude and lifestyle apart from the behaviour which brings about his conviction record. Compared with their non-delinquent peers, 18-year-old delinquents were significantly more likely to report involvement in fights, to express aggressive attitudes, to admit to drinking and driving, to smoke heavily, to have used prohibited drugs, to gamble, to have more sexual experiences than average, to be hostile to authorities, to have poor work records, to make little or no constructive use of their leisure time, and to mix with groups of trouble-makers. A clustering of these anti-social tendencies was especially characteristic of recidivist delinquents, but quite rare among non-delinquents. An anti-sociality score derived from the number of such deviant features, but ignoring actual convictions, proved to be highly predictive of future court appearances (West 1982: 77).

In the United States longitudinal studies have arrived at similar conclusions concerning the personal characteristics and habits of young delinquents. Jessor and Jessor (1977) surveyed successive cohorts of high-school and college students in Colorado, examining their self-reports of socially problematic behaviours and attitudes. A high degree of interrelatedness between different items of behaviour emerged. Marijuana use, precocious sexual experience, problem drinking, and poor attitude to work all tended to go together with delinquent-type acts such as cheating, stealing, aggression, and vandalism. The research was guided by a theoretical concept, namely that behaviour is patterned according to underlying personality structures, that is attitudinal dispositions and moral beliefs, which provide support and continuity for either conformist or deviant ways of life. For example, a low valuation of academic achievement, a jaundiced appreciation of society in general, a concern with personal independence, and a belief in the benefits of transgressions are likely to be associated with a constellation of problem behaviours. There was an obvious connection between anti-social behaviour and personality attributes.

The work of Lee Robins (1966, 1983) provides unusually clear evidence for the existence and chronicity of a syndrome that has become enshrined in the *Diagnostic and Statistical Manual* of the American Psychiatric Association under the rubric of 'anti-social personality'. She followed up after thirty years a sample of former clients of a child guidance clinic in St Louis, Missouri. Those who had been referred originally for behaviour problems, as opposed to those with neurotic complaints or to schoolfellows who had never been to the clinic, were very significantly more likely to evince anti-social features as adults, exemplified by arrests, poor work record, social alienation, drink problems, belligerency, sexual promiscuity, welfare dependency, broken marriages, and the production of children with behaviour disorders. The frequency, seriousness, and variety of the conduct disorder of childhood was quantitatively proportional to the risk of chronic anti-social personality disorder in later life, that is to say the more severe the childhood disturbance the more likely it was to persist.

The evidence is overwhelming that recidivist delinquency is often associated with an array of attributes fittingly described as the 'anti-social' or 'delinquent' personality. The features of aggressiveness, low frustration tolerance, impulsively hedonistic lifestyle (exemplified by lack of restraint in regard to drink, drugs, and sex), indifference to conventional standards, antagonism towards authorities, poor motivation and poor achievement at school and at work, and irresponsibility towards family responsibilities have been repeatedly described by clinicians and are now supported by sound empirical studies. The syndrome is very much a matter of degree. Indeed the concept of anti-social personality has been criticized for its over-inclusiveness and for the arbitrary nature of the cut-off between normal variation and pathological deviance. There is a danger that all young delinquents will be given the label, with the implication that they are necessarily doomed to life-long social disturbance. In fact, the steep drop in incidence of convictions after the age of 21 indicates otherwise.

The majority of delinquents settle down after a few years to become respectable, hard-working, family men. The Cambridge study found that many delinquents who had been rated as in some degree 'anti-social' at 18 ceased being convicted thereafter. By the age of 24 these former delinquents were hardly more 'anti-social' than their social peers who had never been found guilty of crime (West 1982: 80). The population of officially convicted delinquents includes many who appear in court only once or twice. They are not persistent recidivists and their 'anti-sociality', if it exists, is relatively mild and temporary. Radzinowicz and King (1977: 135) referred to three groups of people: those for whom crime was almost unthinkable, those for whom it was all too often irresistible, and those marginal cases who would offend on occasion given sufficient opportunity and encouragement. Many clients of the juvenile courts fall into the 'marginal' category, and their numbers have increased as the net-widening propensities of the modern criminal justice system draws into the clutches of the law mildly troublesome juveniles who would have been dealt with in previous times by teachers, parents, or by informal warning by the police. Nowadays, about a quarter of all males are expected to acquire a criminal record at some time during their juvenile or early adult lives (Farrington 1981). At most, only about a fifth of these are persistent, long-term recidivists or candidates for the label 'anti-social personality'.

The relatively small minority of persistent recidivists should be the main focus of concern. Boys who carry a high risk of becoming a part of this hard core can be identified at an early age. Notwithstanding all the justified criticisms of their exaggerated claims for the near infallibility of prediction, Glueck and Glueck (1950), in their classic follow-up studies, did show that certain deviant features of behaviour and family background were highly predictive of long-term delinquency careers. The Cambridge study also showed that an accumulation of adverse features, notably marked troublesomeness in their primary-school classes, combined with criminal convictions among parents or other family members, often linked with large, low-income families, limited intelligence and poor quality of parenting, were highly predictive of an early onset of court appearances and a delinquency career persisting into adult life. The difficulty is not in identifying the vulnerable group but in deciding what should be done to try to prevent or reduce their criminal tendency.

Attempts to mount intervention of any kind at an early stage meet with serious practical and ethical difficulties. The individuals most at risk are likely to come from families already known to the police and to have parents who distrust and strive to avoid social services and other authorities. Such families are likely to supervise and control their children inadequately and to resent any scheme that involves inspection, interference, or discussion of intimate family matters with controlling agencies. In short, the individuals most in need are the ones most difficult to contact. Moreover, intervention can only be justified if it is benign and effective. There are doubts about the wisdom of measures that involve bringing together groups of difficult children and attaching to them some stigmatizing label, such as educationally retarded, unsocialized or pre-delinquent. The effect may be to generate an oppositional group defensiveness and to reinforce deviant attitudes.

If families with vulnerable children are left to their own devices until their sons have become regular attenders at the juvenile court valuable opportunities for therapy may be lost. By that time the children are already alienated from the mainstream of scholastic life, their social and academic skills are poorly developed, and their friendship networks are concentrated among fellow delinquents and truants. On the other hand, if their earliest appearances at court are made the occasion for singling them out on the basis of their background and general social behaviour in order to apply different and more radical measures than those normally used for casual first offenders, this runs counter to the current preoccupation with formal justice.

The rise of the movement towards *Justice for Children* (Morris *et al.* 1980), interpreted in the narrow sense of just deserts, presents a powerful obstacle to any scheme of compulsory intervention in the lives of delinquents, however benignly intended, that does not take the form of punishment in proportion to the gravity or otherwise of the instant offence. The welfare philosophy that inspired the Children and Young Persons Act, 1969, according to which a finding of guilt would instigate an investigation into the delinquent's treatment needs, and if necessary removal from home under a care order, has been largely abandoned. In fact it was never really put into effect. The transfer of responsibility for the supervision and care of delinquents from the specialized probation and approved-school systems to the social services was followed by a great escalation of numbers of juveniles in penal custody. What should have been the last resort became more like the norm. Between 1971 and 1979 the proportion of male offenders aged 14 to 16 given detention centre orders more than doubled, from 4 per cent to 10 per cent, and the proportion sent to Borstal training also rose sharply, from 2 to 3 per cent (NACRO 1983).

One reason for the increase in the use of custody was the readiness of social workers to find their troublesome young clients unmanageable and to present the courts with reports pointing to the need for restraints. Residential care orders for delinquents became unpopular and the number of expensive places in children's homes occupied by delinquents dwindled, no doubt to the relief of the local authorities who had to pay the bills. More recent political pronouncements and legislative changes have further encouraged the operation of justice, in the shape of the 'short, sharp shock', in place of attempts at treatment. The introduction of youth custody following the Criminal Justice Act, 1982, has not improved the situation. Figures released by the Home Office (1985) comparing the first full year of operation of the Act (i.e. July, 1983, to June, 1984) with the calendar year 1981 show that, although the numbers dealt with by the courts have fallen, the numbers of males aged 14 to 20 received into penal custody have not fallen in proportion (27,050 in 1983–84 against 27,861 in 1981). More important, severer sentences have become considerably more frequent. In 1983–84, 16,210 young males were received into youth custody compared with only 14,200 who received equivalent sentences (i.e. Borstal training and imprisonment combined) in 1981.

A difficulty with the operation of the justice model is that it easily develops into an indefinite extension of punitive sentencing indiscriminately applied, regardless of the fact that in the natural course of events most young offenders will settle down of their own accord. Exclusive attention to the tariff or the instant offence permits no proper distinction between the more problematic cases and the marginal or opportunistic delinquents for whom a period in custody in the company of more dedicated law-breakers can be counter-productive. Giving an ever-increasing proportion of the young male working class a taste of custody could have deleterious effects in the long run, widening the divisions in a society that is already sadly polarized. On the other hand equally unfortunate consequences can arise from the failure to take constructive action about those offenders whose misbehaviour is part of an all-embracing anti-sociality syndrome that is likely to persist unless something is done. By the time a series of increasingly serious offences have appeared on the conviction record it may be too late to alter the course of events.

Recognition of the importance of the individual does not in itself do much to narrow down the nature of the problem of recidivism. The remarkable concentration of anti-social recidivists in successive generations of a small minority of families (West 1982: 72) suggests the possibility of some inherited propensity. A famous Danish study showed that the likelihood of an adopted boy acquiring a criminal record was influenced by whether his biological father had such a record (Mednick, Garbrielli, and Hutchings 1984). The survey was based on a national sample of 14,427 adoptions of male and female infants into unrelated households over the years 1924 to 1947. There was an incremental increase in the prevalence of criminal records among male adoptees, from 13.5 to 14.7 to 20.0 to 24.5 per cent according to whether no parent, an adopting parent, a biological parent, or both kinds of parent had a criminal record. The larger incremental increase was associated with having a biological rather than an adopting parent with a record, an observation highly suggestive of some inherited factor.

Few of the Danish male adoptees, only 4.09 per cent, were chronic offenders with three or more convictions, but these were responsible for 69.4 per cent of all the convictions recorded against the sample. On the assumption that a hereditary predisposition has more relevance to anti-sociality than to casual offending, one might expect a closer connection with biological parentage where chronic offending is involved, and that was what was found. Having a biological parent with three or more convictions, as against having no biological parent with a conviction, trebled a male adoptee's chances of himself acquiring three or more convictions, from 3 per cent to 9 per cent. This may seem a minor contribution to the totality of crime, but the thirty-seven recidivist sons of recidivist biological parentage, although constituting only 1 per cent of the 3,718 male adoptees, were responsible for 30 per cent of their convictions.

The possibility that the biological parents' criminality exerted its influence through the adopting parents being aware of it was ruled out by the observation that, where a biological parent's first conviction occurred after the adoption, when it would be unlikely to be heard about, the adoptee's chances of conviction were not reduced. A majority were placed with adopted parents either immediately after birth or during the first year, but the findings were no different among those who were not placed until somewhat later. The picture was slightly confused by the tendency of adoption agencies to try to match the social class of the adopting parents to those of the biological parents. However, analysis showed that within each category of social class there was an incremental increase in the percentage of adoptees with a criminal record according to the level (high, medium, or low) of the biological parents' social class. The adopting parents' social class made a difference to the likelihood of the adoptee being convicted, but the contribution of the biological parents' social class and criminality was also clearly significant (Van Dusen et al. 1983).

A congenital predisposition towards anti-sociality is rendered more plausible as a hypothesis by the observation among delinquents of features, such as depressed IQ levels, aggressivity, anomalous autonomic responses to stressful stimuli, hyperkinesis, and neurologically based learning difficulties, all of which may have biological determinants. Certain aspects of upbringing commonly classed as environmental causes of anti-sociality might actually be generated by the child's innate temperament. For example, a recent study by Home Office researchers of a representative sample of teenagers and their parents, while confirming the significant association between poor supervision and delinquency, found that the reason might be that difficult boys were more difficult to supervise. Boys who were reluctant to tell their parents what they were up to when they were out were far less likely to be well supervised. When certain characteristics of boys were taken into account, notably choice of delinquent friends and lack of guilt at the idea of stealing, the relationship between low parental supervision and delinquency in boys tended to disappear (Riley and Shaw 1985).

Whatever the contribution of innate predisposition, it can only operate through interaction with the environment. For the infant this means interaction with parents. No one doubts the importance of upbringing in the formation of character, and the earliest years are particularly important in setting the emotional tone that is likely to continue throughout development. The evidence suggests that an affectionate bond between the child and both parents, combined with sensible, caring, and consistent discipline, provides maximum protection against anti-sociality. Rows, recriminations, and outbursts of hostility or violence confuse and frighten, and interfere with the processes of socialization. Children reared in a favourable home atmosphere tend to imbibe readily their parents' standards and values, to apply them in their dealings with peers, and to be highly motivated to please their parents by conformity and achievement. In contrast, the child from a less fortunate background arrives at primary school without preparation, practice, or encouragement for learning, with less urge to please, with greater dependence on leadership from peers, and perhaps with an appearance, demeanour, language, and reputation that invite rejection from teachers and set him apart from better-placed pupils.

Emphasis on the importance of individual character and family background does not mean, as some critics suggest, a failure to recognize wider social influences (Johnstone 1980). The smooth functioning of family units depends upon support from outside sources in society. Under conditions of economic deprivation, unemployment, poor housing, and a neighbourhood lacking in amenities, and with a well-developed delinquent subculture of the streets, the tasks of child rearing and supervision become stressful and difficult (Wilson 1980). In better areas where the delinquency rate is lower the disturbed families who generate chronic delinquents stand out more starkly. Under conditions of severe external stress a much higher proportion of families become chaotic and unsupportive, and many children who would in better circumstances have become normally socialized develop anti-social traits. Although there has not as yet been sufficient time or opportunity for researchers to confirm the trend, there are powerful a priori reasons to expect the increase in permanent unemployment and dole dependency, which inevitably affect most harshly those least able to cope, to exacerbate these problems. Widening the gulf between the poor and the better off may be expected not only to stimulate rationally motivated property offences, but also to produce more of the seriously alienated, anti-social characters whose disruptive influence extends far beyond the commission of petty crime.

It may well be that political change could influence the incidence of anti-sociality more effectively than efforts directed towards individuals at risk, but that does not mean that such efforts are useless. In view of the multiplicity of factors that appear to be involved in the development of anti-sociality, it is not at all clear what form interventions should take. Disillusionment about traditional treatments for individual delinquents has overtaken many leading experts. Sinclair and Clarke (1982: 74), reviewing the state of knowledge on the prediction, treatment, and explanation of delinquency, declared that 'the track records of all acceptable treatments are so poor that to use them to try to reduce reconviction among persistent offenders is to waste resources that could be better directed elsewhere.'

There are good and bad reasons for scepticism about treatments. The majority of projects have to be rejected as evidence for positive effects, not because they are clear failures, but for lack of proper evaluation. Random allocation of subjects into treated and untreated groups is the surest and swiftest way to secure a conclusive result, but it is applied all too rarely, especially in research carried out in England. The most famous large-scale delinquency prevention project using this method, the Cambridge-Somerville Youth Project, involved a large sample of delinquency-prone Boston boys being arranged in matched pairs according to age, intelligence, area of residence, and so forth. They were then divided at random, one member of each pair being allocated to treatment and the other left alone. When followed up after thirty years, the treated group had no fewer criminal convictions and no fewer social problems than the untreated controls (McCord 1978).

The unsuccessful Cambridge-Somerville treatment consisted of lengthy but somewhat unstructured counselling and befriending. More recent work suggests that treatments have a better chance of success if they are directed towards a modification of specific aspects of behaviour, or to overcoming identifiable deficits in social skills or learning tasks. It appears preferable to involve the family and to try to change their ways of interacting rather than to tackle the delinquent in isolation. Soundly evaluated schemes with positive outcomes are few and far between, but Farrington (1982, 1985) has reviewed some of them.

In the Perry project in Ypsilanti, Michigan, the target was a group who might be expected to be highly delinquency-prone, namely 123 black children aged 3 to 4 from a slum neighbourhood, selected from families in poverty, and performing on the borderline of mental retardation on IQ tests. They were ranked by IQ and allocated alternately to one or other of two groups so as to produce similar IQ distributions. Similarly ranked children were exchanged between the groups until the sex distribution was the same. One group was randomly chosen for coaching in cognitive tasks and linguistic expression, given in small classes every weekday morning over one or two years. They were also seen with their mothers at weekly home visits. The idea was to give the group a 'head start' by preparing them for the demands to be met on entering school. On assessment at the age of 14, school achievement was very significantly better among the experimental group than among the controls. At 15 and again at 19 self-reported delinquency was significantly less among the experimental group and by 19 only 31 per cent of the experimental group, compared with 51 per cent of the controls, had been arrested or charged (Schweinhart and Weikart 1980; Barrueta-Clement et al. 1984).

This promising result, which cries out for replication, could be considered a vindication of the belief that amelioration of disadvantage in competition at school, which is such a constant feature of anti-social juveniles, would have a preventive effect. The home visits may have influenced relationships as well as learning, but the concentration on testing and improving abilities no doubt enhanced the acceptability of the programme to the parents.

Another experiment cited by Farrington was the Youth Service Program of the University of California at Irvine. Troublesome juveniles were referred by the police in an effort to forestall their probable progress up the ladder of juvenile justice. A few were given special attention as 'emergencies', because it was thought unethical to do otherwise, but a random selection from all the rest was made to decide who should be admitted to the scheme. The treatment consisted of active interventions directed towards specific goals, such as teaching parents better ways of imposing sanctions and giving rewards, improving communication within families, trying to alter situations that seemed to be provoking trouble, and providing the juveniles with social-skills training and with adult volunteers to act as friends and models. The scheme differed from the more traditional casework of the Cambridge-Somerville Project in recognizing the importance of environmental pressures and trying to engage the adults concerned as well as the juvenile himself. Significant differences between the recidivism rates of the experimental and control groups were observed.

Results such as these give grounds for qualified optimism. Efforts to provide effective treatment for actual and potential anti-social delinquents should continue, but it is essential that they should be subjected to proper control and evaluation. Many causes of anti-sociality are known or suspected, but only controlled experiment will show how far and by what means affected individuals can be helped. The juvenile justice system as presently operated has proved a blunt and ineffectual instrument. The increasing tendency to give young offenders custodial sentences for almost all types of offence may satisfy a particular theory of justice, but it is deplored in a recent report by the Association of Directors of Social Services (Jillings 1985). The report contends that juvenile courts are unsuited to the task of making discriminating decisions as to what to do about young offenders and suggests replacing them with non-judicial tribunals on the lines of the system in Scotland. That might indeed be an improvement, but what is needed even more is investment in the development and testing of interventions directed towards those offenders whose troublesomeness is of a kind unlikely to be changed by conventional penal sanctions.

REFERENCES

Barrueta-Clement, J. R., Schweinhart, L. J., Barnett, W. S., Epstein, A. S., and Weikart, D. P. (1984) *Changed Lives.* Ypsilanti, Mich.: High/Scope.

Farrington, D. P. (1981) The Prevalence of Convictions. *British Journal of Criminology* 21: 123–35.

—— (1982) Randomized Experiments in Crime and Justice. In M. Tonry and N. Morris (eds) *Crime and Justice.* Vol. 4. Chicago: University of Chicago Press.

—— (1985) Delinquency Prevention in the 1980s. *Journal of Adolescence* 8: 3–16.

Fry, L. J. (1985) Drug Abuse and Crime in a Swedish Birth Cohort. *British Journal of Criminology* 25: 46–59.

Glueck, S. and Glueck, E. T. (1950) *Unravelling Juvenile Delinquency.* Cambridge, Mass.: Harvard University Press.

Home Office (1985) Young Offenders in Prison Department Establishments under the Criminal Justice Act 1982: July 1983–June 1984. *Home Office Statistical Bulletin,* 5 February. London: Home Office Statistical Department.

Jessor, R. and Jessor, S. L. (1977) *Problem Behavior and Psychological Development.* New York: Academic Press.

Jillings, J. (1985) *Children Still in Trouble.* Taunton: Association of Directors of Social Services.

Johnstone, J. W. C. (1980) Delinquency and the Changing American Family. In D. Shichor and D. H. Kelly (eds) *Critical Issues in Juvenile Delinquency.* Lexington, Mass.: Lexington Books.

Klein, M. W. (1984). Offence Specialisation and Versatility among Juveniles. *British Journal of Criminology* 24: 185–94.

McCord, J. (1978) A Thirty Year Follow up of Treatment Effects. *American Psychologist* 33: 284–89.

Mednick, S. A., Gabrielli, W. F., and Hutchings, B. (1984) Genetic Influences in Criminal Convictions: Evidence from an Adoption Cohort. *Science* 224(4651): 891–94.

Morris, A., Giller, H., Szwed, E., and Geach, H. (1980) *Justice for Children.* London: Macmillan.

NACRO (1983) *NACRO briefing: Trends in the Use of Custody, 1971–1981.* London: National Association for the Care and Resettlement of Offenders.

Radzinowicz, L. and King, J. (1977) *The Growth of Crime.* New York: Basic Books.

Riley, D. and Shaw, M. (1985) *Parental Supervision and Juvenile Delinquency.* Home Office Research Study No. 83. London: HMSO.

Robins, L. (1966) *Deviant Children Grown Up*. Baltimore, Md.: Williams and Wilkinson.

—— (1983) Continuities and Discontinuities in Childhood Behavior Disorders. In D. E. Mechanic (ed.) *Handbook of Health and Health Services*. New York: Free Press.

Schweinhart, L. J. and Weikart, D. P. (1980) *Young Children Grown Up*. Ypsilanti, Mich.: High/Scope.

Sinclair, I. and Clarke, R. (1982) Predicting, Treating and Explaining Delinquency. In M. P. Feldman (ed.) *Criminal Behaviour*. Vol 1. Chichester: Wiley.

Van Dusen, K. T., Mednick, S. A., Gabrielli, W. F., and Hutchings, B. (1983) Social Class and Crime in an Adoption Cohort. *Journal of Criminal Law and Criminology* 74: 249–69.

West, D. J. (1982) *Delinquency: Its Roots, Careers and Prospects*. London: Macmillan.

Wilson, H. (1980) Parental Supervision: A Neglected Aspect of Delinquency. *British Journal of Criminology* 20: 203–35.

Wolfgang, M. E., Figlio, R. M., and Sellin, T. (1972) *Delinquency in a Birth Cohort*. Chicago: University of Chicago Press.

Wootton, B. (1959) *Social Science and Social Pathology*. London: Allen & Unwin.

14

INNOVATION
IN PENAL PRACTICE
Gordon Trasler

INTRODUCTION

Innovations in ways of dealing with offenders, in the form of new sentences and new regimes, are usually responses to what are perceived as crises: serious overcrowding in prisons, the failure of existing methods to dissuade all but a few convicted offenders from further involvement in crime, or an upsurge of some form of criminal activity, inconspicuous in the past, which seems to pose a threat to social order and tranquillity. For the most part, governments in office assign a low priority to issues of penal reform, and the Home Office, which has responsibility for the administration of the penal system, typically (and understandably) adopts a defensive stance: it responds to the scandals which overtake aspects of the system from time to time, sometimes neutralizing the problem by a delaying tactic – often the appointment of a Royal Commission – or by *ad hoc* action which owes more to political considerations than to the implications of social-scientific research. A Home Office remit which also includes so diverse and sensitive a range of responsibilities as immigration control, practice in the scientific use of animals for experimental purposes, and the prevention of addiction to dangerous drugs, inevitably leads to an emphasis on 'damage limitation', so that the long-term needs of the penal system tend to be set on one side in favour of more immediate problems.

All governments are obliged to respond to public opinion channelled through MPs' assessments of the issues which are currently of concern to their constituents. Government managers and their opposition counterparts use this imperfect information in determining the amount of parliamentary time to be devoted to various issues of policy. In practice, matters concerning the penal system are accorded a comparatively small allocation of parliamentary time (Drewry 1974), though they may be aired rather more generously if the Home Secretary of the day is a figure of seniority and high standing (see Land 1975). Unfortunately, in the British system the Home Office is not in the first rank of ministries, and – at least since the Second World War – some of those who have occupied this post have been men whose prestige in their own parties, and in the country as a whole, has not been high. (R. A. Butler, Roy Jenkins, and William Whitelaw are the most obvious exceptions to this observation.)

Although (as we have remarked) governments seldom give issues of penal policy high priority, 'law and order' is frequently a plank in electoral platforms, and it is generally thought that the undertaking to 'get tough' with offenders is worth a great many votes, as indeed was true of promises to reinstate capital punishment in the 1950s. It is a common assumption among party strategists that the professed intention to impose more severe penalties on those convicted of serious crime (or of particular crimes, such as the murder of policemen or terrorist bomb attacks on prominent people) is highly attractive to the 'floating voter'.

VEHICLES OF CHANGE:
THE ADVISORY COUNCILS

As Barbara Wootton has pointed out the last half-century has brought major changes in the composition and procedures of advisory bodies, in the field of penal policy as elsewhere in the concerns of government. The procedure that was followed in the first two or three decades of this century was to select a group of men, distinguished in their own careers but with no particular claim to knowledge of the matters they were required to study, 'with, in recent years, the addition of the statutory woman'. Not surprisingly, such bodies 'modelled themselves on the procedure of a court of law, and reached their conclusions by "taking evidence" from those who had the knowledge and experience that they themselves lacked' (Wootton 1977: 13).

The substitution of working groups of men and women 'already versed in some aspect of the subject to be investigated' was signalled by the formation of the Advisory Council on the Treatment of Offenders (ACTO) in 1944. Until it was dissolved in 1966, that body produced a series of reports on matters of penal policy, some of considerable technical complexity, such as the merits and drawbacks of the suspended sentence, the case for corporal punishment, the organization of after-care, and the system of preventive detention. But Hood (1974) notes that ACTO's recommendations regarding the suspended sentence were ignored, and at least one major innovation – the parole system – was not referred to that body. ACTO was succeeded by the Advisory Council on the Penal System (ACPS), a smaller body which was similarly composed of people with experience or specialized knowledge of crime and penal policies. The ACPS delegated some of its work to subcommittees, producing in this way a series of reports on particular issues, such as the Widgery Report, *Reparation by the Offender*, and the Wootton Report, *Non-Custodial and Semi-Custodial Penalties* (of which more will be said later). It also conducted a wide-ranging review of provision for *Young Adult Offenders*, under the chairmanship of Sir Kenneth Younger, and the ill-received *Sentences of Imprisonment – a Review of Maximum Penalties*, under Baroness Serota. On the other hand, the short-lived Royal Commission on the Penal System (1964–66) seems in some respects to have resembled the older style of consultation. Its terms of reference were impossibly broad:

> 'to re-examine both penal theory and practice "in the light of modern knowledge of crime and its causes" and "to assess how far the available methods of punishment achieve their objectives and to review the way in which the services actually operate and are administered. In addition it was charged with reporting whether any changes in penal methods were desirable, including "the arrangements and responsibility for selecting the sentences to be imposed on particular offenders".'
>
> (Hood 1974)

(The essay just quoted contains a detailed discussion of the style and significance of advisory bodies, including the Royal Commission.)

COMMUNITY SERVICE ORDERS

In November, 1966 the Advisory Council on the Penal System was asked by Mr Roy Jenkins, the Home Secretary, 'to consider what changes and additions might be made in the existing range of non-custodial penalties, disabilities, and other requirements which may be imposed on offenders'. The council delegated this task to a subcommittee of eight people, chaired by the Baroness Wootton, which proceeded at a rapid pace, through thirty-nine meetings, several visits to other countries, and the study of a number of reports and evaluations of non-custodial penal measures in use elsewhere. The subcommittee included 'three JPs, (one [Lady Wootton] with over thirty years' metropolitan experience) as well as a Q.C. practising in the Criminal Courts, a Chief Constable, a Professor of Psychology with extensive experience with prisoners and an academic criminologist' (Wootton 1977: 19). The central problem, which then seemed urgent (though it had not yet developed into the crisis which has now overtaken the prison system), was to devise ways of restricting the prison population to those offenders who needed to be kept under lock and key in order to safeguard the public. The sub-committee devoted much of its time to studying policies and practices elsewhere (in the United States, Scandinavia, and New Zealand, for example) in the search for schemes which appeared to be no less effective, as measured by the rate of reconviction, than the custodial sentences which they replaced. (The comparison is a difficult one, because non-custodial measures necessarily entail the risk of further offending during the period of the penalty, whereas men dealt with by means of custodial sentences are, for the most part, incapacitated from offending during the period of the custodial sentence.)

The Wootton Subcommittee reported, through the Advisory Council, in the summer of 1970. They commended the Swedish day fine system, but reluctantly concluded that it would be very difficult to transplant the scheme into the different conditions which obtained in England and Wales. They commented on the practicability of introducing various kinds of 'intermittent custody' (such as weekend imprisonment), and of establishing more senior attendance centres: they also made specific proposals concerning the deferment of sentence and the disqualification of individuals 'convicted of a sexual offence or an offence of violence involving a child or a young person' from occupations involving contact with children. The subcommittee saw merit in each of these proposals, but noted that most of them would involve additional expenditure; intermittent custody schemes, for example, would in practice require the construction of additional prisons or camps, since it would not be practicable to use existing prisons for ordinary (continuous) imprisonment and for intermittent custody.

The proposal to which the subcommittee attached the most importance was the introduction of Community Service Orders (CSOs) as a new form of penalty. The nature of the order itself, the need to determine whether the offender was suitable for community service and willing to consent to the order, and the administration of the scheme were set out in some detail. In conformity with its own principle that 'Where our suggestions take the form of completely untried kinds of treatment it would, we think, be a wise precaution to proceed initially by means of controlled experiments', the subcommittee recommended that 'a few pilot schemes should be established to test its practicality.'

It should not be thought that the Wootton Subcommittee simply observed, pondered, listened to submissions, and published their proposals. While the subcommittee was contemplating the introduction of some form of community service scheme, it devoted a number of sessions to discussions with practitioners (such as probation officers, the organizers of various groups of social-service volunteers, members of the Magistrates' Association, the Chief Metropolitan Magistrate, and the Lord Chief

Justice of England) and with civil servants. These discussions were invaluable in tackling several crucial issues: what the relationship should be between the CSO scheme and the voluntary agencies (which agreed wholeheartedly with the suggestion that they should take a major share in the provision of tasks, and that offenders would work side by side with volunteers, in most cases); who should provide the administrative structure for the scheme; whether the court should have the offender's consent to the making of a Community Service Order (as it does in making a probation order); and whether the scheme ought in principle to be available to all kinds of offenders. What was set out in the report thus represented a negotiated scheme, which owed a great deal to these extended discussions with people with experience and expertise in various occupations in the field of criminal justice and work with offenders. The odd, but traditional, custom of describing these discussions as 'receiving evidence' does not capture the nature of these transactions. An extensive critique of the way in which the Wootton Subcommittee approached its task is contained in Hood's (1974) essay, 'Criminology and Penal Change': some of his criticisms have been answered (if not to his satisfaction) in spirited rejoinders by the Chairman of the Subcommittee (Wootton 1977, 1978).

Home Office officials were present at meetings of the Wootton Subcommittee, and were therefore fully conversant with the reasoning which led to its recommendations. A small working party of civil servants, chaired by Mr E. N. Kent, was given the task of drafting legislation which was incorporated in the Criminal Justice Act of 1972. Although in general the draft produced by the working party followed the recommendations of the Wootton Subcommittee, it departed from them in several particulars. First, it restricted Community Service Orders to imprisonable offences, thus excluding two groups of offenders for whom community service might be appropriate: people convicted of traffic offences and fine defaulters. Second, a minimum period of 40 hours and a maximum of 240 hours (twice the upper limit suggested in the Wootton Report) were imposed. Third, the recommendation that 'it should be possible to order community service either as a requirement of a probation order or as a direction unaccompanied by a probation order' (Wootton Report 1970: paragraph 56) was not followed: the terms of the Act preclude the combination of probation and community service. While these changes were apparently made in order to emphasize that a CSO was a serious penalty which made considerable demands on the offender's time and energy, they have produced certain anomalies which are discussed in Wootton 1978: Chapter 7. (A useful account of the implementation of the scheme is contained in Smith (1974).)

The six pilot schemes for community service set up in 1973, and closely monitored by the Home Office Research Unit, showed that this way of dealing with offenders was viable, and within the next four years or so it was extended to the rest of England and Wales. The experience of the first few years of CSOs has been encouraging: a majority of offenders complete the number of hours' work imposed under the order, the numbers of individuals reconvicted during the period of the order are broadly comparable with those for probation (as far as one can judge), and the recidivism rate following the completion of the terms of the order is certainly no worse than that for men discharged from prison.

DETENTION CENTRES

The first detention centres were established some thirty years ago under the provisions of the Criminal Justice Act of 1948. A junior centre (Campsfield House) for youths aged 14 to 16 was opened in 1952, and a senior one for those aged 17 to 20 (Blantyre House) in 1954. The number of young people detained rose steadily year by year, so that by 1977 there were more than 5,000 serving periods of detention. Recidivism rates for the detention centres, like those for Borstals, also increased, so that by 1974 three-quarters of those who were the subjects of detention orders were convicted of further offences within two years of release.

As Hilary Land (1975) points out, the introduction of the detention centre system was prompted by political judgements of a complex kind. There was concern about the practice of sending young offenders to prison, and in particular about the fairly sharp increase in young offenders for whom some suitable penalty had to be found. The use of corporal punishment for young offenders was also at issue, both in Parliament and among the several organizations striving for penal reform. The introduction of detention centres was widely regarded as the price of phasing out corporal punishment. This explains the manner in which the proposal to set up tough, punitive institutions surfaced in the debate on the Criminal Justice Bill which was primarily concerned with the inappropriateness of sending youthful offenders to ordinary prisons and the desirability (or imprudence) of abolishing judicial corporal punishment. Government ministers seem to have been remarkably vague about the sort of regime that one might expect to find in such an institution, save only that it would be tough and intended to be deterrent rather than reformative. But the need to reassure Parliament that the abolition of corporal punishment would not leave society defenceless against the predatory young offender appears to have been the main reason for including, in the Criminal Justice Bill, provision for the building of these new establishments at such time as resources might become available for that purpose. For example, the Home Secretary of the day, Chuter Ede, identified the primary purpose of detention centres as a means of deterring young men who seemed destined for a career in crime – not as a vehicle of 'treatment' or education. The detention centre order was intended to provide a more effective alternative both to short terms of imprisonment and to corporal punishment. The notion of the 'short, sharp shock' was thus rooted in the original conception of the purpose of detention centres, and certainly did not originate in the rhetoric of the 1979 election campaign. (Land (1975) remarks that the expression was used in the Prison Commissioners' report for 1952.) 'Getting tough with young offenders' meant, from the outset, submitting them to Spartan conditions, "brisk" programmes, enforced obedience to exacting, imposed rules about dress, cleanliness and punctuality.'

The fact that convictions of adolescent offenders rose steadily from the middle 1950s ensured that the detention centres continued to be the focus of a great deal of interest – and criticism – in Parliament. There remained a strong lobby in favour of the reintroduction of corporal punishment, both in the House and at Conservative Party Conferences. Successive Home Secretaries were obliged to emphasize the punitive nature of detention regimes in order to deflect demands for the return of birching, which were by this time being given prominence in the national press.

The question of whether detention centres were generally appropriate for young offenders, of whether those to be sent there would be selected according to their personal characteristics, or perhaps the nature (rather than the length) of their criminal records, surfaced from time to time but was never settled. During the debate on the Criminal Justice Bill, in 1947, Chuter Ede referred to:

'the young offender for whom a fine or probation order would be inadequate, but who does not require the prolonged period of training which is given by an approved school or a borstal institution. There is a type of offender to whom it seems necessary to give a short, but sharp reminder that he is getting into ways that will inevitably land him in disaster.'[1]

(House of Commons Debates, vol.444, col.2138)

Chuter Ede later explained:

'What we hope to provide in detention centres is a short, sharp punishment that will cause the young offender clearly to realise the injudiciousness of attempting continuously to flout the law. I want that part of the work to be clearly understood by all concerned. Education and reformative training will, I hope, go on simultaneously; but I do not want these places turned into a kind of junior or specialised approved school. They are entirely different in their purpose.'

(Standing Committee A, 5 February 1948, col.971)

During the Commons debate on the 1947 Bill the Home Secretary described the detention centres as 'experimental', and there was much vagueness about the nature of the regimes which they would offer – except, of course, that they were to be 'brisk' and exacting, demanding unquestioning obedience and high standards of cleanliness, neatness, and punctuality. It is clear, however, that the initial intention, to give young men an unpleasant shock which would have a strongly deterrent effect, in contrast to the training regimes to be found in the Borstals, gradually gave way to a more positive view. Thus Grunhut, who conducted studies of the first detention centres, commented that 'it has been possible to adapt the original conception of the "short, sharp shock" to include a limited, but positive, form of training' (Land 1975: 358). This tentative defence of treatment as an appropriate goal for detention regimes was strongly endorsed by the Advisory Council on the Treatment of Offenders, which noted that 'the system has already shown some flexibility in expanding the original conception of a regime based primarily on deterrence to include elements of positive personal training' (ACTO 1959: 10), and recommended an expansion of the system as a means of countering the rise in adolescent crime. The written evidence submitted by the Home Office to the abortive Royal Commission on the Penal System gives a succinct account of the purposes and nature of detention regimes (Vol.I 1967: 36–9).

TOUGH DETENTION REGIMES

In developing penal policies for young offenders, following the passage of the 1948 Act, successive governments relied to a considerable extent on the advice which they received from various sources. Home Office ministers consulted their advisory councils, ACTO and its successor, ACPS, and they sought the views of a variety of non-governmental organizations, such as the Howard League for Penal Reform and the Magistrates' Association. All governments must take heed of the views of their own supporters, in and out of Parliament. Such was the strength of feeling about the rapidly rising numbers of criminal convictions among youths and young men that annual party conferences – especially those of the Conservative Party – usually included a vigorous debate about 'law and order' issues. It was largely taken for granted that responsible governments should seek advice from bodies and individuals with expert knowledge and experience, in the field of penal policy as in other areas of state activity. One may guess that the advice they received was often conflicting, and the process of consultation was certainly used, on occasion, as a defence of policies that were unpopular among back-benchers and active party members in the constituencies, but the propriety of seeking such advice was seldom questioned – except, perhaps, in relation to the special question of abolition or retention of the death penalty.

All this was to change in the electoral campaign of 1979. As it happened, the Advisory Council on the Penal System had been dissolved a little while before. It was a common practice with other advisory bodies to disband the group from time to time, in order to bring in new members in the place of those who had become stale, complacent, or otherwise ineffective, and it was assumed that the ACPS would be reconstituted after the general election. It was unfortunate that the last report from the ACPS, dealing with the maximum length of custodial sentences, had been widely mis-understood – or perhaps simply misrepresented – in the popular press and elsewhere, as arguing for a general reduction in prison sentences, at a time of anxiety about increasing crime rates. The incident was a striking example of misjudgement by those officials whose job it was to dissemin-ate information about the findings of these deliberations – which had, of course, been commissioned by the Home Secretary – but there is no reason to suspect that this minor fiasco formed the reason for not reappointing the council after the general election. A major change in attitude towards experts and their advice seems to have been the main cause.

The Conservative Party Manifesto for the 1979 general election in-cluded a brief statement of policy for 'deterring the criminal'. In relation to young offenders, this read: 'We need more compulsory attendance centres for hooligans at junior and senior levels. In certain detention centres we will experiment with a tougher regime as a short, sharp shock for young criminals.' William Whitelaw, the Home Secretary, introduced these proposals to the 1979 Conference of the Conservative Party in the following terms:

> 'life will be conducted at a brisk tempo. Much greater emphasis will be put on hard and constructive activities, on discipline and tidiness, on self-respect and respect for those in authority. We will introduce on a regular basis drill, parades and inspections. Offenders will have to earn their limited privileges by good behaviour . . . these will be no holiday camps and I sincerely hope that those who attend them will not ever want to go back there.'

> (Quoted by Thornton *et al.*: 1984: 1)

The task of translating this specification into a practical programme seems to have been undertaken by the Home Secretary himself, presum-ably with the assistance of his junior ministers and senior civil servants; in any event, he does not appear to have sought the views of the Young Offender Psychology Unit in the Home Office or of the Research and Planning Unit of the Home Office about the design and implementation of the experiment. However that may be, the decision was taken to set up 'tougher' regimes in two establishments, Send (a junior detention centre in Surrey) and New Hall (a senior detention centre in Yorkshire). The results of the change in regime were to be evaluated. It might appear that the principle advanced by the Wootton Subcommittee (and strongly advocated by its chairman), that innovations in penal practice should be tested in a few institutions or areas before being adopted by the system as a whole, had been heeded in the Home Office. However, subsequent events suggest that ministers were in no doubt that the experimental regimes would be a success, and simply wished to demonstrate that what they took to be a realistic, common-sense approach to penal problems was to be preferred to the ineffective policies which had been advocated by academics and other advisers during the preceding decade, and which had brought steady increases in the level of adolescent crime and in the rates of reconviction of young people leaving conventional establishments.

As in other aspects of its policies, the first Thatcher administration reflected 'conviction politics' and an impatience with the tradition that the professionals and experts must be consulted before major changes were planned. The 'tougher detention regimes' initiative was certainly a major policy development of a kind which won general approval at the Conservative Party Conference, and had the backing of several members of the Cabinet, including the Prime Minister. But it was a development that would be coldly received by the criminological community, and by many professionals in criminal justice and the penal system. Holloway (1984) notes that the *Report of the Advisory Council on the Penal System in Detention Centres,*

> 'whilst endorsing the confirmed purposive atmosphere of detention centres, had the effect of stressing that the punitive function was met by the incarceration itself without the need for further punishment from the regime itself, that individualisation was important, that some of the more regimented activities were not productive, and that numerous areas such as education and physical education should be further developed . . . and there were to be more opportunities for community work.'

In the circumstances there was little point in consultation: the initiative was in the hands of the Home Secretary who showed no reluctance to use his powers.

Evaluation of 'tougher' regimes

The decision to mount an evaluation of the experiment had already been taken, but deciding who should undertake this task, and what kind of resources and arrangements would be appropriate, presented problems.

The obvious choice was the Research and Planning Unit in the Home Office, but – even setting aside the risk that politicians and criminologists alike might be sceptical of the outcome, especially if it was favourable – there was the problem that the Unit already had heavy commitments, and was about to embark on an extensive programme of research into problems of policing, which were generally thought to be of greater importance at that time. It thus fell to the Young Offender Psychology Unit (YOPU), with help from the statistical branch of the Home Office, to take on the task of evaluation, with the help of a steering committee which consisted of representatives of various divisions of the Home Office (including the Research Unit) and the Department of Health and Social Security (DHSS), and two independent advisers (a distinguished statistician and a criminologist) who might also act as guarantors of the objectivity of the research should this be necessary (in the event it was not). The decision to have the evaluation done within the Home Office, rather than by an independent research team, probably reflected the government's desire to press ahead with all possible speed, and perhaps its distrust of criminological researchers and social scientists generally.

As it was, the evaluation team, led by Vernon Holloway, were in the unusual position of having to design and implement their study at very short notice, when they had not participated in the arrangements for the experiment itself. With commendable prescience, Holloway and his colleagues undertook a thorough study of six detention centres (three junior and three senior), including the two which were to be required to establish 'tougher' regimes, before the identity of the experimental institutions was made known, so that the staff of these establishments, and indeed the researchers themselves, did not know which were the two that would make the change. This made it possible to make before-and-after comparisons in the experimental institutions as well as continuing observations of the four 'control' establishments, and thus considerably extend the research to include studies of the processes of change and adaptation to a new regime imposed from without.

Potential conflicts between political and practical considerations and the demands of the evaluation became apparent early in the experiment. The government, evidently keen to demonstrate its determination to press ahead with measures designed to contain the rising crime figures, extended the experiment to embrace two further 'tougher' regimes without first consulting the research committee or the YOPU evaluation team. This complicated the study considerably, if only because the staff of the second pair of institutions were likely to react rather differently to the change compared with their pioneer colleagues at Send and New Hall. Administrative changes to the catchment areas of two of the detention centres in the experiment were another source of difficulty, and indeed it seems likely that doubts about the representativeness of the intake at Send, which took boys from parts of London and from the immediate locality in proportions which changed markedly during the first year of the study, prompted this new initiative.

It was evident from the outset that the government wanted and expected quick results which could be reported to Parliament, in order to encourage its own back-benchers and to satisfy the impatient questions of MPs with an interest in penal affairs, including particularly those who belonged to the All-Party Penal Affairs Committee chaired by Mr Robert Kilroy-Silk. For their part, the researchers and their steering committee were aware that newly-introduced regimes often show a novelty effect – impressively low rates of post-discharge recidivism, which tend, after a while, to return to the high rates of reconviction that have become characteristic of institutions for young offenders. There was anxiety that the first batch of results might give rise to unjustified optimism about the effectiveness of the 'tough' regimes, and so to premature pressure to impose them throughout the detention centre system.

The results of the first phase of the study (Thornton *et al.* 1984) indicated that the 'tough' regimes were no more – or less – effective than those in the control establishments in preventing post-release recidivism; nor was there any sign that the prospect of being sent to a 'tough' detention centre was deterring young men in the locality from engaging in crime. In short, the primary purpose of the experiment – to demonstrate that 'getting tough' with young offenders would reduce crime – had failed; nor was there any support for the contrary belief, that strict regimes have a negative effect upon the behaviour of those who experience them. More detailed study of the report shows that relations between boys and staff in the 'tough' regimes remained fairly good, despite the irritations of frequent inspections and changes of clothes. On the whole the parade-ground drill and the extra physical education which were to be central features of the regimes (being borrowed, as William Whitelaw observed, from military training) proved enjoyable, and a welcome diversion from periods of hard work, which had to be curtailed to make time for these new activities. There were costs, especially to the education programmes, but these were felt more keenly by the staff than by the boys.

The findings of the first phase of the experiment and the publication of the report, *Tougher Regimes in Detention Centres* (Thornton *et al.* 1984) were announced by the Home Secretary, Mr Leon Brittan, in a written answer to a question put down by a former Home Office minister, Mr Mark Carlisle, on 24 July, 1984. It was a carefully constructed reply. He said:

'I am now putting in hand a programme of work to establish a consistent regime for the whole detention centre system – including those establishments which have been operating the experimental regime – with a view to enhancing the role of detention centres as a distinctive feature of the penal system commanding the confidence of the courts. The experiment will now be concluded [a rather surprising comment, since the evaluation was to continue to study longer-term reconviction rates of the young men in the original sample, and to follow through those who comprised the second wave of inmates]. . . . Formal drill sessions and extra physical education will not be continued: many trainees came to find them undemanding and their inclusion would leave less time for other features – notably work – which the new regime will emphasise. . . . The evaluation report finds that the experimental regime had no statistically significant effect on the rate at which trainees were reconvicted: while it was right to test whether any such effect would be produced this conclusion is not surprising against the general background of research findings on the identifiable deterrent effect of particular sentences.'

A similar comment was made by Lord Elton (a Home Office minister) in *The Times* on 13 March, 1985. Lord Elton was replying to a letter from the Chairman of the Howard League, Mr Andrew Rutherford, which was published in the same newspaper on 8 March. Mr Rutherford wrote:

'The Home Secretary's decision to extend the "tougher" regime to all detention centres as from March 6 is to be deplored on two counts. Firstly, it rejects the principle that the custodial sentence is intended as a punishment and not for punishment. Secondly, Mr Brittan's decision rejects research findings provided by his own department. Honouring a manifesto commitment, Lord Whitelaw announced in October 1979 that two experimental "tougher" regime detention centres would be evaluated. A careful and expensive study was published in July, 1984. . . . The research demonstrated that the tougher regimes had no discernible individual or general deterrent effect. Nothing in the research indicated that the tougher regime would reduce the 70 per cent reconviction rate (over 24 months) of detention centres. It is probable that Lord Whitelaw would have used the research findings to disarm the shrill punitive elements within his party. For Mr Brittan and his advisers, image appears to take precedence and this bodes ill for rational policy on criminal justice.'

Lord Elton responded to these criticisms in the following terms:

'Andrew Rutherford . . . wrongly claims that we have ignored the evaluation findings. The narrow point that reconviction rates were not significantly affected by the experimental regime hardly came as a surprise. The structured initial two-week programme, the emphasis on standard setting, the sharpening of the grade system, the way in which inmates will progress from the most basic kinds of work to less unpopular tasks – these all respond to the research evidence, as well as to management experience of running detention centres and the comments of the prison service unions. . . .'

It is hard to reconcile these comments with the stated purpose of the experiment at the outset. None of the trainees in the two experimental establishments, Send and New Hall, was sentenced to more than three months' detention, although their populations had previously included a minority of youths serving the maximum of six months. The researchers observed that the first two or three weeks were stressful for new-arrived trainees, but that:

'by about the third week of his sentence a significant acclimatisation has taken place. Much of the uncertainty about the institution has been resolved, [the trainee] now feels more "at home" with the routine which is no longer seen as particularly demanding or stern, and his general mood is much lighter. His increasing confidence in his ability to manage his surroundings is expressed in a more forward and positive attitude to staff (with reservations), and also by a growth of deviant behaviour.'

(Thornton et al. 1984: 171–72)

This was presumably what prompted the Home Secretary to write:

'The report's confirmation of the impact on inmates of the first few days of sentence is especially important. We shall build on this finding – and on the changes made by detention centres in May 1983 to accommodate the new two week minimum effective sentence – to make a brisk and structured initial two week programme a key feature of the new regime. This will highlight basic and unpopular work such as scrubbing floors; increased emphasis on parades and inspections, and minimal privileges and association.'

(Weekly Hansard, Issue 1320, 24 July, 1984: cols 578–80)

CONCLUDING COMMENT

The examples reviewed in this essay serve to show that innovations in penal practice come about by diverse means, usually involving legislators, organized pressure groups (such as the Howard League and the National Association for the Care and Resettlement of Offenders), the predominant values and policies which characterize governments (especially incoming governments), and sometimes (as in the case of capital punishment – or, to take a more recent example, deliberately punitive regimes) the personal convictions of ministers and Members of Parliament. These considerations often conflict, especially when issues of party policy are dominant, as during election campaigns and party conferences, and have to be resolved by a kind of bargaining, so well illustrated by Land's account of the development of detention centres and the really rather extraordinary use that has been made of the most recent experiment in 'tough' regimes – especially the use of data relating solely to young men serving three-month sentences to support a scheme in which many of those detained will spend no more than two weeks in custody. The role of scholars and researchers in the generation of policy is particularly difficult to assess. The weight of academic opinion was firmly against the introduction of the suspended sentence; but that device was introduced in defiance of such views. On the other hand the deliberations of the Wootton Subcommittee clearly did influence civil servants and (perhaps mainly through them) ministers, and that was true not only of the major innovation of the Community Service Order, but also of the less dramatic but nevertheless valuable introduction of the principle that individuals convicted of sexual or aggressive assaults on children should be debarred from occupations which involve contact with children. The processes through which our penal system develops are difficult to trace and harder still to predict. Change is often the achievement of many hands, sometimes aided by some fortuitous event, so that it is seldom possible to identify the circumstances and the people who brought it about. There is, happily, no doubt about the parentage of Community Service Orders: Barbara Wootton will long be remembered for the advent of 'the most imaginative and hopeful' development in penal practice for half a century.

NOTES

1 Land (1975) mistakenly attributes this comment to Kenneth Younger, but the records of the Parliamentary debate on the second reading and the transactions in committee do not support this suggestion.

REFERENCES

ACTO (1959) *The Treatment of Young Offenders: A Report of the Advisory Council on the Treatment of Offenders*. London: HMSO.

Choppen, V. (1970) The Origins of the Philosophy of Detention Centres. *British Journal of Criminology* 10: 158–68.

Drewry, G. (1974) Parliament and Penal Policy. In L. Blom-Cooper (ed.) *Progress in Penal Reform*. Oxford: Clarendon Press.

Holloway, V. P. (1984) The History of detention centres. (Unpublished paper presented at a conference of the British Psychological Society in London.)

Hood, R. G. (1974) Criminology and Penal Change: A Case Study of the Nature and Impact of Some Recent Advice to Government. In R. G. Hood (ed.) *Crime, Criminology and Public Policy*. London: Heinemann.

Land, H. (1975) Detention Centres: The Experiment which Could not Fail. In P. Hall, H. Land, R. Parker, and A. Webb, *Change, Choice and Conflict in Social Policy*. London: Heinemann.

Ryan, M. (1983) *The Politics of Penal Reform*. London: Longman.

Serota Report *Sentences of Imprisonment – a Review of Maximum Penalties*.

Thornton, D., Curran, L., Grayson, D., and Holloway, V. (1984) *Tougher Regimes in Detention Centres*. London: HMSO.

Wootton, B. (1978) *Crime and Penal Policy*. London: Allen & Unwin.

Wootton Report (1970) *Non-Custodial and Semi-custodial Penalties – A Report of the Advisory Council on the Penal System*. London: HMSO.

Younger Report (1974) *Young Adult Offenders – A Report of the Advisory Council on the Penal System*. London: HMSO.

15

SOCIAL ENQUIRY REPORTS TWENTY-FIVE YEARS AFTER THE STREATFEILD REPORT

Anthony E. Bottoms and William McWilliams

The Report of the Interdepartmental Committee on the Business of the Criminal Courts (Chairman: Mr Justice Streatfeild) was published in February, 1961 (Home Office 1961), so it is now possible to look back upon it with the hindsight of a quarter-century. Such a review is of special interest for this volume since Barbara Wootton was a member of the Streatfeild Committee, this being the first of a succession of official committees on criminological topics to which she gave unstintingly of her time from 1958 onwards (see Wootton 1978: 17).

The Streatfeild Report falls into two quite distinct parts. Part A, which is now only of historical interest, was concerned with arrangements for bringing accused persons to trial. Part B was rather clumsily entitled 'Arrangements for providing the courts with the information necessary to enable them to select the most appropriate treatment for offenders'. These two subjects appear to be very different, and were treated separately by the committee, though we know from the writings of Hugh Klare (1962: 137–42; 1964) that there was in fact an intended connecting link.[1]

In retrospect, Part B of the Streatfeild Report is notable for its quality of scientific optimism. It begins by observing that 'sentencing used to be a comparatively simple matter' (para. 257), by which is meant that sentencing had habitually been based upon straightforward 'tariff' principles. But,

> 'in a considerable, and growing, number of cases the "tariff system" can no longer be relied on to fit all the considerations in the court's mind. The need to deter or reform the offender, the need to protect society and the need to deter potential offenders may in a particular case be

conflicting considerations. These objectives have an importance of their own and have a separate effect on the decision of the court.'

(Home Office 1961: para. 262)

This had consequences in the matter of information for the courts. 'In our view the key to advance in this field is to recognise the fundamental difference between assessing culpability and pursuing the other objectives of sentencing' (para. 269). This is because assessing culpability looks backwards to the seriousness of the offence, and is by definition not susceptible to a test of efficacy, whereas the other objectives are all 'seeking to control future events' (para. 269), and the success or otherwise of attempts to exercise this influence can be measured. Research should therefore be carried out, since 'unless the results of this observation are properly marshalled and systematically made available to the courts, sentences aimed at controlling future events are largely speculative' (para. 270).

At least two things should happen, the committee thought. First, courts should be made aware of the general results of relevant research (there is a notably optimistic paragraph on prediction studies, clearly influenced by the then very prominent Mannheim and Wilkins' (1955) study of borstal trainees: para. 278). In this connection a handbook for sentencers should be developed, incorporating appropriate research results; this should be revised every few years, and 'supplemented every six months, say, by information about national trends in crime, together with additional research information as it becomes available' (para. 300).

Second, courts should be supplied with fuller and better information about individual offenders. Here, in by far the longest chapter in Part B, careful attention is given to the different information sources available about individuals – police antecedents, prison reports, medical reports, and social enquiry reports prepared by the probation service – and recommendations are made about each.

With the benefit of hindsight we can see that the committee's hopes for a more scientific information base for sentencing have scarcely been fulfilled. A rather slim 'handbook for courts on the treatment of offenders' was produced, and some other relevant research has been conducted, but much of this research is open to differing scientific interpretation, and it has probably had little influence on sentencing decisions.[2] Certainly six-monthly research supplements have not seemed necessary.

By contrast, there is no doubt that the Streatfeild Committee's work has been extremely influential in the matter of reports upon individual offenders, and most particularly as regards social enquiry reports by probation officers. This influence has taken two forms. First, administratively the publication of the Streatfeild Report, followed by the relevant Home

Office Circular in 1963 (138/1963) led to a considerable growth in the volume of social enquiry reports in the 1960s and afterwards (see Davies 1974: 18–20), a growth which has only recently come into question in an era of much greater cost-consciousness.[3] Second, the analytic discussions in Streatfeild on the nature and purpose of social enquiry reports, the scope of their contents, and whether or not they should make recommendations to sentencers have proved of lasting influence and worth, even if not necessarily followed in detail by subsequent writers or official circulars.[4] Thus for example Curran and Chambers (1982: 34), while rejecting some aspects of Streatfeild as 'based upon a specific philosophy of science which viewed the achievements of the social sciences as accumulative', nevertheless conceded that 'the clearest guidance [on social enquiry reports] remains that given in the Streatfeild Report'.

Against this background there is a clear case for celebrating the silver jubilee of the Streatfeild Report with a special discussion of social enquiry reports. We do not, however, intend to examine here such matters as the changing historical nature of social enquiry practice, nor what form these reports should ideally take. This is partly because we are both, in different ways, tackling such matters elsewhere (McWilliams 1985; Bottoms and Stelman, forthcoming). More importantly, it is because we want to focus specific attention upon the empirical research on social enquiry reports, of which there has been a good deal in Britain during the last quarter-century.[5] Streatfeild was very keen on research and the need for courts to keep abreast of it; this scientific approach can, however, be applied not only to particular matters relevant to courts when sentencing individual offenders, but also to broader aspects of social and penal policy. Hence, within the scientific spirit of Streatfeild one can, paradoxically, turn a critical research gaze upon the Streatfeild Committee's own main policy achievement, namely, the development of a modern and greatly expanded service of social enquiry reports to the courts.

A critical look of this kind is congruent not only with the spirit of Streatfeild, but also with that of Barbara Wootton. In *Crime and Penal Policy* she refers briefly to a small piece of social enquiry research by Wilkins and Chandler (1965), and comments that, as a magistrate,

> 'I find that I welcome social enquiry reports because they make me feel cosy, inasmuch as they transform a "case" into a human being; but, sadly, I am driven to the conclusion, reinforced by Wilkins and Chandler, that except in [certain] limited contexts . . . , they do little to make me (or anybody else) in any sense a better sentencer.'
>
> (Wootton 1978: 45)

Is this pessimistic conclusion justified? What exactly *is* the research evidence on the achievements and limitations of social enquiry reports

(SERs) twenty-five years after the Streatfeild Report? We shall examine these issues in the remainder of this paper, focusing upon the following six questions:

1 What effect do SERs have on courts' ability to choose effectively reductionist sentences?
2 What effect do SERs have on courts' sentencing decisions?
3 What effect do SERs have in diverting offenders from custodial sentences?
4 What is known about the content of SERs?
5 What influences recommendations in SERs?
6 What do sentencers think about SERs?

These questions do not exhaust the possibilities of kinds of research into SERs,[6] but they do perhaps cover most of the central issues. In considering them, we shall try to look at the main research studies relevant to each question, but in the space available we necessarily cannot provide a fully comprehensive review.

WHAT EFFECT DO SERs HAVE ON COURTS' ABILITY TO CHOOSE EFFECTIVELY REDUCTIONIST SENTENCES?

In the last of Barbara Wootton's Hamlyn Lectures, delivered at the University of Sheffield in 1963, she expressed the view that 'the primary function of the criminal courts is to discourage crime', and that the object of a sentence should be 'to take the minimum action which offers an adequate prospect of preventing future offences' (Wootton 1963: 95). In the second edition of this work she reaffirmed what she called this 'reductionist' approach to sentencing policy (Wootton 1981: 117).

For a 'reductionist', the key test of social information presented to a court is whether or not it helps the court to make a better decision, 'better' being here defined as 'more likely to reduce crime'. The Streatfeild Committee went some way towards such a view, declaring that the two main kinds of information in a social enquiry report should be, first, information that is 'relevant to the court's assessment of [the defendant's] culpability', and second, that which is 'relevant to the court's consideration of how [the defendant's] criminal career might be checked' (para. 335).[7]

Despite this reductionist thrust in Streatfeild, there has been remarkably little research interest in the comparative reductive efficacy of sentences passed with or without the benefit of social enquiry reports. There is, in fact, only one research study which has centrally addressed this topic, namely that begun by Hood (1966) and completed by Hood and Taylor (1968) in Sunderland Magistrates' Court.

The first part of this project compared the reconviction rates of a sample of 100 male offenders aged between 17 and 21 years appearing between June 1959 and June 1961 (a period 'when the Bench remanded for inquiries simply when they felt them to be needed' (Hood 1966: 305): Sample A), and a sample of 100 male offenders in the same age group appearing between September 1961 and September 1963 (a period during which it had been 'decided that . . . reports should be obtained for all offenders under twenty-one convicted of indictable offences and certain other offences' (Hood 1966: 303): Sample B). The object of the research was to make a comparison of reconviction rates as between the samples, but it also had the subsidiary aim of comparing reconviction rates of those offenders for whom a remand for enquiries had been made with those for whom such a remand was not considered necessary.

The samples were considered to be equivalent in terms of initial risk of reconviction, and in respect of the main objective (the comparison of reconviction rates between the samples) the finding was one of no difference. From this Hood (1966: 309) concluded that the 'policy of the Sunderland justices in implementing the recommendations of the Streatfeild Report has not, as yet, led to a significant drop in the number of boys being reconvicted'. It is important to be clear, however, that it is the general implementation of the policy which is identified here, and *not* the provision of social information by probation officers in specific cases. The opportunity existed in the research to examine the latter, but it was not taken. This is clear from an examination of the manner in which the subsidiary objective (to compare those offenders for whom a remand for enquiries had been made with those for whom it had not) was pursued.

In Sample A, only 8 of the 100 offenders had enquiries made about them, of which 4 were reports of suitability for borstal training. In Sample B, 49 remands for enquiries were made, of which 6 were suitability for borstal reports. Because of the small number of enquiries in Sample A, Hood restricted his analysis to Sample B and found no difference in reconviction rates between those who were remanded and those who were not. The comparison, however, was between *remands* and not *reports*. Of those 51 youths who were *not* remanded a probation officer had submitted a report in 20 cases and given information (presumably verbally) in a further 7 cases. Had those 27 cases been placed in the 'remand' category in the analysis the outcome might have been different. Thus, because of the rather curious conventions that were used in relation to the subsidiary aim, we are unable to draw any conclusions about the value of social enquiry reports in reducing recidivism from the intra-sample (Sample B) analysis. We can, of course, conclude that *remands* for enquiries had no effect in reducing reconviction, but it is difficult to see any grounds for expecting them to do so.

In the second part of the study Hood and Taylor (1968) took a further sample of 100 male offenders, Sample C (ages were not given but presumably were similar to Samples A and B) and compared their reconviction rates with those of the earlier samples. The differences were not significant: 35 per cent of Sample C members were reconvicted of an indictable offence compared with 36 per cent for Sample A and 30 per cent for Sample B. However, the authors then compare Samples A and C in terms of the number of members of the samples who have two or more previous court appearances for indictable offences, and show that in Sample C 39 per cent fell into this category, as against only 28 per cent in Sample A. From this they conclude that:

> 'although similar proportions are reconvicted, those in Sample C started off with a worse record. In other words, the proportion reconvicted in Sample C is lower than would be expected if the scheme were making no impact. This result could only appear by chance in one sample in a hundred. This . . . clearly alters the rather pessimistic conclusion of the previous report and appears to suggest that what could only be called "an encouraging trend" has continued.'
>
> (Hood and Taylor 1968: 432–33)

There are, however, technical difficulties in accepting this conclusion at face value, since it is not clear what statistical test has been applied to give the apparent $p < .01$ result, and moreover the proportionate difference between Samples A and C in the number of those with two or more previous convictions appears, from the data presented, to be not statistically significant.[8]

Various commentators have reacted in different ways to this evidence. Martin Davies (1974: 21), though clearly aware of the Sunderland study, nevertheless concludes that 'there is no evidence that the growth in the use of social enquiry reports has occurred simultaneously with any significant improvement in the "effectiveness" of sentencing as measured by its success in reducing the level of crime'. Nigel Walker (1985: 31), on the other hand, accepts the Sunderland evidence and believes that, given the complex interactions involved, a slight positive result should not be regarded as disappointing, since 'all that could be expected was a small improvement'. Our own conclusion is that, given the technical complications to which we have alluded, it is difficult to draw firm conclusions from the Sunderland evidence; rather than continue to debate this evidence, the case for a fresh study of the topic seems overwhelming.

WHAT EFFECT DO SERs HAVE ON COURTS' SENTENCING DECISIONS?

From the previous discussion, the possibility that social enquiry reports help courts to choose reductively better sentences cannot be ruled out. However, it is important to notice that such an effect can exist only if in fact SERs actually do alter sentencers' decision making in a reasonable proportion of cases: this is a necessary though not sufficient condition for the reductive efficacy of SERs.

Whether SERs affect sentences is therefore a topic of some importance. One frequently adopted approach to this question is to look at the agreement rates between probation officers' recommendations and the sentences given; when this is done high agreement rates are typically found. To take two recent studies, Stanley and Murphy (1984), in a survey of cases in Inner London found an overall rate of agreement of 62 per cent in cases where a specific recommendation was made, though with much lower agreement rates in the Crown Court than the magistrates' courts. (However, no specific recommendation was made in a quarter of their cases.) In a comprehensive Scottish study, Curran and Chambers (1982: 85) report a 'take-up' rate overall of 69 per cent for 'firm' recommendations, though with variations from 92 per cent for custodial recommendations to 12 per cent for recommendations that sentence should be deferred.[9]

However, it is now generally recognized that these high agreement rates tell us little in themselves about the influence of social enquiry reports on sentencing. In a much-quoted discussion, Carter and Wilkins (1967: 509) suggested that four factors may be operating independently or in combination to produce agreement between report-writer and sentencer, of which only the first betokens an influence by the report-writer. The four suggested factors are (a) that sentencers may agree with probation officers because of their high regard for their professional qualities and competence; (b) that there may be many offenders who are 'obviously' cases for either probation or prison; (c) that probation officers may make recommendations which they anticipate the court would like to receive; or (d) that probation officers and courts place similar emphasis on the same factors in selecting particular sentences.[10] Some years later Davies (1974: 28–30) placed some emphasis upon the third of Carter and Wilkins' factors; he hypothesized a 'closed loop' situation in which the probation officer perceived the magistrates' likely sentence and usually recommended in agreement with it (perhaps in order to maximize credibility with the bench), although leaving open to himself the possibility of recommending outside the magistrates' likely range of sentences in particular selected cases. The points which Carter and Wilkins and Davies make are, of course, open to empirical investigation, and two studies in particular have attempted to disentangle at least some of the factors involved (Mott 1977; Hine, McWilliams, and Pease 1978).

In Joy Mott's study of 133 male offenders in one juvenile court the sentencing process was divided into three stages: first, magistrates were given certain basic background information about the offender (age, sex, type of offence, number of offences taken into consideration, and the visible characteristics and responses of the offender and his parents in court) and were asked to make a provisional sentencing decision acting independently of their colleagues on the bench; second, magistrates were given the social enquiry report, where this was available, together with any other reports which had been prepared, and then recorded a second provisional decision; and third, after discussion between the members of the bench, a third and final sentencing decision was recorded, and this was the sentence awarded to the offender.

The overall finding in respect of the 111 cases in which a social enquiry report was available and the probation officer had made a specific recommendation was that in 10 per cent of cases there was no agreement between the officers' recommendations and the sentences imposed; in 65 per cent of cases there was agreement as to sentence between probation officers and magistrates before the reports were seen (that is, the second, third, or fourth of Carter and Wilkins' explanations of agreement could have applied); and in 25 per cent of cases the magistrates actually changed their original decision in the direction of the probation officers' recommendations. In general terms, therefore, the probation officers' influence was limited to a quarter of the cases, whereas in most of the 'agreement' cases the agreement was not as a result of such influence. Of course, influence over sentences in 25 per cent of cases is not negligible, and could form the basis for a (necessarily rather small) reductionist effect. Equally – and to anticipate the next section of our discussion – such a level of influence does at least open the door to a possible policy of diverting appropriate offenders from custodial sentences by SER recommendations, if such a policy is thought desirable. The latter point depends, however, on the *direction* of officers' influence in their recommendations; that is, do they tend to divert offenders away from or towards custodial sentences? Unfortunately, this is a question that Mott did not address in her research; from her data we can know only that the probation officers' influence existed, but not the direction which it took.[11]

The second study to be considered, that by Hine and her colleagues (1978), did tackle the issue of the direction of probation officers' influence in their recommendations, but unlike that of Mott it was based on a sentencing exercise rather than real cases in a court. In the study 89 magistrates were asked to sentence 12 cases which were presented to them in three different experimental conditions. In condition A sentencers were given only basic information consisting of the details of the offence and the police antecedents; in condition B there was added to the basic information the social information contained in a social enquiry report but without the probation officer's recommendation; and in condition C the sentencer was given the basic information, the social information, and the officer's recommendation. Comparisons were made of the sentences passed under each of the three conditions. The general finding was that the levels of agreement between recommendations and sentences increased in line with the amount of information presented; thus comparing conditions A and B, condition B resulted in significantly more sentences in line with the recommendations than did condition A; and condition C resulted in more sentences in line with the recommendation than did condition B. There were however differences in the magnitude of the movement between the conditions. In condition A only 31 out of a possible maximum of 220 sentences were in line with the recommendation; this increased to 65 in condition B and 175 in condition C, with the increased congruence substantially greater between conditions B and C than between conditions A and B. The authors conclude therefore that recommendations 'had a substantially greater influence in attracting "sentences" than did [the provision of] social information alone' (Hine, McWilliams, and Pease 1978: 97).

In this study Hine and her colleagues did record the direction of change as between their three conditions in respect of recommendations for probation and custody. In relation to probation they found a significant movement towards the acceptance of recommendations for probation as between conditions A and B, but the addition of the recommendation in condition C then did not add significantly to the acceptance rate. From this they conclude that social information is a prerequisite for sentencers to begin to consider a probation order. In respect of custodial sentences the researchers found no significant differences as between the experimental conditions. However, they did show that as between conditions A and C 24 cases were diverted from custody, but that at the same time 24 cases were diverted into custody by the probation officers' recommendations; and they found that where the probation officers had recommended custody a custodial sentence was given in all but one instance. When the cases in which custody had been recommended were excluded they found that in condition A 41 custodial sentences were given; in condition B it fell to 34 and in condition C it was only 17. They conclude that social information plus a recommendation, although not social information alone, does seem potentially able to divert from custody, but they were unable to show that the differences involved were significant because the numbers of cases were too small for testing.

Overall, these two studies do show fairly clearly that report writers can and do have an influence upon sentencers, though probably only in a minority of cases; however, that influence can apparently be both away from *and towards* custodial sentences. The fact of influence provides a necessary precondition for a possible reductionist effect of SERs (see pp. 248–50), though the small proportion of cases influenced necessarily places limits upon any such effect.

WHAT EFFECT DO SERs HAVE IN DIVERTING OFFENDERS FROM CUSTODIAL SENTENCES?

In some of her later writings Barbara Wootton emphasized research findings showing the ineffectiveness of custodial sentences in reducing subsequent criminal behaviour, and the potentially damaging effects of custody, even under an enlightened regime (Wootton 1978: 184, 188). It is reasonable to suppose, therefore, that she would be interested in the issue of how far social enquiry reports can influence courts to divert offenders from custody, even though that was not an objective which the Streatfeild Report espoused. Certainly this potentially 'diversionary' effect of SERs has been the subject of much interest within the probation service in recent years, and the recent Home Office national statement of objectives and priorities for the probation service suggests a concentration of effort in social enquiry work on, *inter alia*, cases where 'the court may be prepared to divert an offender from what would otherwise be a custodial sentence' (Home Office 1984).

Walker (1985: 32) claims it can 'safely be said' that if courts did not have social enquiry reports 'they would make much more use of custodial measures than they do'. He might be right, but in fact there is no conclusive evidence to support this view.

Jennifer Thorpe (1979) carried out a study for the Home Office Research Unit in which, *inter alia*, she examined, on an areal basis, the relationship between sentences given and the average rate of report provision per probation officer in the different areas. Overall her finding was that there 'was no conclusive evidence . . . to support the view that variations in sentencing were caused by differences in the rate of provision of reports'; and, specifically in relation to our present concern, that there 'was no evidence . . . to suggest that the number of custodial sentences passed is affected by the more routine provision of reports' (Thorpe 1979: 31). She also found that high report-provision areas made proportionately fewer specific recommendations in magistrates' courts (though not in the Crown Court); hence, 'if it is the recommendation in a social enquiry report which influences sentencing, the potential increase in influence due to the preparation of a high rate of reports for magistrates' courts in certain areas is unfulfilled, to a greater or lesser extent, because of the lower rate of specific recommendations made' (Thorpe 1979: 26). However, there were a number of technical difficulties with these area-based comparisons, and Thorpe regarded her conclusions as tentative.

In a study similar to that of Thorpe, but based on improved statistical material, Roberts and Roberts (1982) likewise concluded that there was 'no evidence that increasing the provision of social enquiry reports affects the courts' use of custodial sentences' (1982: 91). They reached the 'inescapable conclusion . . . that the level of use of custodial sentences is strongly rooted in local sentencing practices, and not readily influenced by the provision of reports' (1982: 77). By contrast, there was 'clear evidence of a link between a higher provision of reports and a higher level of use of probation and community service orders' (1982: 91); the greater use of these measures was, however, at the expense of other non-custodial measures rather than custodial disposals.

The foregoing conclusions do not imply of course, that the various non-custodial measures never attract offenders who, in the absence of social enquiry reports, would have been locked up. Rather the central message of both Thorpe and Roberts and Roberts is that, given the present form of social enquiry practice, and in particular the extent to which probation officers are currently recommending non-custodial measures, a simple increase in the provision of reports seems to have little or no effect on the proportion of offenders incarcerated.

Some further light on this point may be obtained from Stanley and Murphy's (1984) extensive study of social enquiry practice in Inner London, based on a 'census' of 3,735 reports and a more intensively studied sub-set of 941 of those reports. Stanley and Murphy examined in detail the recommendations made in adult cases finally sentenced to imprisonment, and found that in a high proportion of such cases the probation officer had not recommended a non-custodial measure, but had either recommended prison or made no recommendation. Moreover, this was true regardless of the length of prison sentence imposed: immediate custodial recommendations or no recommendations were made in 56 per cent of long prison sentence cases (more than twelve months), 48 per cent of medium prison terms (three to twelve months), and 59 per cent of short sentence cases (less than three months) (Stanley and Murphy 1984: 28). While a high percentage figure for long sentences is perhaps not unex- pected (report-writers 'bowing to the inevitable', etc.), the fact that so few non-custodial recommendations were made in short-sentence cases sug- gests that, if the probation service's aim is diversion from custody, officers are perhaps not maximizing their opportunities. Stanley and Murphy then went on to examine in detail the kinds of cases recommended for pro- bation or other supervisory orders, and concluded that:

'probation officers were directing their recommendations for supervision not only towards offenders with short or non-existent criminal records but also towards those whose needs were perhaps more immediate, and easier to meet, at the expense of those with longer lasting difficulties and criminal records.'   (Stanley and Murphy 1984: 34)

Overall, the authors therefore felt able to conclude that probation officers had in general been 'cautious rather than adventurous' (1984: 37) in their recommendations, and that this had created 'definite limits to the efficacy of reports in diverting offenders . . . from custody' (1984: 36).

Again however it does not follow from this that social enquiry reports never have the effect of diverting from custody. Indeed, Stanley and Murphy themselves estimated that 'the process of preparing SERs succeeded in diverting from a custodial sentence just over a quarter of their subjects' (1984: 33), though, as they admit, this estimate is based upon inferences which may or may not be correct.[12]

Finally in this section we may return briefly to the study by Hine, McWilliams, and Pease (1978); the finding here, it will be recalled, was of *some* diversionary effect from custody, but statistical significance could not be demonstrated. The central message, however, in relation to the role of social enquiry reports in keeping offenders out of custody was that they acted as a double-edged sword: they appeared to divert some offenders away from custody, but they simultaneously appeared to divert an equal number of offenders *into* custody. The import from this and the other studies is clear; if the probation service wishes, for whatever reason, to pursue a policy of diverting offenders away from incarceration some means would need to be found *both* to encourage the more active recommending of non-custodial options by probation officers, *and* to discourage custodial recommendations. This would be far from easy to achieve, of course, and obviously there could be no guarantee of what the results might be. The present balance in recommendations as between custodial, non-custodial, and no recommendation at all has been achieved over a lengthy period of time and involves complex relationships between probation officers, sentencers, and offenders. A sharp change by one of those parties (i.e. probation officers) might not necessarily produce expected or desired results.

WHAT IS KNOWN ABOUT THE CONTENT OF SERs?

The Streatfeild Report enunciated as a 'cardinal principle' that sentences should be based upon 'reliable, comprehensive information relevant to what the court is seeking to do'. It was important, the committee went on, that reports should be on a 'sound factual basis' and not 'speculative and based on vague impressions' (para. 292). At the same time, 'information should not be proliferated for information's sake', as the key test was *relevance*. 'Irrelevant information is not only useless, but possibly harmful . . . it may cloud the issue before the court and induce a cosy feeling in which the absence of really useful information passes unnoticed' (para. 293).

The earliest systematic content analysis of SERs was carried out by Perry (1974). Although recognizing the importance of relevance as opposed to comprehensiveness (1974: 41), the thrust of Perry's research method and interpretive comments in fact emphasized the comprehensiveness issue. For example, the author comments that he 'did not find any reason for the exclusion [in a minority of cases] of the basic facts about the subject, such as where he was born and the number of other children in the family' (1974: 43), but place of birth is surely likely to be irrelevant information in most cases for most of the purposes of court sentencing, while number of siblings may also be irrelevant, especially in an adult sample. (Perry's content analysis was made from a sample of 200 reports presented to the Crown Court, so the great majority will have been prepared on adult defendants.)

Perry is most famous for the summary statement in which he declares that the average social enquiry report contains,

> 'NO statement about receipt of police
> antecedents;
> NO mention of the amount of contact upon
> which the report was based . . .'

and so on down a list of sixteen 'NO' items, followed by:

> 'ONLY a mention of the members of his present household;
> SOME facts about his educational/work record;
> a mention of the subjects' account of the offence,
> but no comment on it;
> a recommendation;
> the basic facts regarding parents or siblings with
> either a statement about or assessment of relationships;
> CERTAINLY the name and age of the subject.'   (Perry 1974: 64)

Perry concludes that it would be premature to regard SERs as a technical or scientific tool, that they are 'idiosyncratic and selective' documents, and that there is evidence of 'hack-work' in them (1974: 65–6). Not surprisingly, his analysis did not meet with universal acclaim in the probation service (see e.g. Pearce and Wareham 1977).

Though Perry may have overemphasized comprehensiveness at the expense of relevance, it is important to make clear that some later research which has not made this mistake has been just as unflattering to report writers. For example, Martin, Fox, and Murray (1981) in an analysis of reports presented in 300 cases before children's hearings in Scotland,[13] concluded that: 'in more than half of all the cases examined, the reports did not provide the hearing with information on basic features of the child's growth and development which, in terms of current professional opinion, might be held essential to any realistic discussion about his future' (1981: 156).

Moreover, while there was considerable variation in the quality of reports, the authors considered that 'the general impression conveyed is of a high frequency of rather piecemeal statements which in a substantial proportion of cases fails to organise and integrate the observations into a balanced whole' (1981: 156).

Jennifer Thorpe's (1979) Home Office research included a content analysis of some 500 reports which were prepared in 1975 for both the Crown Court and magistrates' courts. Like Perry, she found a high rate of absence of information, but was less willing than Perry to draw conclusions of poor practice from such absence. Also like Perry, she found that reports 'differ substantially in terms of content and format' (Thorpe 1979: 30). An interesting analysis was conducted (1979: 41, Table 2) in which items of information, where present, were classified as having been presented in a 'positive, favourable or good' context, or a 'negative, unfavourable or bad' one. Of the nineteen subject headings examined in this way, only four were more likely to be mentioned in unfavourable than favourable terms: these four were intelligence, employment prospects, delinquent friends, and ability to form relationships, which suggested to the author that 'even where the report was more "negative" in content, the defendant was viewed sympathetically, being characterised as a person of poor intelligence, who found it difficult to form relationships, and had delinquent friends and poor employment prospects' (Thorpe 1979: 18–19). Thorpe added speculatively that perhaps some of the cases where particular topics were not mentioned in reports were because 'officers had selectively omitted unfavourable details', in which case 'the impression of defendants gained from these reports could be unreliable' (1979: 19). Most informed observers would agree that selective omission of unfavourable detail does sometimes occur;[14] but the overall tenor of Thorpe's interpretation of her findings is open to criticism in that she appears to suggest that reports will always tend to present defendants in a predominantly favourable light, which is certainly not the case (see Bean 1975, 1976: Chapter 5).

Perhaps the most sophisticated research analysis of SER content to date comes from Curran and Chambers' (1982) Scottish Office study of 180 reports, mostly prepared for Sheriff Courts. In a key summary sentence,

Curran (the author of Part I of the study) concludes that SERs 'read either as rather bland descriptions . . . expressed in neutral, non-committal language, or, more frequently, as lay accounts of "good" or "bad" characters' (1982: 100). This requires some explanation, as it is based on two different kinds of research.

First, Curran carried out a quantitative content analysis similar to those of Perry (1974) and Thorpe (1979), and tabulated the results in such a way as to facilitate easy comparison with their earlier work (1982: 152, Appendix III). As before, many items were frequently not mentioned. More interestingly, each item was rated, as by Thorpe, according to whether it was presented in a positive or negative way, except that this time a 'neutral' category was also introduced. For some items (particularly intelligence, personality, leisure activities, previous employment, and school behaviour or performance) the neutral category was of considerable numerical importance. This analysis therefore makes more complex the picture presented by Thorpe, and justifies the view that at least some parts of many SERs read as 'bland descriptions . . . expressed in neutral, non-committal language'.

Second, Curran also examined the reports qualitatively. Here two further findings may be stressed. In the first place, in the discussion of family relationships in reports 'an analysis of the kinds of "facts" used, and the ways in which they are presented, suggests some tendency for particular kinds of *value judgements* to be made as if they were *professional assessments*' (italics in original) (1982: 48). Equally, in relation to personality assessment, 'social work discourse reflects a lay system of value judgements, expressing itself in everyday notions such as "weak-willed", "immature", "complacent", "arrogant" and "likeable"' (1982: 75).

But as well as showing the value-laden content of many social enquiry reports, Curran (1982: 75) also stresses that they are 'notable for their failure to utilise, in any explicit form, the theories and research findings developed by criminologists and other social scientists'. Even where a social science theory or finding is hinted at, it is usually in isolation from current behaviour: 'no link is forged and the facts take on the appearance of being potentially interesting but presently irrelevant.' Why is this so?

'That social workers are playing it cautiously, not wishing to over-commit themselves to a particular interpretation and not wishing to bring down the wrath of the court because of an overly-technical report, can not be discounted. Unfortunately, such a stance leaves the social worker vulnerable to accusations of discussing irrelevancies, being self-contradictory and not professional.'

(Curran and Chambers 1982: 75)

Hence, the qualitative analysis reveals social enquiry reports as very often 'lay accounts of "good" or "bad" characters' (our italics) (1982: 100). But Curran has a final twist to his argument. Rather than being straightforwardly critical of this as bad professionalism (as, for example, Martin, Fox, and Murray (1981) were), perhaps the point is, suggests Curran, that social enquiry reports are a different kind of document from that which many researchers have implicitly assumed: perhaps the content and shape of reports is powerfully influenced by what the report-writer thinks (a) is wanted by the court, and/or (b) may persuade the court towards a particular result. In short, perhaps SERs are 'strategic documents involved in "persuasive communication" with the courts' (Curran and Chambers 1982: 100).

Two things perhaps emerge clearly from this discussion of research into the content of SERs. First, whatever else it is, the typical social enquiry report seems not to be what two very experienced senior members of the probation service declared it to be, namely, 'a comprehensive and objective document prepared by the professionally trained social worker of the court to assist the court in a more effective sentencing practice' (Herbert and Mathieson 1975: 11).

Second, it is quite clear that, as other writers have also stressed, research analysis of SER content cannot avoid becoming involved with the question of the purpose of preparing such reports (see Pearce and Wareham 1977: 101; Curran and Chambers 1982: 32). And if, for example, the purpose of reports is seen as being 'strategic documents involved in persuasive communication', their content will be judged very differently than they would be in terms of the Streatfeild Committee's test of 'reliable, comprehensive information relevant to what the court is seeking to do'.

WHAT INFLUENCES RECOMMENDATIONS IN SERs?

The research by Wilkins and Chandler (1965) which impressed Barbara Wootton (see p. 247) was a decision-board analysis carried out in the United States, though published in Britain. A probation case history was subjected to content analysis, and its contents classified under 49 headings. Probation officers were asked to select from these 49 items sequentially, and to decide whether or not to recommend probation as a suitable treatment. As Barbara Wootton (1978: 45) puts it, 'the result showed that the methods of gathering and utilising information had no consistent effect upon the type of decision reached, but were apparently more characteristic of the persons concerned in the operation'. However, this research has been criticized for the artificiality of the decision-board method, and for promoting 'an over-simplified approach to a complex subject' (Davies 1974: 27; see also Pearce and Wareham 1977: 100). Its results have also been to some extent contradicted and superseded by subsequent research into the way in which probation officers make SER recommendations (see p. 262).

An interesting recent study of the shaping of recommendations was made by Martin, Fox, and Murray (1981: 158–63) in the context of children's hearings in Scotland. They carried out two separate analyses, the first a statistical exercise designed to show what factors correlated with what recommendations, and the second an interview study of social workers to find out the reasons given for particular recommendations. Thus for example recommendations for residential supervision (or continued residential supervision) were shown in the statistical analysis to be particularly associated with the number of times the child had previously been before the children's hearing; with irregular school attendance; and (surprisingly) with coming from a *non*-manual family background or being of above average intelligence. From the interview analysis residential supervision recommendations were shown, in three-quarters of the cases, to be associated with three kinds of social work reasoning (in roughly equal proportions): these are described as 'care' ('to pursue special help', 'to benefit the child', etc.); 'positive control' ('to prevent further trouble', 'to provide a structured environment', etc.); and 'negative control' ('no alternative', 'total lack of co-operation', etc.). Unfortunately there is no cross-analysis between the two kinds of data, but the authors have shown that the rigorous pursuit of these separate types of analysis, preferably then brought together, does hold promise for future studies.

But by far the most important and influential work on the shaping of recommendations in social enquiry reports has been carried out by Pauline Hardiker. Unfortunately this is difficult to deal with adequately in short compass, partly because of the extensive and rather scattered nature of Hardiker's work (Hardiker 1975, 1977a/b, 1979; Curnock and Hardiker 1979; Hardiker and Webb 1979), and partly because it has been the subject of controversy (Paley and Leeves 1982; Webb and Hardiker 1983). We can only try to sketch in the main issues as we see them.[15]

At the time when Hardiker began her work, in the early to mid-1970s, accounts were being offered of social enquiry practice which 'stressed either the idiosyncratic and individualistic nature of the probation officer's recommendation . . . or relied on a crude idealism which put everything down to treatment ideologies' (Webb and Hardiker 1983: 215). These accounts had no adequate empirical backing. Hardiker's own initial interest lay in the extent to which different probation officers differentially subscribed to 'treatment model' assumptions, and she did indeed find some individual differences between officers of this kind. However, in her research, 'when it came to their social enquiry practices, there seemed to be no difference between officers in this respect; *every* probation officer held a treatment orientation towards some of his cases and not to others, and this appeared to be *related to the circumstances of the case*. Treatment orientations tended to be held when the offender had a relatively serious criminal record, severe personal/social problems, and the recommendation was for either probation or custody' (our italics).

(Hardiker 1977b: 152)

Two things are critical here. First, there is the stress on the generality of the findings ('every probation officer . . .'), and second, what seemed to determine the approach taken by the officer was the context – that is, the circumstances of the case. Philip Bean (1975) had suggested that offenders should choose their probation officer carefully; Hardiker and Webb (1979: 13) explicitly challenged this, saying rather that, 'given the legal and social work parameters which inform probation practice, we would say "choose your offence and your social problems". It is these which appear to be crucial factors in explaining how probation officers think about offenders' actions.' These emphases on generality, and on the circumstances of the case in shaping the recommendation, have remained prominent in Hardiker's work on SERs.

The phrase 'choose your offence and your social problems' in the above quotation is not accidental, and reflects the two key dimensions of Hardiker's analysis, usually described respectively as 'tariff' and 'need'. In an empirical study of the social enquiry recommendations of an intake team in Leicester, an (admittedly crude) measurement of 'low' or 'high' offender need was shown to be highly significantly associated with recommendations. For example, probation recommendations were much more likely to be associated with high than with low need cases, while fine recommendations were associated with low need (Hardiker 1979: 119). However, 'need' was not the only relevant consideration, and a second dimension added was that of 'seriousness of criminal history' or 'tariff', which was also (not surprisingly) significantly associated with recommendations. Although 'need' and 'tariff' were themselves significantly associated statistically (Hardiker 1979: 122), they were by no means identical; hence it became possible to plot a two-dimensional matrix encompassing 'tariff' (divided into 'low', 'medium', and 'high') and 'need' ('high'/'low'). A table was then prepared showing, for the Leicester intake sample, the recommendations made in relation to the six cells of this matrix (Hardiker 1979: 123). This is reproduced here as *Table 1(a)*.

Clearly there are significant differences in the recommendations as between the six categories. Hardiker (1979: 122–23) claims that this is therefore a 'relatively precise means of pinning down the association

Table 1a   *Recommendations, criminal history, and offender need in a Leicester sample (%)*

recommendation	low need			high need		
	low tariff	medium tariff	high tariff	low tariff	medium tariff	high tariff
conditional discharge	44*	7	—	29+	4	—
fine	27	48*	11	2	8+	3
probation	1	4	1	53	58*	28+
custody	2	8	42	—	8	36*
other	16	23	29	4	14	21
no recommendation	10	10	17	12	8	12
	100	100	100	100	100	100
N =	99	325	76	49	262	117

* = dominant 'reverse tariff' disposal (see *Table 1b*)
+ = secondary 'reverse tariff' disposal (see *Table 1b*)
Source: Hardiker (1979: 123).

Table 1b   *A 'reverse tariff'*

need	tariff		
	low	medium	high
low	conditional discharge	fine	
high	(conditional discharge)	probation (fine)	custody (probation)

Source: Curnock and Hardiker (1979: 71), modifying Hardiker (1979: 123).

between recommendations, personal problems, and criminal histories'; she goes on to postulate what she calls a 'reverse tariff rank' in the following words:[16]

> 'The sentencer through the medium of the social enquiry report determines *where on the continuum of tariff and social need the offender stands*. If tariff and need are minimal, a conditional discharge will be recommended; if the tariff is moderate and needs are minimal, a fine will be indicated; if the tariff is moderate and needs are evident, probation will be suggested; a maximum tariff and serious personal and social problems will be a pointer to custodial measures.' (italics in original)
>
> (Hardiker 1979: 122–23)

This 'reverse tariff rank' is shown diagrammatically in *Table 1(b)*, together with (in parentheses) some modifications introduced later because the original 'simple formula does not exhaust the parameters of recommendations' (Curnock and Hardiker 1979: 70–1). In *Table 1(a)* the suggested dominant sentence for each category in the 'reverse tariff rank' has been shown by an asterisk, and the later, less dominant, modifications (recommendations supposedly sometimes made in some cases) by a cross. It will be seen that in four of the five columns for which the 'reverse tariff rank' offers a solution, at least 40 per cent of the recommendations fall within the suggested framework.

Webb and Hardiker (1983: 216) have recently pointed out, correctly, that 'Hardiker herself has never made the claim that the reverse tariff is the *sole* explanatory variable in her work' (italics in original). Nevertheless, they do claim 'theoretical and empirical primacy for the reverse tariff concept: empirically because of its ability to explain much of the variation in probation officers' recommendations (see p. 262), and theoretically since 'need and tariff compose (*sic*) central elements in the officers' world-view as it bears on particular problems with which he has to deal' (1983: 216).

Actually there are some obvious difficulties with the 'reverse tariff rank' which means one should not rush to defend every detail of it too quickly. In the first place, it makes no mention of community service recommendations, largely because there were very few of these when Hardiker's empirical work was originally carried out in the mid-1970s; the few that there were were difficult to characterize in a uniform way (Hardiker 1977a: 49–53). Second, Hardiker's (1977a: 9) empirical analysis classifies suspended sentence recommendations as custodial recommendations, which is undoubtedly correct in law (Powers of Criminal Courts Act 1973, s.22(2)) but almost certainly does not reflect accurately the way in which most probation officers think of the suspended sentence when recommending it, which is what matters for present purposes. These points are not negligible in statistical terms. By 1980 in Inner London, probation officers in the Crown Court recommended community service for 18 per cent of the cases, and suspended sentence for 12 per cent, with the corresponding figures for magistrates' courts being 14 per cent and 7 per cent (Stanley and Murphy 1984: 62). Over and above all this, it is clear from Hardiker's own data that there are very many (not just a few) recommendations which do not fit the reverse tariff categories (see *Table 1a*); indeed, even Hardiker's (1979: 125) own claim that 'the majority of social enquiry recommendations probably fit into' the reverse tariff does not quite square with the data in that table, certainly if only the dominent reverse tariff possibilities are taken into account.

Nevertheless, any fair assessment of Hardiker's research cannot be simply negative. Despite certain problems (see p. 265) her analysis does have some empirical strength, and discussions we have held while teaching on courses for experienced probation officers suggest to us that Webb and Hardiker are probably right in saying that 'need and tariff comprise central elements in the officer's world view'. Perhaps, therefore, it is best to regard Hardiker as having made a notable contribution to understanding what influences SER recommendations, but to be prepared to modify her contribution where appropriate. In what follows we shall argue that this suggested approach makes sense in the light of subsequent research and writing: we concentrate in this respect on the three separate aspects of 'tariff', 'need', and 'individual/agency/court differences'.

Paley and Leeves (1982: 370–72) in a critique of Hardiker's work, have suggested that her concept of 'tariff' is oversimplified. The concept 'tariff', they suggest, embraces the three distinct matters of (a) the offender's past criminal history, (b) the seriousness of the current offence, and (c) the risk of future offending; the three need to be distinguished, they argue, particularly because when formulating recommendations there may be some tension between them (notably where future risk is high but the current offence is not serious; or where risk is low but the current offence is serious). Moreover, they say, there may be an important difference between the probation officer's own judgement of these three elements and his view of how the court may assess them (this is perhaps especially so as regards seriousness of the offence, although Paley and Leeves do not explicitly make this point). Hardiker has accepted this critique (Webb and Hardiker 1983: 208, 212–13), and in doing so clearly accepts some need for future empirical development of the 'tariff' dimension of her work.

The concept of 'need' in Hardiker's work also requires some clarification. In the Leicester intake analysis, from which Table 1a is derived, 'need' was measured in terms of probation officers' answers to the question 'how would you rate this offender's personal/social need?' (Hardiker 1977a: Appendix 1); this clearly poses some problems of reliability which should be addressed in future work. Subsequently, Curnock and Hardiker (1979) seemed to use the concept 'need' in a rather unfortunately free-floating way, and not simply by reference to 'social/personal need'.[17] The importance of further clarification and elaboration has been particularly well shown in the recent work by Stanley and Murphy (1984) in Inner London. In a content analysis of social enquiry reports, they coded 63 per cent of cases as containing one or other of a list of specific items 'identified as indicating a present need for supervision' (1984: 13); the list included matters such as problems in social functioning, addiction, being affected by aspects of family pathology, etc. However, they also compiled another specific list of 'indicators against supervision', including 'unlikely to succeed under supervision', 'having problems for which another agency would be more appropriate', etc. Later, when looking specifically at recommendations for supervision, they say (fully in line with Pauline Hardiker) that 'the great majority . . . for whom supervision was recommended had some present needs' (Stanley and Murphy 1984: 33). But, they continue, 'the influence of "need" . . . is weaker than at first appears', for while 63 per cent of the whole sample had present needs, less than half of these were recommended for probation, usually because (a) the report also contained some of the contra-indicators to supervision, (b) the need related to especially deep-seated problems, or (c) the subject had several previous convictions (1984: 34). The third of these is well catered for in Hardiker's theory (by the 'tariff' dimension); the other two less easily so.[18] The general lesson is that just as 'tariff' needs to be broken down into its constituent and perhaps (from the point of view of a recommendation) competing elements, so also does 'social/personal need'.[19]

Finally, there is the issue of individual, agency, or court differences. Hardiker's work, as we have seen, stresses the *generality* of the 'tariff' and 'need' dimensions in accounting for social enquiry recommendations even when considering officers with different personal ideologies and approaches; her critics accuse her of thus minimizing important differences between individual officers, particular social work/probation areas or teams, or particular local court situations (Paley and Leeves 1982); Hardiker responds that her work has always shown the existence of such features (e.g. Hardiker 1975, 1977a) but that they are empirically less important than the generalities (Webb and Hardiker 1983: 214). The debate seems to have at least something in common with the legendary argument as to whether a bottle is half-full or half-empty. Be that as it may, it is very important that issues like court or agency differences are not lost sight of. Their importance is strikingly demonstrated in a recent analysis of social enquiry reports in one juvenile court (Osborne 1984) which showed that although social workers serving the court were dealing with a significantly greater proportion of minor offenders than were the probation officers at the same court, nevertheless the social workers were making significantly more custodial recommendations and significantly fewer recommendations for 'minor' disposals (such as a fine or discharge) than were the probation officers.

In summary, then, it looks as if Hardiker's work has made some important discoveries, but that (a) the concepts of 'tariff' and 'need' require greater clarification and elaboration, and (b) we also need to know more, empirically, about the ways in which these concepts are operationalized by different agencies, teams, or individuals and before different kinds of court (e.g. Crown Court versus magistrates' court). Only then may something like a full explanation of what influences SER recommendations become available. In all this, one general point perhaps requires to be stressed. There seems to be a tendency to assume (Webb and Hardiker 1983: 209, 214) that to defend the 'tariff-need calculus' is necessarily to defend the 'reverse tariff rank' as an explanatory device. But this is surely not so, for it is one thing to insist that tariff and need are central and generally applied elements in formulating SER recommendations, and quite another to defend some of Hardiker's specific suggestions, such as for example 'high need × high tariff = custodial recommendation'. Our own hunch is that an elaborated version of the 'tariff-need calculus' will prove of lasting value,[20] but that the specific hypotheses of the 'reverse tariff rank' will require revision, perhaps drastically, after future empirical research.

One final point needs to be made. We noted at the end of the previous section a suggestion in Curran and Chambers (1982: 100) that SERs perhaps need to be seen above all as 'strategic documents involved in "persuasive communication" with the courts'. With all the discussion above about deriving more precise research indices of the constituent parts of the 'tariff' and 'need' dimensions, and so on (necessary though all this undoubtedly is), we may be in some danger of forgetting that this section is about *recommendations* in social enquiry reports, and that if 'persuasive communication' is to be attempted by the officer anywhere in the report, it is most likely to occur in the shaping of the recommendation. With this point in mind, and having explicitly read and referred to Hardiker's work, Curran and Chambers (1982: 142–45) essay an interesting alteration to her 'reverse tariff' formulation. They note evidence in Perry (1974: 27) that in most cases the report-writer recommends a lesser sentence than he anticipates the court will actually give. Perhaps, then, the report-writer decides what sentence he thinks the court might pass, and then (because of his commitment, as a social worker, to his client) usually – though not always – argues, on a social work basis, for a penalty which is just below that anticipated sentence level. This approach is described by Curran and Chambers 'a "pitch" for a *tariff-minus-one* disposal' (italics in original), though one which, because of the social work skills which underlie it, is 'not simply a plea for leniency' (1982: 144). This is a most interesting suggestion which requires careful testing through further research.

WHAT DO SENTENCERS THINK ABOUT SERs?

Social enquiry reports are not general, abstract documents. They are written for a very specific occasion (a court appearance), and for very specific reader(s) (the sentencer(s)). Other people may see the reports afterwards (see Shaw 1981), but that probably influences the report-writers very little. It is the court with whom they are seeking to communicate.

All this being the case, an obvious research topic is 'what do courts think of SERs?'. Yet, surprisingly, this question has scarcely been asked by researchers. We have been able to locate only three studies, all rather small-scale. What is more, none of these studies sought to discover what sentencers thought about *particular* SERs on individual defendants; all simply asked sentencers in general terms for their views and impressions concerning SERs.

Burney (1979: 107–73) asked a sample of 59 English lay magistrates about SERs. Almost all were favourable in their replies; only one had any detailed criticisms. 'Excellent', 'helpful', 'full and explicit' were among the views expressed. The few criticisms that were made concentrated on the 'unrealistic' nature of some recommendations (see below), and on the 'jargon-ridden language of reports' (1979: 169). However, Horsley's (1984) small study on SER language suggested that actually jargon in the strict sense was rare.[21]

Joanna Shapland (1981: 130–34) interviewed a small sample of barristers, and of professionally qualified sentencers (judges and recorders). (The views of the two groups were not very clearly distinguished.) Both groups seemed to be very favourable about SERs, which were 'uniformly held to be valuable' and were of a 'generally high standard'. The major criticisms were (a) that there was insufficient distinction between the information provided and the probation officer's own opinion, and (b) that although the presence of recommendations in the reports was generally welcomed, '60 per cent considered that recommendations were often unrealistic'.

The 'realism'/'unrealism' issue, thrown up by both these samples, raises one of the most important unresolved issues about SER practice. The Streatfeild Report (para. 346) thought the probation officer could express a professional opinion on what was most likely to stop the offender from offending again, but that it was for the court to assess the nature of the offence and the public interest. The Court of Appeal has on occasions taken a similar view, but on other occasions has said that the probation officer's recommendation must be sufficiently 'realistic' to take account of public safety and public reaction (see Walker 1985: 30). As Walker comments, 'this question is so important that it needs to be answered less equivocally' (see also p. 270, note 4).

The third research study of sentencers' views of SERs comes from Scotland, and was based on interviews with twelve Sheriffs (Curran and Chambers 1982: 105–14). Once again the predominant tone was complimentary about SERs: nine of the twelve Sheriffs said they were satisfied with the overall standard of reports. An interesting point was that Sheriffs welcomed information in the report about the offender's attitude to the offence, but they did not, in general, approve of social workers commenting on the circumstances of the offence. Finally, it is perhaps of great importance that there was very little unity among the Sheriffs on the *purpose* of SERs: the three main views on purpose expressed were 'to assess the character of the offender', 'to assess suitability for probation', and 'to provide an objective or factual background report'. If sentencers in Britain generally are as divided as this about the proper purpose of reports, it should not be too surprising that probation officers and social workers sometimes become confused about what SERs are for.

Perhaps the most striking point about these three small studies is their uniformly favourable view of SERs. As Burney (1979: 167–68) wryly points out, this high level of satisfaction about reports among sentencers contrasts rather oddly with the research literature on the subject. Perhaps an explanation of this lies in Barbara Wootton's view (1978: 45) that the objective achievements of SERs are slight, but that they nevertheless appeal to sentencers because they 'transform a "case" into a human being'.

Curran and Chambers (1982: 145) regard current social enquiry practice as a negotiated compromise between the report-writer and the court, and suggest that: 'given the current level of satisfaction by the primary client in this affair – the courts – one would need to seriously question any movement which might disrupt the present compromise'.

It is a comment far removed from the spirit of the Streatfeild Committee; for them, the test was not the satisfaction of the sentencer, but 'whether the information can help the court to reach a better decision' (para. 293). 'It is not', they insisted, 'simply a matter of providing the courts with the fullest possible information about offenders' (para. 293) – even if that does make the courts happy.

CONCLUSION

'The high hopes of . . . the Streatfeild Committee seem far removed from current practice' (Moore 1984: 103). Few would disagree. Barbara Wootton certainly would not. Reflecting in 1981 on her 1963 Hamlyn Lectures (written very much in the spirit of Streatfeild), she commented:

> 'My final lecture ended on a relatively optimistic note, still cherishing the hope . . . that more refined methods of investigation together with the rapid growth of electronic mechanisms for handling more complex data, may make sentencers better aware of the results of their own decisions, and more competent to achieve whatever it is they want to achieve. But I have to confess that over the years since these lectures were delivered, I have been increasingly haunted by the image . . . of the whole penal system as in a sense a gigantic irrelevance – wholly misconceived as a method of controlling phenomena the origins of which are inextricably rooted in the structure of our society.'
>
> (Wootton 1981: 119)

This comment is obviously influenced by the depressing results of treatment studies in penology, and by theoretical critiques of the 're-habilitative ideal' (for a summary see Bottoms 1980). In the light of all this, and of the research reviewed in this paper, are social enquiry reports (along with much else done in the courts) indeed a 'gigantic irrelevance'? None of the research reported in this paper shows clearly that they are not, but, equally, it does not prove that they are. The challenge, perhaps, is to report-writers, and to the courts they serve, to evolve a better social enquiry practice twenty-five years after the Streatfeild Report: and to decide more clearly what 'better' might mean in this context.

NOTES

1 The link lay in the suggestion put to the committee for a greatly expanded network of permanent Crown Courts, similar to those then existing at Liverpool and Manchester, which it was hoped would improve the possibilities of courts receiving information before sentencing, notably through the creation of a number of 'observation and classification centres [for adults] . . . adjacent to the remand centres to be set up for young persons and [using] the same diagnostic staff' (Home Office 1959: para. 59). The Streatfeild Committee however rejected permanent Crown Courts (chapter 5), with only a brief look at the links to improved information (paras 134–35); the Prison Commissioners then felt unable to pursue their plans for adult observation and classification centres.

2 The 'handbook for courts' is *The Sentence of the Court*, which has been through three editions in 1964, 1969, and 1978 (Home Office 1978), but is now badly outdated. All three editions are mostly a description of available sentencing measures, with only brief concluding discussions of research. For a much more comprehensive approach, perhaps more akin to what Streatfeild had in mind, and summarizing all the main research results, see now Walker (1985); note, however, the tentative and/or disputed nature of much of the research evidence.

3 Evidence of cost-consciousness is apparent in Thorpe's Home Office Research Unit study, which referred to 'limited resources and increasing pressure of work', and had as one of its background policy considerations 'whether . . . the number of reports written could be reduced for certain categories of offender' (Thorpe 1979: 2). See also the Home Office national statement of objectives and priorities for the probation service (Home Office 1984).

4 A particularly important example of the way in which some subsequent official circulars have gone beyond Streatfeild is the celebrated

issue as to whether 'opinions' or 'recommendations' by probation officers in their social enquiry reports are appropriate. The matter is well discussed in Harris (1979).

5 To keep the review within practicable bounds we have confined it to research carried out in Great Britain, though that does include Scotland where the Streatfeild Report necessarily had a much more diffuse and indirect effect than in England and Wales (see Moore 1984: 108–09). For a consideration of some aspects of pre-sentence reports in other jurisdictions see Perry (1979).

6 Other possible kinds of research include research on offenders' perceptions of SER contents; prospective research with probation officers on how they go about shaping a social enquiry report from the moment of receiving the initial notification; and research into the uses to which social enquiry reports are put after the court hearing (on which see Shaw 1981).

7 The committee went on to point out that 'at present' these two kinds of information are usually treated as one, but said it was important to recognize the distinction: 'as the results of further research become known, it may be found possible to define more precisely those aspects of the offender and his background which are relevant to the success or failure of particular forms of penal treatment' (Home Office 1961: para. 336).

8 There is a printing error in footnote 2 on p. 433 of the paper which means we do not know what statistical test was applied: it presumably cannot be chi-squared, since chi-squared with one degree of freedom cannot handle the three-way interaction here between (i) reconviction, (ii) Sample A/Sample C, and (iii) number of previous convictions. The absence of statistical significance in the proportion of those with two or more previous convictions is not necessarily fatal to the result reported by Hood and Taylor, but does give one pause. More generally, as Hood (1966: 309) correctly stated in his first paper, 'it is extremely difficult completely satisfactorily to "match" the two samples; the results should therefore be interpreted with some caution'.

9 Curran and Chambers (1982) are particularly careful to distinguish between what they call 'firm recommendations', 'tentative recommendations', and 'no recommendation'; in a sentenced sample of 176, the numbers in these three categories were respectively 120, 35, and 21.

10 Despite its widespread acceptance, this categorization is not beyond criticism. It is, for example, not clear why category (b) does not collapse into category (d). As regards category (a), probation officers may have influence over sentencers for other reasons than sentencers' regard for their professional qualities and competence: as Davies (1974: 30) suggests, these reasons might include a sentencer's wish not to

disappoint the probation officer, or the fact that a sentencer honestly doesn't know what to do with the offender anyway.

11 In their earlier study Hood and Taylor (1968: 433–34) set up a scheme not dissimilar to that of Mott; they reported 174 cases dealt with in the relevant period, amongst which 92 remands for enquiry were made; in 44 of these 92 cases (48 per cent) the magistrates changed their provisional decision recorded at the time of remand, apparently mostly in the direction of the probation officers' recommendations. This was a higher proportionate change than in Mott's study, but is restricted specifically to cases where the magistrates felt they needed more information, so this is not surprising.

12 Stanley and Murphy's estimate is, overall, that 28 per cent of offenders on whom SERs were prepared were diverted from custody; of these, it is estimated, 10 per cent were sentenced to probation or supervision, 5 per cent to community service, 6 per cent to a suspended sentence, and 7 per cent to other disposals. The authors point out, however, that their calculations should be accepted only 'if it is true that the proportion of failed recommendations resulting in an immediate custodial sentence can be taken as an indicator of how far the disposal recommended is in fact an alternative to custody' (Stanley and Murphy 1984: 32). This use of failed recommendations resulting in immediate custody as an indicator of diversion from custody is derived from research into community service by Pease (1980); however, it really should be more widely tested before it can be used generally as an indicator, especially for disposals other than community service.

13 Martin, Fox, and Murray's (1981) analysis of report contents includes school reports and other available reports (e.g. from assessment centres and child guidance clinics), as well as social enquiry reports. However, it is clear from the context that the criticisms cited in the text refer mainly to social workers' reports.

14 Indeed, it is sometimes advocated: 'Report writing is about getting a result, and getting results involves the use of strategies. These . . . all involve the selective use of information and the careful choice of words and concepts to get a desired result. When the explicit recognition of such strategic writing is felt to be unwise or potentially embarrassing, it can easily be justified in terms of "keeping it relevant" or "personal style"' (Powell 1985: 27). This clearly has strong links to the question of the purpose of report-writing, discussed at the end of this section.

15 The reader who is seeking a simple and rapid approach to Pauline Hardiker's work is advised to concentrate initially upon Hardiker (1979).

16 There are two small linguistic oddities here. First, the 'reverse tariff' formulation does not seem to be a very accurate way of describing

Hardiker's model, as she has now conceded (Webb and Hardiker 1983: 208). Second, in this key quotation the first sentence refers, surely erroneously, to *the sentencer*; as the rest of the quotation makes clear, it is the report-writer's recommendation which is really under consideration.

17 This point was picked up by Paley and Leeves (1982: 373) with particular reference to a case where Curnock and Hardiker (1979: 62) seem to say that a defendant 'needed' custody precisely because he was, in personal and social terms, 'a fairly stable young man'. Webb and Hardiker's (1983) reply to Paley and Leeves offers no adequate defence on this point (see p. 213).

18 Hardiker could point here to the additional 'resources' dimension which is introduced into her work especially in Curnock and Hardiker (1979); the argument would presumably be that in the first and second type of case there is no adequate resource to meet the need, so supervision is not recommended. But this poses dilemmas for the 'reverse tariff' theory particularly, which has never (unlike Curnock and Hardiker's work) formally introduced a resources dimension. Moreover, a case could be argued that what is involved here is a refinement of the 'need' concept, not a needs vs. resources conflict.

19 It should be noted in this connection that Stanley and Murphy's (1984) 'contra-indicators to supervision' seem not to be functionally equivalent to Hardiker's 'probation inappropriate' category, since in 62 per cent of the latter conditional discharge or a fine were anticipated (Webb and Hardiker 1983: 212). The three main elements in Stanley and Murphy's 'contra-indicator' dimension were 'not in need of supervision', 'unlikely to succeed under supervision', and 'having an adverse attitude to supervision'. The first of these would of course not be a 'contra-indicator' in a 'high need' case; interestingly, of the other two 'unlikely to succeed' was related to number of previous convictions, while 'adverse attitude' was not (Stanley and Murphy 1984: 16, 47).

20 It is of interest here that Paley and Leeves (1982), in their critique of Hardiker, do not seek to abandon these concepts, though they do seek to formulate the relationship between them differently from Hardiker (pp. 374–75), and in a way that she finds unconvincing (Webb and Hardiker 1983: 213–14).

21 This study by Gail Horsley (1984) was an innovative and fascinating examination of the language of SERs: the author found that the complexity of both vocabulary and syntax in the reports was often such that the defendant, given his reading age, stood little chance of understanding what was being said about him.

REFERENCES

Bean, P. T. (1975) Social Inquiry Reports: A Recommendation for Disposal. *Justice of the Peace* 139: 563–64, 585–86.

—— (1976) *Rehabilitation and Deviance*. London: Routledge & Kegan Paul.

Bottoms, A. E. (1980) An Introduction to 'The Coming Crisis'. In A. E. Bottoms and R. H. Preston (eds) *The Coming Penal Crisis: A Criminological and Theological Exploration*. Edinburgh: Scottish Academic Press.

Bottoms, A. E. and Stelman, A. (forthcoming) *Rethinking Social Enquiry Reports*. Farnborough: Gower.

Burney, E. (1979) *J. P. Magistrate, Court and Community*. London: Hutchinson.

Carter, R. M. and Wilkins, L. T. (1967) Some Factors in Sentencing Policy. *Journal of Criminal Law, Criminology and Police Science* 58(4): 503–14.

Curnock, K. and Hardiker, P. (1979) *Towards Practice Theory: Skills and Methods in Social Assessments*. London: Routledge & Kegan Paul.

Curran, J. H. and Chambers, G. A. (1982) *Social Enquiry Reports in Scotland*. Edinburgh: HMSO.

Davies, M. (1974) Social Inquiry for the Courts. *British Journal of Criminology* 14: 18–33.

Hardiker, P. (1975) Ideologies in Social Inquiry Reports. Unpublished Research Report: Social Science Research Council.

—— (1977a) A Probation Intake Team in Action. Unpublished Research Report: Leicestershire Probation Service and Social Science Research Council.

—— (1977b) Social Work Ideologies in the Probation Service. *British Journal of Social Work* 7(2): 131–53.

—— (1979) The Role of Probation Officers in Sentencing. In H. Parker (ed.) *Social Work and the Courts*. London: Edward Arnold.

Hardiker, P. and Webb, D. (1979) Explaining Deviant Behaviour: The Social Context of Action and Infraction Accounts in the Probation Service. *Sociology* 13(1): 1–17.

Harris, B. (1979) Recommendations in Social Inquiry Reports. *Criminal Law Review*: 73–81.

Herbert, L. and Mathieson, D. (1975) *Reports for Courts*. London: National Association of Probation Officers.

Hine, J., McWilliams, W., and Pease, K. (1978) Recommendations, Social Information and Sentencing. *Howard Journal* 17: 91–100.

Home Office (1959) *Penal Practice in a Changing Society*. Cmnd 645. London: HMSO.

—— (1978) *The Sentence of the Court: A Handbook for Courts on the Treatment of Offenders*. London: HMSO.

—— (1984) Statement of National Objectives and Priorities for the Probation Service. London: Home Office.

Home Office and Lord Chancellor's Office (1961) *Report of the Interdepartmental Committee on the Business of the Criminal Courts* (Chairman: Mr Justice Streatfeild). Cmnd 1289. London: HMSO.

Hood, R. (1966) A Study of the Effectiveness of Pre-Sentence Investigations in Reducing Recidivism. *British Journal of Criminology* 6: 303–10.

Hood, R. and Taylor, I. (1968) Second Report of the Study of the Effectiveness of Pre-Sentence Investigations in Reducing Recidivism. *British Journal of Criminology* 8: 431–34.

Horsley, G. (1984) *The Language of Social Enquiry Reports*. Social Work Monograph No. 27. Norwich: University of East Anglia.

Klare, H. J. (1962) *The Anatomy of Prison*. Harmondsworth: Penguin.

—— (1964) The Problem of Remand in Custody for Diagnostic Purposes. In M. Lopez-Rey and C. Germain (eds) *Studies in Penology*. The Hague: Martinus Nijhoff.

McWilliams, W. (1985) The English Social Enquiry Report: Development and Practice. Unpublished PhD Thesis: University of Sheffield.

Mannheim, H. and Wilkins, L. T. (1955) *Prediction Methods in Relation to Borstal Training*. Home Office Studies in the Causes of Delinquency and the Treatment of Offenders No. 1. London: HMSO.

Martin, F. M., Fox, S. J., and Murray, K. (1981) *Children Out of Court*. Edinburgh: Scottish Academic Press.

Moore, G. (1984) *The Practice of Social Inquiry*. Aberdeen: Aberdeen University Press.

Mott, J. (1977) Decision Making and Social Inquiry Reports in One Juvenile Court. *British Journal of Social Work* 7(4): 421–32.

Osborne, S. (1984) Social Inquiry Reports in One Juvenile Court: An Examination. *British Journal of Social Work* 14(4): 361–78.

Paley, J. and Leeves, R. (1982) Some Questions About the Reverse Tariff. *British Journal of Social Work* 12(4): 363–80.

Pearce, I. and Wareham, A. (1977) The Questionable Relevance of Research Into Social Enquiry Reports. *Howard Journal* 16(2): 97–108.

Pease, K. (1980) Community Service and Prison: Are They Alternatives? In K. Pease and W. McWilliams (eds) *Community Service by Order*. Edinburgh: Scottish Academic Press.

Perry, F. G. (1974) *Information for the Courts: A New Look at Social Inquiry Reports*. Cambridge: Institute of Criminology.

—— (1979) *Reports for Criminal Courts*. Ilkley: Owen Wells.

Powell, M. (1985) Court Work. In H. Walker and B. Beaumont (eds) *Working with Offenders*. London: Macmillan.

Roberts, J. and Roberts, C. (1982) Social Enquiry Reports and Sentencing. *Howard Journal* 21: 76–93.

Shapland, J. (1981) *Between Conviction and Sentence: The Process of Mitigation*. London: Routledge & Kegan Paul.

Shaw, R. (1981) *Who Uses Social Inquiry Reports?* Institute of Criminology Occasional Papers No. 7. Cambridge: Institute of Criminology.

Stanley, S. J. and Murphy, B. (1984) *Inner London Probation Service: Survey of Social Enquiry Reports*. London: Inner London Probation Service.

Thorpe, J. (1979) *Social Inquiry Reports: A Survey*. Home Office Research Study No. 48. London: HMSO.

Walker, N. (1985) *Sentencing: Theory, Law and Practice*. London: Butterworths.

Webb, D. and Hardiker, P. (1983) Some Answers About the Reverse Tariff: A Reply to Paley and Leeves. *British Journal of Social Work* 13(2): 207–18.

Wilkins, L. T. and Chandler, A. (1965) Confidence and Competence in Decision Making. *British Journal of Criminology* 5(1): 22–35.

Wootton, B. (1963) *Crime and the Criminal Law: Reflections of a Magistrate and Social Scientist* (1st edn). London: Stevens.

—— (1978) *Crime and Penal Policy: Reflections on Fifty Years' Experience*. London: Allen & Unwin.

—— (1981) *Crime and the Criminal Law: Reflections of a Magistrate and Social Scientist* (2nd edn). London: Stevens.

16

CRIMES: PUNISHMENT AND PREVENTION
Louis Blom-Cooper Q.C.

For the last twenty years Barbara Wootton has continued to irritate, if not to infuriate English criminal lawyers by her denunciation of the traditional concept of criminal responsibility. By her impeccable logic she has consistently demonstrated the internally inconsistent philosophies of the criminal justice system which seeks to reconcile the irreconcilable, namely, punitive and preventive purposes. Less professional hostility, although well short of any agreement, would have been aroused had she followed her argument to a logical conclusion in advocating (as do most criminologists) the abolition or, at very least, the positive and substantial reduction of the criminal justice system. Instead she opted for a hopelessly optimistic prediction that there would be a gradual withering away of the system, that no doubt has served the country well enough in the distant past but ceases to fulfil any socially useful purpose in contemporary society.

In her Hamlyn Lectures for 1963 *Crime and the Criminal Law*, subtitled *Reflections of a Magistrate and Social Scientist* (a second edition appeared in 1981), she provoked the debate that simmers on and evokes the decorous chidings of Professor John Smith in this commemorative volume of essays. Lady Wootton identified the punitive concept with the historical concept between crime and sin (or, to use a less fundamentalist notion, the conventional morality) and the preventive concept with a system whose primary purpose is to reduce the occurrence of offences, on the basis that they are so socially harmful as to require defensive action by the institutions of the state. (I pause only to note the difficulty in defining the terms of the state's ability and competence to reflect the moral pluralism of our society.)

The former concept involves *mens rea* (the guilty state of mind) as a prime element in criminal offences. Far from the concept declining in importance, the courts are giving it an increasing significance. No less a figure than the Lord Chancellor has acknowledged this judicial approach as a 'thoroughly praiseworthy development' (*R* v. *Lawrence* [1982] A.C. 210). The latter concept involves *mens rea* only to the extent that it is relevant to the treatment (or disposal of offenders) in a preventive system. The offender's state of mind (or absence of it) in a preventive system will serve only as an indicator in evaluating the degree of state intervention in a person's liberty, in imposing restriction on his freedom of movement, or in assessing the amount of any monetary penalty.

Those who favour the punitive system not merely welcome its judicial reinforcement but actively oppose its erosion by statutory extension of the list of crimes of strict liability. They do so on the thoroughly respectable grounds that strict liability removes the moral obloquy from many acts that are individually despicable and socially opprobrious. Lady Wootton favoured the strict liability notion, without ever grappling with the consequences of the abandonment of a guilty state of mind. And this is her Achilles heel. She acknowledges that there are difficulties beyond any question of reconciliation, such as those of definition, in suggesting that the code of criminal offences should immediately be transferred to the category of strict liability. The existing division between these two categories of criminal offences is illogical and haphazard, depending on natural causes, the obscure draftsmanship of Acts of Parliament or statutory instruments, and judicial interpretation reflecting at different times different policy attitudes. While the debate rages, at least the legislature can insist that its draftsmen should use unequivocal language when creating crimes of strict liability or not; and also if the liability is strict and not absolute, what specific defences are available to an accused.

Barbara Wootton's analysis was correct. The contemporary system of criminal justice in its penal segment of the whole criminal process, more pointedly than in the past, has been riding two horses simultaneously in opposite directions. The courts traditionally exist to punish offenders (and inferentially to demarcate the boundaries of behaviour in more general and symbolic terms).[1] They do so more severely for graver offences and more lightly with lesser ones, or less severely where there are mitigating factors. This approach is quintessentially backward-looking. It gauges the seriousness of past events and measures the commensurate penalty. Increasingly, at least since the Second World War, emphasis has been laid upon objectives that look to future conduct. Even if rehabilitation of the individual offender is no longer espoused, there is a powerful element in all sentencing of deterring potential offenders and of protecting the community. Conflicts between the claims of the past and of the future are thus made manifest in the daily sentencing practice of the courts.

Lady Wootton pointed to two spheres where this conflict has been most marked. The first involves those persons adjudged by the law not to be fully responsible for their acts. The concept of diminished responsibility in the law of homicide, which reduces what would be a crime of murder to that of manslaughter and allows the court to view the offender as semi-responsible and deserving not of punishment but of treatment in a hospital setting, or at least a reduced amount of punishment, is juris-prudentially unsound. The concept of diminished responsibility, Lady Wootton wrote in a devastating attack on it in a Cambridge lecture in 1960,[2] 'represents, in fact, an attempt to smuggle into an essentially punitive system ideas and aims which are totally incompatible with such a system. The results have been in a limited degree humane, and for that we may well be thankful; but they would be far more humane if modern conceptions of treatment did not have to be dressed up in the outmoded fashions of responsibility.' This is what the Gowers Commission on Capital Punishment called the search for the chimera.[2] Now that the death penalty for murder has gone – one anticipates, for ever – there is no need to mitigate the rigours of that irreversible penalty. Were Parliament to go one step further and remove the mandatory element from the sentence of life imprisonment, giving the judges at the time of conviction a discretion to impose a sentence appropriate to the particular homicide, that juris-prudential blot could at a stroke be confined to the legal history museum.

The other, more perceptible conflict concerns the delinquent child. The attempt to give pre-eminence to considerations of welfare in the structure of juvenile courts within a fundamentally penal structure, accentuated by the changes wrought by the Children and Young Persons Act 1969, poses even more glaring anomalies. The continued admixture of criminal offences and the need for care and control confuses the difference between right and wrong and the need for help and guidance for those under seventeen, and exhibits the law's ambivalence about responsibility. Lady Wootton's argument from the particular of juvenile delinquency to the general of adult criminality stemmed from forty years' experience as a magistrate in the juvenile courts. Without taking up a determinist position she felt compelled to argue that the whole criminal process should refrain from raising the issue of responsibility at all.[3] In this way and only in this way, she concluded 'can all the contradictions be resolved'. Discard ideas of responsibility and the law can ask sensibly, not whether an offender *ought* to be punished but whether he is likely to benefit from punishment. All the agencies for treatment – psychiatrists, probation officers, and social workers – need no longer masquerade as moralists but apply their proper role of applied scientists and carers indicating their methods of control and influence of future behaviour.

It has been the inability, not to say futility of penal sanctions that has led criminologists to question the whole process. What is the purpose of an elaborate system of investigation, analysis, and decision-making if the remedy applied fails palpably to remedy, even inflicts harm on the individual, and does little or nothing to assuage the victim and the aroused public? Lady Wootton's own contribution to penal reform – and few will fail to associate her name with the one innovative sanction of modern time, the Community Service Order – should have led her to join as a leading proponent of the dismantling of the criminal justice system. Yet, so far as I am aware, she never publicly joined the chorus of criminological icono-clasm. Had she done so, her assault on the lawyer's adherence to the principle, no penal sanction without a finding of a guilty state of mind to legitimize state intervention in the individual's freedom, would have made more impact.

In one respect Lady Wootton did point the way. 'Crime', she was fond of reminding her audiences, did not exist, save as a socially meaningless abstraction. There are, of course, 'crimes' listed in the notional calendar of criminal offences. But here again the lawyers have distracted the rest of us by assigning human conduct into definitional offences. What matters to society is not the label given to a class of acts but the particular criminal event, for which the legal system must prescribe some appropriate response. What has an affray by a large number of youths in the local village hall in the country got in common with the deliberately concocted defrauding of the Inland Revenue by a company director, or the battering by a distraught parent, with a low threshold of tolerance, of its fractious child? The answer in terms of sensible social response is: nothing. Yet each of these criminal events is squeezed into the unitary system of criminal justice and is differentiated only when it comes to the appropriate disposal. Lady Wootton has been right, therefore, to point the legal profession in the direction of the outcome of the criminal process, and indirectly to call for a system that best achieves the ultimate aim, that of assuaging the feelings of victims and restoring so far as possible social equilibrium. Criminal responsibility needs to be redefined in terms of penal disposal and liability for human conduct. The lawyers have indeed got, and still get, *mens rea* in the wrong place.

NOTES

1 The clearest exposition of this motion came from Viscount Simonds in *Shaw* v. *Director of Public Prosecutions* (The Ladies' Directory Case) (1962) A.C.220: 267. 'I entertain no doubt that there remains in the courts of law a residual power to enforce the supreme and fundamental purpose of the law, to conserve not only the safety and order but also the moral welfare of the state. . . .'

2 Seventh Biennial Lecture in Criminal Science of the Cambridge Institute of Criminology in February 1960 (reproduced in Volume 76, *Law Quarterly Review*, pp. 224–39).

3 Yet if the model of adult criminal process is abandoned it leads to the state of affairs that had to be rectified in the reform of practice in the US following the Gault decision: in *Re* Gault 387 US 1 (1967).

© *1986 Louis Blom-Cooper Q.C.*

BARBARA WOOTTON
– A SELECT
BIBLIOGRAPHY

1920 Classical Principles and Modern Views of Labour. *Economic Journal* 30: 46–60.

1929 Shavian Socialism. *Economic Journal* 39: 71–7.

1933 *Twos and Threes*. London: Howe.

1934 *Plan or No Plan*. London: Gollancz.

1936 *London's Burning*. London: Allen & Unwin.

1938 *Lament for Economics*. London: Allen & Unwin.

1940 Some Aspects of Social Structure in England and Wales. *Adult Education* 13 (2): 97–116.

— *Should Socialists Support Federal Union?* (Report of a debate between Federal Union – Mrs Barbara Wootton – and the Socialist Party of Great Britain – Mr E. Hardy). London: SPGB Library No. 14.

1941 *End Social Inequality*. London: Kegan Paul.

1942 Chaos in the Social Services. *Sociological Review* 34: 1–11.

1943 *Full Employment*. London: Fabian Research Series 14.

1945 *Freedom Under Planning*. London: Allen & Unwin.

1950 *Testament for Social Science: An Essay in the Application of Scientific Method to Human Problems*. London: Allen & Unwin.

1952 The Contribution of Science to Democracy. *The Plain View*, August: 136–43.

— Reflections on Resigning a Professorship. *Universities Quarterly* 7(1): 36–49.

1954 Social Prestige and Social Class. *British Journal of Sociology* 5: 371–74.

1955 Holiness or Happiness? *The Twentieth Century*, November: 407–16.

— *The Social Foundations of Wage Policy: A Study of Contemporary British Wage and Salary Structure*. London: Allen & Unwin.

1956 Why not Change the Schools? *Highway*. March.

— Sickness or Sin? *The Twentieth Century*, January: 433–42.

— The Ethics of the Wage Structure: Retrospect and Prospect. *Hibbert Journal*, January.

1958 Sex and Society. *The Twentieth Century*, January: 5–15.

— The Puzzling Politics of Ghana. *The Twentieth Century*, May: 416–26.

1959 *Social Science and Social Pathology*. London: Allen & Unwin.

— Daddy Knows Best. *The Twentieth Century*, October: 248–61.

— *Contemporary Trends in Crime and Its Treatment*. London: Clarke-Hall
. Fellowship.

1960 Diminished Responsibility: a Layman's View. *Law Review Quarterly*,
April: 224–39.

— The Image of the Social Worker. *British Journal of Sociology* 11: 373–85.

1961 *Remuneration in a Welfare State*, Eleanor Rathbone Memorial Lecture.
Liverpool: University Press.

— The Juvenile Courts. *Criminal Law Review*, October: 669–77.

1962 *The Future of the Social Sciences*. Canberra: Australian National
University.

— Socrates, Science and Social Problems. *New Society* 1: 16–17.

— A Social Scientist's Approach to Maternal Deprivation. *World Health
Organisation Public Health Paper* 14: 63–73.

1963 Is There a Welfare State? A Review of Recent Social Change in
Britain. *Political Science Quarterly* 78(2): 179–97.

— *Crime and the Criminal Law: Reflections of a Magistrate and a Social
Scientist*. Hamlyn Lectures. London: Stevens. (Second edition 1981 with
postscripts to each chapter.)

— Sentencing: Art or Science? *New Society* 24: 18–19.

— The Law, the Doctor and the Deviant. *British Medical Journal* 5351:
197–202.

1967 *In a World I Never Made: Autobiographical Reflections*. London: Allen &
Unwin.

1968 Social Psychiatry and Psychopathology: a Layman's Comments on
Contemporary Developments. *Proceedings of the American Psychopatho-
logical Association* 57: 283–99.

— Crime and the British Penal System: Reflections of a Long-service
Magistrate. *Proceedings of the Royal Society of Medicine* 61: 317–24.

— The White Paper on Children in Trouble. *Criminal Law Review*,
September: 465–73.

1969 British Medical Practice as Seen Through the Eyes of a Layman.
Journal of the Royal College of General Practitioners 17 Supp. 1: 15–24.

1970 The Management of Staff in General Practice – Chairman's Summary. *Journal of the Royal College of General Practitioners* 19 Supp. 3:
20–22.

— Deviance: Criminal and Other. *New Society* 423: 812–16.

— Report on Non-Custodial and Semi-Custodial Treatment of Offenders. *Probation* 16, March: 69–70.

1971 *Contemporary Britain: Three Lectures.* British Humanist Association Voltaire Lectures 1. London: Allen & Unwin.

1972 The Place of Psychiatry and Medical Concepts in the Treatment of Offenders: a Layman's View. *Canadian Psychiatric Association Journal* 17: 365–75.

1973 Spot the Winner. *New Society* 545: 599–600.

1974 *Incomes Policy: an Inquest and a Proposal.* London: Davis-Poynter.

— *Fair Pay, Relativities and Policies for Incomes.* University of Southampton.

1975 A Philosophy for the Social Services. Rita Hinden Memorial Lecture. *Socialist Commentary* January: ii–iii.

1976 *In Pursuit of Equality.* Blanche Colebrook Memorial Lecture. London: Fabian Tract 443.

1977 Some Reflections on the First Five Years of Community Service. *Probation Journal* 24/4: 110–112.

— The End of the Peers. *New Society* 787: 232–33.

— Aubrey Lewis's Paper on Health as a Social Concept Reconsidered in the Light of Today. *British Journal of Psychiatry* 131: 243–48.

1978 *Crime and Penal Policy: Reflections on Fifty Years' Experience.* London: Allen & Unwin.

— The Uses of Sociology. *New Society* 805: 553–54.

— The Right to Die. *New Society* 838: 202–03.

— Reflections on Crime and Penal Policy in Contemporary England. *Current Legal Problems* 31: 1–13.

1979 Towards a Rational Pay Policy. *New Society* 860: 735–37.

1980 Psychiatry, Ethics and the Criminal Law. *British Journal of Psychiatry* 136: 525–32.

— Death – Whose Right to Choose? *Midwife, Health Visitor and Community Nurse* 16 (5): 205–06.

1981 When is a War not a War? *New Society* 980: 339–41.

1983 Reflections on the Welfare State. In P. Bean and S. MacPherson (eds) *Approaches to Welfare.* London: Routledge & Kegan Paul.

1985 The Moral Basis of the Welfare State. In P. Bean, J. Ferris, and D. Whynes (eds) *In Defence of Welfare.* London: Tavistock.

NAME INDEX

SUBJECT INDEX

Note: the abbreviation 'B.W.' is used for Lady Barbara Wootton throughout.